Ai

CW00539216

Pocket Book

Author and Publisher
Major (Retd) John Hobbis Harris
Technical & Creative Production
John (Jnr) & Rachel Harris

ISBN 1-874528-09-8

i

CONTENT

CONTENT

CONTENT

CONTENT

PERSONAL DETAILS

Surname ....

Other Names ....

Home Address ....

.... Post Code ....

Date of Birth   /   /   Nat Insurance No ....

Blood Group .... Home Telephone No ....

Next of Kin Relationship .... Tel No ....

Address   ....

.... Post Code ....

Religious Denomination ....

Relevant Medical Information, Allergies, etc ....

....

School Attending/Employer ....

Date Joined Corps.................................... Date Left Corps ....

Enrolled on .... at ....

Signed .... Officer i/c

Unit.. Date ....

Chapter I

INTRODUCTION

Although, there is no substitute for good instruction given by an experienced instructor, your Pocket Book is designed for you to be able to refer to it at any time.

Should you find any mistakes, in-correct detail or would like to make some constructive comments on its content, the publishers would be very pleased to hear from you - their address is shown on the inside of the front cover.

Your time and that of your instructors, when you **are** 'on parade', is very limited for them to teach you a full lesson on a topic.
Technical subjects are impossible to cover in detail, we have attempted to arouse your interest by short explanations, expertly written, by members of the Air Training Corps officers and instrutors.

It will make it easier for both you and your instructors if you use your Pocket Book for the purpose for which it has been produced - to refresh your memory and remind you of important facts.

NCO's will find it an invaluable aid when revising or planning lessons. With its help, you will gain a great deal of knowledge and improve your training and at the same time fulfil the Aims of the Air Training Corps, thus making you a good cadet and a better citizen.

Studying your Air Cadets Pocket Book does not absolve you from attending your Squadron parades, the reward for your OC is to see you regularly (on parade), perhaps better (turned-out), better prepared to play your part in the Squadron and hopefully more knowledgeable.

THE BANNER OF THE AIR TRAINING CORPS

In 1962 the first Banner of the Air Training Corps was presented by (His Royal Highness), The Duke of Edinburgh on the occasion of the 21st Anniversary of the Corps.
A new Banner was again presented by (HRH) The Duke of Edinburgh in 1979, and the old Banner was Laid Up in St Clement Danes Church, Holborn London in 1980.

The Air Cadets Promise
This is to remind you of your own Enrolment Ceremony and your obligations as a cadet.

"I hereby solemnly promise on my honour
To serve my Squadron loyally",
"And to be faithful to my obligations
As a member of the Air Training Corps".
"I further promise to be a good citizen,
And to do my duty to God and the Queen
My Country and my flag".

**Your Record of Service Book
(RAF Form 3822)
must be carried by you whenever taking
part in any ATC activities.**

GENERAL INFORMATION

ORGANISATION OF THE AIR TRAINING CORPS

The Air Training Corps is a National voluntary youth organisation aimed at encouraging a practical interest in aviation, adventure and sport. It was established by Royal Warrant on the 5th February 1941. The age at which the cadet joins as a probationer is 13 and normally they leave at the age of 18. When you reach the age of 18 and if you are successful enough to become a SNCO (i.e. Sgt or above) you may stay in the Cadets until your 20th birthday.

Upon completion of your probationary period you are then enrolled at the minimum age of 13 years and 3 months.

Should you gain promotion and eventually become a Cadet Warrant Officer you may then be selected to remain a member of the ATC until you are twenty years old.

HEADQUARTERS AIR CADETS

The Headquarters of the Air Cadets is the National Headquarters and administrative centre for the Air Cadet Organization in the UK based at Royal Air Force College Cranwell in Lincolnshire.

It is home to both Air Training Corps and the Combined Cadet Forces' RAF Sections as well as the University Air Squadrons, Volunteer Gliding Schools and Air Experience Flights.

The Corps is commanded and controlled by a full - time RAF Air Commodore, with staff of Regular and Reserve officers plus Civilian staff based at Headquarters Air Cadets (HQAC).

DEPARTMENTS WITHIN HQ AIR CADETS

Administration Dept

Covers the role of personnel, accounts/finance, works services, providing pay and allowances to all adult volunteers as well as dealing with the payment of all bills liable on the ACO public account.

Also included is the responsibility for the Finance and General Purpose Fund, which is a registered Charity.

Staff working with the Reserve Forces & Cadet Associations in the Counties provide maintenance and new work services for the Corps 1000 units.

GENERAL INFORMATION

Corporate Business Dept

The staff appointed to this branch have a major responsibility to develop the Air Cadet Organization (ACO) Management Plan. Drafting reports, preparing briefs, studies and staffing papers on corporate matters. Developing and carrying forward initiatives concerning planning and future strategies.

Organizes meetings of Regional Commandants and the Annual ATC Convention. Provides the ADC to Commandant Air Cadets, is the HQ Security Officer, the HQ Training Liaison Officer and custodian of the Corps Trophies and Corps Banner.

Logistics Dept

The Department is responsible for many of the support functions required to maintain the activities undertaken by the Air Cadet Organization. These include; Glider Maintenance Policy, Information Technology Support, Equipment Supply and Small Arms Range Inspections.

Support Equipment

There are many vehicles used to support the Glider function. The most complex being the Munster Van fielder Winch, which offers a 6-drum capacity giving high launch rates for conventional Gliders. Support Equipment also deals with; fire fighting trailers, aircraft refuellers, cable retrieve trailers and an assortment of passenger carrying vehicles.

The Supply role is faced with tight budgetary limits and increasingly stringent health and safety controls. They have a constant challenge to ensure Cadets are properly clothed and equipped.

Shooting: Logistics Branch plays its part by ensuring that miniature rifle and air rifle ranges are constructed and maintained to the highest possible standards in order that all aspects of safety are taken into consideration and that Cadets have every opportunity to produce good results.

Shooting is a very popular part of Air Cadet Training and to increase the interest changes are being made to the firing positions for the Cadets to adopt three positions namely the prone, kneeling, and standing positions. It will open up greater challenges and opportunities for competitive shooting events.

The Air Training Corps has always been well represented and has shown a high degree of marksmanship at the Cadet Inter Services Skill at Arms Competition held at Bisley every year.

The CCRS (Council for Cadet Rifle Shooting) promote and supervise major Postal Shooting Competitions for the Cadet Forces and the Combined Cadet Force. These small bore competitions allow shooting to be part of the training syllabus throughout the year.

NOTE: Skill at Arms and Shooting are not included in this Pocket Book but the subject is fully covered in **The Cadet Force Skill at Arms & Shooting Pocket Book** - see details www.milpkbk.co.uk.

Corporate Communications

This Department led by a MOD Information Officer and their staff have access to RAF Photographers. This team is responsible for producing Publicity Material for the organisation, providing information requested by the media and internal communications. Your Air Cadet Magazine is also produced by this team.

Physical Education (ATC)

The team in this department include the staff based at the two Corps National Adventure Training Centres at Llanbedr in Wales and Windemere in the Lake District. They arrange courses in outdoor activities to qualify adult staff and SNCO Cadets to national governing body approved standards.

The Department also arrange special Cadet courses for parachuting, hang gliding, offshore sailing, outward bound, Nordic skiing, basic winter training and community sports leaders.

Organising the major Corps sports events, schemes and competitions and advise the six Regional Physical Education Officers.

AIR CADET REGIONS

The UK is divided into six Regions, each Regon is controlled by a Group Captain who is a Retired Officer and is referred to as the Regional Commandant, who is assisted by a Regional Staff Officer (RSO) and civilian Staff

AIR CADET WINGS

Each Region is divided into a number of Wings which cover one or more Counties. Wings are controlled by a Wing Commander based at Wing Headquarters. Staff who are responsible for the many Squadrons and Detached Flights report to the OC of their respective Wing. The Wing Commander is directly responsible to the Regional Commandant for the command, discipline, training and the efficiency of the units in the Wing. See 'wiring diagram on page 1-7.

GENERAL INFORMATION

Wing Staff Officer (WSO) is the direct link between your Squadron and the Wing HQ, apart from their normal 'staff duties they may also carry out specific roles such as Training Officer (Trg Off), Physical Education Officer (PEdO}, Corporate Communications Officer (CCO), or Adventure Training Technical Officer (WATTO)

AIR CADET WING LOCATIONS

Glasgow & West Scotland Wing
The Cadet Centre 65 Hawkshead Road Paisley PA 10 3NE
Tel: 0141 887 311 1
Kent Wing
Yeomanry Cottages Boxley Rd Maidstone Kent ME14 2AP
Tel: 01622 754754188
South & West Yorkshire Wing
Air Training HQ Headfield Road Castleford WF 1 0 4SF
whq-swyorksaa @atc.raf.mod.uk
South & East Midlands Wing
Wittering , Peterborough PE6 6HB
Tel: 01780 783838 ext 7297
Welsh Wing
Building 29a RAF SU Sealand Welsh Road Deeside Flintshire CH5 2RD
TEL: 01244 847502 or 01244 847531
Dorset & Wilts Wing
RAF Boscombe Down Salisbury Wilts SP4 OJE
Te101980 622014

THE AIR CADET COUNCIL

The Air Cadet Council acts as an advisory group on all matters that will affect the well being of the Air Training Corps and of the cadets in particular.
All civilian committees, Wing Committees and Regional Councils are represented by the Air Cadet Council.
The Council meets twice a year under the presidency of the Parliamentary Under Secretary of State for Defence for the Armed Services.

AIR CADETS OVERSEAS

The ATC have Squadrons located overseas in Cyprus, Germany, and also in Gibraltar.
Over the years many cadets from the UK have visited ATC Squadrons in these locations and there is no reason why you should not be one of them in the future, provided you are up to the required standard to be selected.

GENERAL INFORMATION

WHERE YOU FIT INTO THE ORGANISATION

COMMANDANT AIR CADETS

CHIEF OF STAFF AIR CADETS

Wing Cmdr, Sqn Ldr, Fl Lt, Fl Sgt, Sgt, Civilian Admin Staff

CIVILIAN STRUCTURE

AIR CADET CHAPLAIN COMMITTEE

AIR CADET COUNCIL

REGIONAL HEADQUARTERS (6)

Group Captain

Sqn Ldr (Regional Admin Officer), Regional Staff Officers, Civilian Admin Staff

CIVILIAN STRUCTURE

CHAPLAINS COMMITTEE

REGIONAL COUNCIL

WING HEADQUARTERS

Wing Commander (Wg Cdr)

Sqn Ldr (Wing Admin Offr WgAdO), Wing Staff Offrs, Civilian Admin Staff.

CIVILIAN STRUCTURE

WING CIVILIAN COMMITTEE

CHAPLAINS COMMITTEE

SQUADRONS

Squadron Leader (Sqn Ldr)

Flight Lieutenant (Fl Lt)

ATC Positions: Adult Warrant Officer (AWO), Civilian Instructor (CI)
Cadet Positions: Cadet Warrant Officer (CWO), Flight Sergeant (F/Sgt), Sergeant (Sgt), Corporal (Cpl), Cadets, Probationers.

CIVILIAN STRUCTURE

Civilian Committee | Parents & Friends | Sqn Chaplain

GENERAL INFORMATION

WHO PAYS FOR THE RUNNING OF THE ATC?

The money to support the ATC comes from three sources:-
I. Ministry of Defence (Air).
2. The General Purpose Fund.
3. Squadron Welfare Fund

Ministry of Defence (Air)

This is known as Public Money and therefore can only be used for official purposes and is strictly audited every year.

Training, accommodation, and flying are paid for by this money. At squadron level it pays for your uniform, rent of your accommodation, community charge, electricity and repairs. Limits are put on the amount of Electricity your Squadron is allowed to consume, after which the Squadron has to pay,

A special grant called the 'Annual Grant' is paid to each squadron depending upon its performance and strength. This grant can only be spent on administration costs and the provision of approved training items.

GENERAL PURPOSE FUND (GP Fund)

As a cadet you will be paying your monthly subscription which is split into several parts as follows:-

I. A contribution to the General Purpose Fund.

2. A levy to the Squadron Welfare Fund.

3. A small levy to both Wing and Regional Welfare Funds.

The General Purpose Fund is controlled by trustees elected by the Air Cadet Council and pays for sports activities at Inter-Wing, Inter-Region and National Corps events.

Grants are also made to replace equipment at the Adventure Training establishments at Windermere in Cumbria and Llanbedr in Wales. The Squadron's Civilian Committee have their portion of the levy and use it within their Squadron for welfare projects.

The Wing spend their levy on the provision of hired sports facilities, sports kit and prizes/medals for contestants.

Region use their portion of the levy for the provision of Adventure Training Equipment.

IMPORTANCE OF YOUR SUBSCRIPTIONS

From the information above you will now see how important it is for every cadet to pay their weekly subs. It might not seem to be very important to you as an individual, but when you multiply it by all the cadets in the Corps it will add up to a useful amount.

GENERAL INFORMATION

AIR CADET SQUADRON

When you join the ATC you will no doubt become a member of a Squadron, this is the most important basic "unit" of the Corps throughout the country, as it is where you - the cadet - is to be found. It is normally commanded by an officer of the **Royal Air Force Volunteer Reserve (Training Branch) (RAFVR(T))** whose rank is that of a Flight Lieutenant.

If the Squadron has more than 130 cadets the officer commanding would be a Squadron Leader.

Other adult instructors will form the staff of your squadron. Civilian instructors are also appointed to the ATC, they are people who will have a particular skill while serving and instruct cadets in that particular discipline or skill.

SQUADRON CIVILIAN COMMITTEE

Each Squadron has a civilian committee comprising of five members of whom the Chairman, Honorary Secretary and Honorary Treasurer are to be elected officers of the Committee. The Squadron Commander and the Honorary Chaplain will be additional members.

Other members, are people from your community, such as a member from your local Royal Air Force Association Branch Committee, parents of some cadets and representatives from other organisations involved with youth and citizenship training, such as the Education Authority, local Police, Fire Brigade.

Your Squadron programme involving non-service type activities will have been sponsored by your Civilian Committee. No doubt there will be many occasions when you are helping at events planned by them to raise funds for the Squadron.

This committee does a great deal of work on behalf of their cadets. This does not only apply to raising funds, but in assisting your Squadron Commander to run an efficient squrdron, such as finding extra instructors, getting good publicity, building good relations with the community, helping with welfare problems, finding local projects for the cadets, assisting with the Duke of Edinburgh Award, providing adventure training equipment and many more. They will always rely on your support in their projects.

GENERAL INFORMATION

THE ENROLMENT CEREMONY

The first few weeks you parade at your Squadron you will take part in your Basic Training. Providing you attend regularly, you will be ENROLLED in about six to eight weeks. You are then officially allowed to wear the Cap Badge of the Corps.

The Enrolment Ceremony is personal to the Cadets taking part. Usually not more than two cadets are enrolled at a time. It is not a photo opportunity for the PRO or local press to be involved in a publicity stunt, it is very much a personal matter for all the Cadets. The format of the Enrolment Ceremony varies, but usually your OC will have invited your parents or guardians, and possibly the Padre to help officiate in the ceremony.

Normally, each Cadet being enrolled has two friends from the Squadron who are appointed as his/her 'sponsors'. They will help you through this milestone in your Cadet career. The Enrolment Ceremony serves as a reminder to the other Cadets of their commitments to their Squadron and the ATC.

RESPONSIBILITY FOR STANDARDS

Your understanding of personal resonsibility for standards is part of your development as a cadet and as a member of the Corps, you will be expected to maintain constant high standards, if standards should fall then you wll be reminded of your commitment to the unit.

EXPECTATIONS OF YOUR OFFICER COMMANDING

The following notes deal with some of the expectations of your Squadron Commander. You must remember at all times that all adults like you, are volunteers, their hobby, again like yours, is the Air Training Corps.

They can run a good squadron if you all work together as a team, bearing in mind that you and they will also have other interests and commitments to work, school, family etc.

THEY WILL EXPECT YOU TO :-

Attend parades at least twice a week or let your OC know if you are not able to attend.

Be on time - five minutes before parade.

Be smartly turned out both in uniform and in your normal clothes.

Read and comply with notices and orders put up on the notice board.

GENERAL INFORMATION

Obey orders - if they seem to be unfair, obey them and complain afterwards.

Have good manners , behave as would be expected of a cadet.

Treat with respect other peoples property, prevent damage and vandalism.

Have a smart bearing, when in uniform wear it correctly at all times.

Keep yourself fit, play and work hard, take part in organised sports and games.

Clean up behind you, put things away - be tidy, don't rely on others to clear up for you.

Never be afraid of doing more than you've have been asked to do.

(Try to be a full and active member) of the squadron - whenever events, parades, weekend exercises are planned or the time of the year gets round to Annual Camp - remember that a lot of people from your Wing Commander to your own officers and instructors have put a lot of time into planning your programme, especially Annual Camp.

It has all been organised for your benefit. This means that if your OC is to rely upon your support as a member of the squadron, you will be expected to take an active part in the life of the squadron and make the progress required of you.

Help others who may be less able than you - especially new recruits.

Bring in new members when the squadron is open to recruit, be sure that you are credit to the Corps.

ANNUAL CAMP

For many years the Air Training Corps and the Combined Cadet Force have enjoyed the training camps provided by the Ministry of Defence. Annual Camp has always been the highlight of the cadet year.

You should always make a special effort to attend. It is a time when all the training you have received during the year is put into practice, by taking part in exercises and expeditions. You will be a full time Cadet for the duration of camp and is an ideal opportunity to make new friends and learn new skills.

Another opportunity Annual Camp offers you is the chance to be in a very different part of the country, perhaps for the first time in your life. Try and find out as much as you can, what the area is famous for, what is made there, local customs and history.

Many wings, depending upon the location of the camp have open days, when parents and friends visit the camp. The day is often planned as a

GENERAL INFORMATION

Sports Day, with demonstrations and displays, many of which are organised by the Cadets. Some events are set up to involve visitors to make it an entertaining day.

WHEN AT CAMP DO NOT:-

1. Drop litter anywhere. Leave your dirty plates on the meal table.
2. Ensure you leave toliets and sinks clean for others to use.
3. Behave as you would be expected as a member of the Air Cadet.
4. Hitch-Hiking in uniform is not allowed.
5. Touch or pick up strange objects on a training area, report anything you find out of the normal to your instructors.

EN ROUTE TO CAMP - DO NOT:-

1. Leave litter, sweet wrappings, drink cans, or any other rubbish on coaches or transport, you only have to clean it up later.
2. Disobey instructions or orders given to you by your instructors.
4. Cause problems for any of the staff who are transporting you to your camp.

WHEN AT CAMP DO THE FOLLOWING:-

1. Read all orders daily and comply with them.
2. If the facilities are provided for safe keeping of your cash, you must use it as set out in your camp instructions.
3. Lock you locker with a secure padlock.
4. Ensure you maintain a healthy diet while at camp, this can cause health problems which can spoil your time away..
5. If you are not feeling well see your instructor who will tell you how to get medical help.
6. Ensure you uniform is pressed and clean daily, if washing facilities are available at Camp use them it will save your taking home dirty laundry.
6. Do your fair share of cleaning of your living and sleeping area.
7. When doing duties your been tasked to do, don't whinge and whine as they have to be done.
8. Phone or text home to let your parents/guardian know you ok and enjoying yourself.

GENERAL INFORMATION

9. Help others - especially those who are at Annual Camp for the first time.
10. Be polite to the people you meet, especially the civilian staff and those who help to run the canteens etc.
11. Be security and safety conscious at all times, be alert, report any suspicious activity or event.
12. If you are ever in doubt about anything while at camp always talk to your adult instructors

MEDICAL CERTIFICATE

You will be given a Medical Certificate for your parent/guardian to complete and sign before you go to annual camp. Procedures vary; you may have to hand it back to your Squadron Commander, or hand it to the Adult in charge of your coach. (See page 1-20 for example of a Certificate) The reason for this form being a requirement is that the Ministry of Defence cannot entertain certain risks and these must be eliminated by regulations, for example:

1. Condition - Epilepsy. Not allowed to undertake such activities as Rock Climbing, Swimming, Shooting, Canoeing, Orienteering, and Expeditions in Wild Country etc.
2. Condition - Asthma. Whether or not they are receiving any form of therapy is not allowed to undertake activities involving strenuous activity.
3. Condition - Diabetes. Those dependent on Insulin, treatment may not undertake activities involving irregular meals or long periods of exertion.
4. Condition - Heart problems. These are of such a variable nature that a cadets' medical practitioner must judge them individually. Should any doubts exist on a Cadets' ability to undertake all the activities listed below, a doctor should be consulted by the parent or guardian before the certificate is signed.

EXAMPLES OF PHYSICAL & SPORTING ACTIVITIES

Rock Climbing, Canoeing, Hang Gliding, Hill Walking on Expeditions, Life Saving, Parachuting, Para ascending, Sailing, Rafting, Offshore and Windsurfing.
Skiing: Cross Country and Downhill, Water Skiing, Caving, Sub-Aqua Diving. Athletics, Boxing, Circuit Training, Cricket, Cross Country Running, Cycling, Mountain Biking, Football, Rugby, Hockey, judo, Orienteering, and Swimming.

GENERAL INFORMATION

THE CADET AND THE COMMUNITY

A part of the Aims of the Air Training Corps reads:
"To foster the spirit of adventure and develop qualities of leadership and good citizenship".
As an individual, a Cadet, you are a citizen. You live in this country, in your own town, city or village. You have family, friends and are part of the community you live in. Every community depends upon people who are prepared to work towards making it a better place to live. During your training, depending on how your Squadron staff plans it, you should be taking part in various projects and activities in your local community. If you are taking part in the Duke of Edinburgh's Award Scheme, you may chose to undertake community project work as part of your award.
Getting involved in the community can often be difficult and demanding, but it can also be great fun and very rewarding.
You may find that you continue working in the community long after you have left the Air Training Corps.

INSURANCE

You will be aware that your parents will have your home, furniture, television, video camera and a whole host of other items insured. If you have a Motor Cycle or a Car it is a legal requirement to have it insured — just incase you have an accident.
Most sports clubs, youth organisations and others all have "insurance cover" for their members, usually while taking part in club activities etc. It is costly to provide insurance cover, but you would be very foolish to belong to an organisation that did not have proper insurance cover for their members.
The Air Training Corps has an insurance scheme for their cadets, **but read carefully the important notice below.**

INSURANCE COVER.
THE ATC INSURANCE SCHEME.
ALL CADETS ARE COVERED BY PERSONAL ACCIDENT INSURANCE
"WHILST ENGAGED ON OFFICIAL ATC ACTIVITIES OR WHILST
TRAVELLING TO & FROM SUCH ACTIVITIES".
THIS INSURANCE IS FREE TO ALL CADETS AND PROBATIONERS.
FULL DETAILS OF THE COVER PROVIDED ARE CONTAINED
IN A BOOKLET ENTITLED "AIR TRAINING CORPS
INSURANCE SCHEMES" A COPY OF THIS IS AVAILABLE
FOR YOU TO READ IN YOUR SQUADRON.
MAKE YOURSELF FAMILIAR WITH IT
- IT IS FOR YOUR PERSONAL BENEFIT.

GENERAL INFORMATION

YOUR WELFARE AND SAFETY

The purpose of the following information is to make you aware of what laws there are for your protection and how they are put into action.

Welfare

The Children Act 2004
This Act is designed to ensure that children (up to the age of 16 years) and young persons (up to the age of 18 years) are treated properly.

What does it mean within the ATC?

Firstly, it means that Adults who express an interest in working with the Cadets are vetted to try and prevent people who might wish to harm young persons physically or mentally from joining the ATC
Secondly, it means that the adults in the ATC must think at all times of your welfare and safety. It is termed "Duty of care".
How does this work? There are systems and procedures in place on a Wing or Squadron level that provide a 'listening ear' for any problems there may be. It is confidential, but you should be aware that serious problems will be passed on to trained personnel for further action.

What do you do?

If something has happened that makes you feel really bad, share it; talk to an Officer or Adult Instructor you get on well with, it is pretty certain that they will have experienced something similar.

- If you feel that you are not being treated properly, talk to a person you can trust. Be truthful, enlarging on the truth will not help you.

- In your cadet activities, there could be some training that you feel you just cannot cope with; you know you will fail. Give it your best, you've tried and that is not failing.

GENERAL INFORMATION

SAFETY

All Officers and Adult Instructors have to comply with official safety requirements. There are strict safety rules all cadet activities. If these rules are followed, the risk of someone being injured is reduced. Failure to follow the safety rules can lead to disciplinary action and possibly court proceedings particularly if someone is injured.

How does this work?

Your Training Syllabus contains safety training where required. When you are out on exercise, there are briefings to inform you of how, what, when and where. Before you receive your briefing, the Adult Instructors and Officers have carefully planned the activity and have had their briefings, including the safety aspects.

What do you do?

- Remember your safety rules ALWAYS follow them

- Watch the more junior Cadets, ensure they follow the safety rules

- Listen, (take notes if necessary), when you have your briefing

- Do not fool around at the wrong time

- Know the telephone numbers of your Squadron Commander and all other Adult Instructors in your Squadron your Wing Commander and the Cadet Wing Headquarters.

- When out on exercise - the mobile numbers to call in an emergency, a Route Card with estimated timings and map references.

If you were to decide to organise an expedition or exercise WITHOUT AUTHORITY and as a result someone is injured, they would NOT be covered by insurance - the best advise is don't do it

---

GENERAL INFORMATION

"WHO'S WHO" IN YOUR WING & SQUADRON

It is an essential part of your knowledge as an efficient cadet to know the names and ranks of your officers and instructors. The next two pages are to record the names and ranks of those Wing and Squadron officers and instructors that you will come into contact with during your cadet career. It is advisable to write this information in **Pencil**, as appointments change quite frequently.

SQUADRON STAFF APPOINTMENTS

Appointment	Name	Rank
Officer Commanding		
Adjutant		
Warrant Officer		
Equipment Officer		
Training Officer		
D of E Officer		
Squadron Padre		

GENERAL INFORMATION
WING STAFF APPOINTMENTS

Appointment	Name	Rank
Wing Commandant		
Wing Staff Officer		
Wing Supply Officer		
Wing Training Officer		
Wing Shooting Officer		
Wing D of E Award Officer		
Wing Medical Officer		
Wing Padre (C of E)		
Wing Padre (RC)		
Wing Padre (other denominations)		
Wing Public Relations Officer		
Wing Warrant Officer		

ANNUAL CAMP KIT CHECK LIST

COMBAT TROUSERS	
COMBAT JACKET	
SHIRTS TWO	
JUMPER	
BUNGEES (6)	
BRASSARD	
BERET	
BELT - WORKING	
BOOTS & CLEANING KIT	
THICK SOCKS (AT LEAST 3 PAIRS)	
SPORTS KIT (INCLUDING SWIM KIT)	
TROUSER ELASTICS (TWO SETS)	
KNIFE, FORK, SPOON AND MUG	
CIVVIES	
WASHING KIT (INCLUDING SHAMPOO & SOAP)	
HAIR GRIPS, SCRUNCHIES, HAIRNETS, MAKE UP ETC.	
TOWELS (1 LARGE, 1 HAND)	
PILLOW SLIP	
UNDERWEAR	
WASHING POWDER/LIQUID (WRAP TO PREVENT LEAKS)	
POCKET NOTEBOOK AND PENCILS	
NEEDLE AND COTTON	
STRONG PADLOCK AND 2 KEYS	
WEBBING	
TORCH	
SCISSORS AND STRING	
POCKET MONEY	
PERSONAL FIRST AID KIT	
ANY MEDICATION YOU MAY NEED	
YOUR FFI (Free From Infection~FORM (Duly Signed)	
GIRLS - Toiletries	
BOYS - Toiletries	

Example of *Free From Infection Form (FFI) Reduced in size*

Billet No .... Flight ....

| Administration |
| Purposes |

Name ....Age .... Date of Birth ....

Address ....

.... Post Code .... Tel No ....

Next of Kin: Name .... Tel No ....

Address..

Other Contact: Name .... Tel No ....

Address ....
Does the above named have any known conditions e.g., Asthma,

allergies etc. ....

Are they allergic to penicillin .... or Surgical Plasters ....

Are they a vegetarian .... Allergic to any particular food ....

Any other allergies ___._____

Name and dosage of prescribed medications the cadet will have······

brought with him/her _____

Name of Cadets General Practitioner ....

Surgery Address .... Tel No ....
This is to certify that my Son/Daughter/Ward has not been in
contact with any infectious diseases) during the previous two weeks.
I also certify that I have read the above information and answered
the questions correctly.

Signed ....

Dated .... Parent/Guardian (Please delete as appropriate)

BADGES OF RANK

ROYAL AIR FORCE

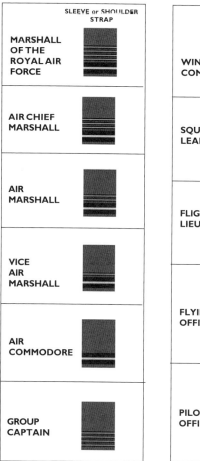

SLEEVE or SHOULDER STRAP

MARSHALL OF THE ROYAL AIR FORCE

AIR CHIEF MARSHALL

AIR MARSHALL

VICE AIR MARSHALL

AIR COMMODORE

GROUP CAPTAIN

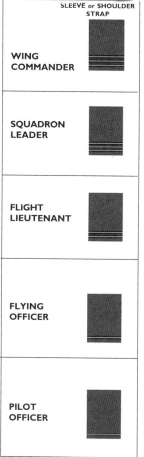

SLEEVE or SHOULDER STRAP

WING COMMANDER

SQUADRON LEADER

FLIGHT LIEUTENANT

FLYING OFFICER

PILOT OFFICER

SELF TEST QUESTIONS

1. When was the first Air Cadets Pocket Book published?
2. Are your Officers and Instructors full-time employed in the ATC?
3. What is the training you do in your first few weeks as a Recruit?
4. When do you get 'Enrolled' and what does it mean to you?
5. How soon can you wear your beret badge?
6. What does your beret badge represent?
7. At the enrollment ceremony who will have been invited?
8. What are 'sponsors' and what is their purpose?
9. What should the enrollment ceremony mean to other Cadets?
10. What is important to you personally about the ceremony?
11. What are the aims of the Air Training Corps?
12. How does your Squadron support your community?
13. What is the main purpose of the Children Act 2004?
16. If you have a problem who do you report it to?
17. You will often be briefed on safety procedures, whose telephone numbers should you know?
18. Why is your FFI Form important for going to camp?
19. As a Cadet, when are you NOT insured for accidents or injury?
20. What is the form when travelling to camp by coach or public transport?
21. There are some Rules about being at Camp what you should do, make a list of them?
22. Is it wise to use an Annual Camp Kit Check List?

Chapter 2

AIR CADET TRAINING

STAGES OF TRAINING

The training syllabus is designed for you to be able to fulfil the aims of the Corps.

First Class Cadet Training

Training at this stage is to enable you to learn how to look after and correctly wear your uniform and to show your officers and instructors that you are becoming interested in all activities in the Squadron and taking part in them.

Leading Cadet Training

Taking between six and nine months, your training at this stage widens your interest in aviation subjects and introduces you to your first practical projects.

Senior Cadet Training

Your training now starts to take on some of the more technical aspects, and over a period of six to nine months your instructors will take you through specific aviation subjects to be studied. You will also continue with your project work.

Staff Cadet Training

Designed to cover a period of six to nine months, this level of training on its successful completion, should see you helping to run the Squadron under the supervision of your Squadron officers. You will be expected to take on some measure of responsibility for various activities within the Squadron. As a Staff Cadet you will wear a yellow lanyard.

AVIATION SUBJECTS

Training in Aviation subjects are a compulsory part of your training and includes training in general service subjects. They cover a wide range of skills and knowledge, many of a technical nature.

PROJECTS

Projects are a compulsory part of your training which you start at the Leading Cadet Level. It is important to note that your OC will not be allowed to enter you for your written examination in the Aviation subjects of each stage until a minimum of twenty five hours has been devoted to Project work in either one or a combination of subjects has

AIR CADET TRAINING

been completed. Projects are a part of the Duke of Edinburgh Award Scheme, and provided you have entered the scheme correctly, and your Project is acceptable, then it could count towards your award.

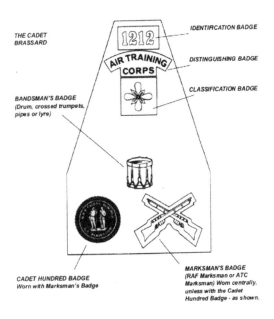

THE CADET BRASSARD

IDENTIFICATION BADGE

DISTINGUISHING BADGE

CLASSIFICATION BADGE

BANDSMAN'S BADGE
(Drum, crossed trumpets, pipes or lyre)

CADET HUNDRED BADGE
Worn with Marksman's Badge

MARKSMAN'S BADGE
(RAF Marksman or ATC Marksman) Worn centrally, unless with the Cadet Hundred Badge - as shown.

AIR CADET TRAINING

THE CADET NCO
Duties and Responsibilities.

Initially as a Cadet NCO you must learn how to instruct the basic subjects you have been taught and also how to take command and control a squad of cadets.

With other NCOs in the squadron you are responsible to your Squadron Commander to assist with the organisation and smooth running of the squadron at the level of your rank.

As a part of your training you will be given specific duties and responsibilities with authority to carry out the tasks allotted to you. Be sure they are carried out correctly.

Remember - with authority goes responsibility

As you progress and are promoted, you will be given additional responsibilities which are yours at all times, both on and off parade, even when engaged in other activities where cadets are involved or it is known that you represent the Air Training Corps.

You will be directly responsible to your Squadron Commander and at the same time be responsible to your OC for the Cadets in your squadron.

To become an NCO not only must you have a good knowledge of the training syllabus subjects, but you must be able to instruct correctly to others, holding their interest and earning their respect.

Every cadet has the opportunity to earn promotion. The skills and ability you require can only be developed by training and practice through the cadet ranks during your time in the Corps.

DELEGATION OF RESPONSIBILITY.

For you to be an effective Cadet NCO - no matter what rank you hold, will require a great amount of understanding and skill on the part of your Officers and Civilian Instructors.

It is very difficult to understand, but it does mean that those adults in your squadron will have to have had the training and experience for them to be prepared to share some of their authority in `running the squadron'.

This is not as bad as it sounds, what it means is that they must be seen to give you the backing or authority to carry out tasks within the squadron, to leave you alone to no doubt make mistakes, but at the same time to start on the ladder of promotion.

AIR CADET TRAINING

Once this is done — it's up to you to prove they made the right decision in promoting you. Only if you have the right qualities and the ability to develop and use them will you be successful.

SOME OF THE ESSENTIAL QUALITIES ARE:-

Loyalty and pride in the Corps , your Wing, and Squadron.

Enthusiasm in all that you do and your cadets imitate you, copying your good example.

Help and encourage those who you are responsible for.

A good Sense of humour — especially when things go wrong.

Knowledge of your subject - giving others confidence in your ability.

Initiative to always have your cadets doing something interesting/ active.

Instructional ability — always having well prepared and planned activities.

Disciplinary powers — ability to control Junior NCO's, who with the cadets perform tasks correctly and to the standards set by you.

Physical fitness - as a leader to set the example from the front, making allowances for those not as old or fit as you.

Appearance - you must maintain the highest standard of personal turnout.

Ensure that you and others maintain the Air Training Corps image in "the eye of the public" — as others see the ATC — such as:-

Good Manners, be an influence on and insist that others have good behaviour and manners in the Squadron, public places, especially on public transport, in shopping precincts etc.

Be helpful, efficient, alert, well turned out, both on and off duty.

Have patience with those that are 'slow' to learn.

Encourage your cadets to 'get on', to take an active part in the Squadron.

Not lacking in responsibility to bring before your OC or Squardon Warrant Officer any cadet(s) or NCOs who are in breach of established good conduct and discipline.

AIR CADET TRAINING

BULLYING

Most of us have been subjected to bullying at one time or another. It is a duty of every individual to immediately report any form of bullying that comes to their notice.

You will often find that the issuing of `threats' or `promises' in one form or another is a common method of bullying.

The constant `picking' on an individual makes them very unhappy, they **are** being bullied, they feel threatened and leave, taking with them all those bad feelings about the Corps.

You must never `turn a blind eye' to BULLYING, no matter what rank or age you are, YOU have a responsibility to bring it to the notice of more senior ranks, don't take no for an answer, don't stop until the bully has ceased.

ABOVE ALL - DON'T TAKE ANY ACTION YOURSELF — OR WITH OTHERS.

FIRST PROMOTION

When you first get your Corporal stripes, it is a milestone in your cadet career. You MAY think you have arrived, and as a result are inclined to throw your weight about, the first to know about it are your mates who yesterday were quite happy to have a laugh with you, but today - you are a Corporal and they seem to be less friendly.

This could mean that they respect your promotion, now you have to get their confidence to prove that you are worthy of it.

So now would be a good time to consider some of the actions and failings of **bad cadet NCOs.**

Be sure you **Do Not** follow their example.

1. Intimidate individuals by shouting at them, especially if standing close up to them face to face.

2. Making personal contact (touch) an individual when addressing them.

3. Use foul language or offensive remarks to an individual, or make threats of what might become of them.

4. Make an example of an individual, such as punishing them without due cause or reason.

5. Using first names when `On Parade'. Difficult, but when `ON PARADE' be `ON PARADE', when `OFF PARADE', then be `OFF PARADE'.

AIR CADET TRAINING

6. Borrowing money or ask favours of cadets.
7. Keep `picking' on an individual in front of others. If they are persistently disruptive, then let to your Squadron Warrant Officer or OC discipline them.
8. Not sharing duties or `chores' fairly, not having a `duty roster' displayed.
9. Being late with orders/information in time for all to respond.
10. Asking cadets to clean, press etc, personal kit or equipment.
11. Not read Orders, un-informed of programme, duties and events, not aware of standing orders.
12. Fails to check untidy cadets and or their rooms.
13. Is always late for parades and duties.
14. Puts off dealing with complaints and problems immediately reported to them.
15. Does not give any encouragement or praise for good work.
16. Passes on responsibilities to others, lacks personal discipline.
17. Fails to report, serious breaches of conduct and discipline, drugs, smoking, theft, cadet out of bounds, security, safety, etc.
18. Sets a bad example by untidy appearance in their own clothes.
19. Mannerisms or bad habits, always saying "OK" or "RIGHT" after a sentence, pulling your ear or scratching your nose, etc.

You will think of many other points to add to the list of **'DON'TS'**, so long as you are **NOT** guilty of them, you may - hopefully, with experience - become a **GOOD NCO.**

YOUR EXAMPLE

If you are to become an NCO, then discipline - *SELF DISCIPLINE* - is your guide.

Your self-respect, self control, sense of purpose and pride in your ability to do properly what ever you do, will ensure that you become reliable and efficient.

Discipline is the pride that we should have in ourselves and "our team" and the fear that by not carrying out orders and instructions to the best of our ability - we will be letting down our own high standards and also our friends.   Surely discipline is something to be proud of.

AIR CADET TRAINING

OPPORTUNITY for PROMOTION

Now that you have read the previous paragraphs in this section, you will realise that qualifications in themselves are not qualifications in self discipline, pride, respect etc, although it will have helped you to become disciplined in the learning of those subjects

You will have an opportunity to be trained as an Instructor in the Methods of Instruction, and later attend the Senior NCO's Leadership course at Frimley Park and other courses, but these alone will not make you a good NCO. With practice you may become a very good instructor, with experience and practice you will develop all the qualities and skills which will go towards making up your character as a person, it is something that you will have to develop.

Only you will know how well you are performing by the way that others respond and the results you are able to achieve with them.

Watch and listen to all those that you come in contact with who are considered to be good NCOs; are they GOOD NCOs and GOOD INSTRUCTORS, or are they JUST good instructors.

You must learn how to judge the difference, to help you gain experience making sure you are a good NCO as well as being a good instructor.

PROMOTION

It is recognised that promotion must be related to your qualifications, as well as your ability, plus the recommendation of your Officer Commanding and Instructors, they will have been watching your development during your time in the Squadron.

They will be considering you and asking themselves *"is this really the sort of cadet we want to be one of our NCOs"*, like so many things, you will find out — it's down to you.

PROMOTION IS NEVER AUTOMATIC

To become a CORPORAL you would normally be expected to have passed your Senior Cadet exam.

To become a SERGEANT or FLIGHT SERGEANT you would normally be expected to have passed your Senior Cadet exam.

To become a CADET WARRANT OFFICER you would normally be expected to have passed your Staff Cadet exam.

You will always have to achieve the standards required and more importantly be selected by your Squadron Commander for ranks up to Flight Sergeant and your Wing Commander for appointment as a Cadet Warrant Officer.

AIR CADET TRAINING

Promotion is always a very important 'milestone' in your life, especially your first promotion.

Most ATC Wings run promotion courses similar to the RAF, and are called **NCO Courses.**

They are usually organised over a weekend when potential NCOs are brought together and given the opportunity of showing how they have developed, not only in their skills, but to see how they behave, if they have any manners, the example they set and if they can gain the respect of those working with them.

This usually follows the form of; planning and taking lessons, command exercises, lecturettes, leadership exercises and other activities.

Those cadets who take part always say it's great fun and a good method for their instructors to find out their strengths and weaknesses, also to see how you behave under different conditions, before making a final decision as to your suitability as an NCO.

If you have a chance to go on an NCO COURSE - jump at it

THE FUTURE OFFICERS and INSTRUCTORS

Many Cadets having reached the age of 20 (or 22 in the case of a Cadet Warrant Officer) apply to stay on in the Air Training Corps as an adult CIVILIAN INSTRUCTOR or (CI).

After service as a CI, providing there is an established vacancy, and providing you meet the criteria on maturity, smartness and age, you may be considered for appointment as an ADULT WARRANT OFFICER (or AWO).

Similarly, if you are suitable and there is an established vacancy, you may be eligible to apply for appointment as an OFFICER by being awarded a Queens Commission in the Royal Air Force Volunteer Reserve (Training Branch).

AIR TRAINING CORPS SYLLABUS OF TRAINING

FIRST CLASS CADET	LEADING CADET	SENIOR CADET	STAFF CADET
BASIC TRAINING Eight subjects: APC31-1 Air Training Corps APC31-2 The Royal Air Force. APC31.3 The Rifle. APC31.4 In tial Expedition Trg APC31.6 Communications. APC32.1 Map Reading APC 33.1 History of Flight. APC34.1 Airmanship I First Aid (optional)	Three Subjects ACP 32.2 Basic Navigation ACP 32.4 Principles of flight ACP 34.2 Airmanship 2 Note: Additionally, ACP35 Vol 2 (Communications Manual) may be studied whilst preparing for Leading Cadet. It is NOT part of the Leading Cadet exam.	Two subjects chosen from : ACP32.1 Air Navigation ACP32.4 Pilot Navigation ACP33.3 Propulsion ACP33.4 Airframes ACP34.2 Aircraft Handling ACP34.3 Operational Flying APC35.3 AdvRadio & Radar APC35.4 Satellite Communications	Two different subjects chosen to Senior Cadet from : ACP32.1 Air Navigation ACP32.4 Pilot Navigation ACP33.3 Propulsion ACP33.4 Airframes APC34.2 Aircraft Handling APC34.3 Operational Flying ACP35.3 Adv Radio & Radar APC35.4 Satellite Comms
RANGE COURSES Initial course followed by annual continuation courses throughout all stages in accordance with ACTI No 43.			
CITIZENSHIP TRAINING Training at and away from the Squadron Headquarters throughout all cadet service.	Examples: Talks Public Speaking Debating Visits to, Talks by, Demonstrations by Local Bodies eg Councils, Airport Authorities, Police, Fire and SENIOR CDT Ambulance Services, Coastguards. Organised Assistance to Local Establishments eg Hospitals, Children's Homes, Old People's Homes.		
EXTRA-MURIAL ACTIVITIES Training at ar d away from the Squadron Headquarters throughout a t cadet service.	Examples: Air Experience Flying Glider Pilot Training Familiarisation Gliding Annual Camps Opportunity Flights Overseas Flights LACE Visits Abroad Leadership Courses throughout all cadet service. Visits to Affiliated Stations Visits to the Aircraft Industry Adventure Training		
PROJECTS For each classification above First Class Cadet, at least 25 hours or projects selected by the Squadron.	Examples: Aircraft Recognition Aeromodelling Engineering Communications Band Training Building and Maintenance Projects Cockpit Trainers projects selected by the Squadron. Construction of Canoes, Hovercraft, Radios, Training Aids		

AIR CADET TRAINING

Self Test Questions

1. When and by whom was the first Banner presented to the Air Training Corps

2. What do you understand by being a MEMBER of your squadron.

3. When must you have a Medical Certificate.

4. When you get to camp, what must you do about your folks at home.

5. What type of Discipline do we have in the ATC.

6. How should you wear your uniform and when.

7. What must you read every day at camp.

8. For promotion to Corporal you would normally have passed your ...... exam.

9. As an NCO, what goes with authority.

10. When are you NOT insured for accident injuries.

11. You MUST be SAFETY and .... conscious at ALL TIMES.

12. As an instructor what is a 'mannerism'.

13. If an NCO uses bad language, what does he/she lose.

14. What are the Foundations of Good Relations.

15. At what `time' should you always be 'On Parade'.

16. When can you go on a Promotion Course.

17. What should you know about the area where your next Annual Camp is being held.

18. If given an order that seems unfair, what do you do about it.

Chapter 3

THE COMBINED CADET FORCE

ORGANISATION

The Combined Cadet Force (CCF) will be found operating in many of the larger schools which continue education to 17 years and above. Historically many of these schools had OTC (Officer Training Corps) that were formed before and during the first world war.

They changed the name of OTC's early in the 1939-45 war to JTC's Junior Training Corps, this in turn was again changed to the CCF, Combined Cadet Force. During the early years of the war there was a need to have young men who were to be trained as air crew in the shortest possible time to meet the needs of the Royal Air Force and the Fleet Air Arm.

It was during this period that the Air Training Corps was established. Many of the schools already had Army and Naval Cadets, it was a natural development to form Air Cadet units in the schools.

The principal difficulty was to find sufficient volunteer teachers from the staff of the school to run the Corps for all three service disciplines. This has always been a problem and as a result some school CCF have suffered.

COMMAND & CONTROL

The AOC Air Cadets is responsible to the Director General Training (RAF) at the Ministry of Defence for the control of training within the RAF sections of the CCF. The policy for the development of the CCF is the responsibility of the Inter-Services Cadet Committee and is regulated by the Joint Cadet Executive.

THE COMBINED CADET FORCE

Located at Air Cadet Headquarters there is a CCF Branch with senior officers, who control a team of RAF liaison officers and senior NCO's who carry out a programme of visits to the schools on a regular basis. There are more than 245 schools that have CCF (RAF Sections).

As a cadet you may have to join the CCF at your school or it may be voluntary or in some cases optional, depending upon the school rules. The amount of time and the training activities carried out have to be fitted in with the general activities of the school and within the curriculum as decided by the school's Head Teacher.

The minimum number of cadets required to establish an RAF Section is twenty five, although a number of schools have over one hundred cadets in their units.

TRAINING PROGRAMME

Each service section within a school CCF share the same accommodation and equipment where applicable, giving each similar facilities and opportunities.

The training programme is similar to that of the Leading and Senior Cadet in the Air Training Corps.

The training carried out concentrates more time on leadership and adventurous training and less cover of the more academic subjects in the syllabus.

Flying training is carried out at thirteen different RAF Stations for Air Experience Flights, at the Air Cadets Central Gliding School and Volunteer Gliding Schools at different locations around the country. Membership of the CCF is open only to boys or girls who are pupils of the school.

Boys and girls join their school contingent and membership is usually voluntarily these days - because they enjoy, or think they will enjoy, a combination of the activities available. They will not initially focus too much on the qualities set out in the Charter, but ill have an awareness of the ultimate purpose of their training. A CCF Cadet has to leave the organisation on leaving school, typically at the age of 18.

CCF CORE ACTIVITIES

A central core of (activities now common to all three Service Sections, is laid down by the Joint Cadet Executive (it the Ministry of Defence at basic Proficiency level. These include drill without rifles), map reading, shooting and the safe handling of weapons, self-reliance training which in turn includes camp craft, first aid, knowledge of the

Country Code and a short camping expedition. Satisfactory completion of the Basic Pro-ficiency marks the progress from recruit to cadet.

ADVANCED PROFICIENCY

Thereafter, at Advanced Proficiency level, activities will be chosen from very flexible Service Syllabi which take account of the different factors which affect a Contingent's situation proximity to Sponsor units of the three Services, training areas, ranges, water, mountains and availability of school resources. Service, Adventurous and Duke of Edinburgh Award training are all authorised activities at this level.

DEVELOPMENT OPPORTUNITIES

It is certainly the case that mere participation in such activities will allow certain qualities to emerge but really a more deliberate and structured approach is needed. This involves the Contingent in creating and arranging the opportunities - such as exercises, camps and expeditions - which will provide the testing experiences required for assessment purposes at different levels, so that training and quality development are linked.

Matching a cadet to an appropriate challenge, graded for difficulty yet controlled for safety, is a worthy art form and the very stuff of Cadet Force officering! A cadet's progress should reflect in their promotion up the ladder of leadership.

SCHOOL SUPPORT and INPUT

The extent to which a Contingent can positively engage in the development of leadership potential - an educational process which of course runs parallel to other formative influences in a school, such as prefectorial duties, society official, team captain, etc - will differ considerable from one school to another, depending on resources, facilities time available, but the key factor is the number, expertise, and calibre of the Contingent officers.

Unless a Headmaster has on his staff enough teachers who are willing and - much better - keen to take on this sort of work in addition to their teaching commitments, then, in spite of support from the Services, a Contingent sooner or later start to fail in its obligation to the fulfillment of the CCF Charter, and hence to the concept of the 'educational partnership'.

THE COMBINED CADET FORCE

NATIONAL YOUTH MOVEMENT

The CCF is a part of the national youth movement in the United Kingdom and is administered by the Ministry of Defence. However, the CCF is not part of the Armed Forces and its members are not liable for service or compulsory training in the Armed Forces. (This does not absolve officers and School Staff Instructors from service if they have such a liability in other ways.)

By the turn of the century there was about 100 school cadet units, spurred on no doubt by the Boer War.

The War Office (MOD today) was however concerned at the serious shortage of officers for the Army. As a consequence, in 1908, the Officers Training Corps (OTC) was established with the senior division in the universities the junior division in schools.

Any school which could produce one officer and 30 cadets could form a contingent and 100 immediately did so. Meanwhile. the 'Volunteers' became the 'Territorial Army'.

World War I took a dreadful toll of the cadets, most of whom, with their officers, rushed to join up and many, including virtually complete ex-cadet battalions, perished on the Somme.

LARGE REPRESENTATION

CCF Contingents are to be found in 245 schools, of which some 50 are in the Maintained Schools Sector.

The earliest contingents date from 1860, but whatever their reason of origin as shooting clubs or as a school's response to menacing European rulers, from the Emperor Napoleon III to Hitler their current raison d'etre, more particularly since the ending of National Service in 1962, has been as a form of educational partnership between these schools and the Ministry of Defence.

STARTING A CCF CONTINGENT

For schools that wish to run a contingent, the Services Offer: uniform, weapons and ammunition, training advice and assistance in both Service und Adventurous Training forms, the loan of stores and equipment, transport, and finance covering per capita grant and pay for teacher-officers. They also offer, for both officers and cadets, various courses of instruction during the holidays of which the following are examples:

Royal Navy & Royal Marines Weapons, powerboats sailing, navigation, Submarine familiarisation.

THE COMBINED CADET FORCE

Army	Mechanical and automotivengineering, signals, electronics. cookery, first aid, parachuting and artillery.
Royal Air Force	Gliding, flying instruction, navigation.

If suitable - all cadets can be recommended for leadership courses. This consists, mainly of a positive acceptance on the part of the Headmaster to have a contingent in his school, coupled with an equally positive resolve to afford it the means, within reason of operating successfully.

This will certainly include:
The appointment of contingent commander
Help with persuading a number of teachers to become officers or assisting adults.
Authorising the time for cadet corce activities.
Providing accommodation and allowing use of school vehicles.
Giving the contingent a place in the school budget.
Better resourced schools or contingents of long standing will certainly wish to acquire the services of a School Staff Instructor (SSI) and currently about 150 schools do so.

THE VOLUNTARY SPIRIT

The Combined Cadet Force is a voluntary part-time force organised in schools and colleges, including sixth form colleges, which normally continue education to the age of 17 years or above.
Its organisation is based on the Contingent, which may consist of up to three Service Sections representing the Royal Navy, Army and Royal Air Force.
The activities of the School CCF are of course subject to the policy of the Headmaster who is responsible for:
1. Deciding whether or not there should be a CCF Contingent and, if so, what Service Sections should he/she included in it.
2. Nominating a Contingent Commander and, in consultation with the Contingent Commander, the officers in the Service sections.
3. Defining the policy for service in the CCF within the school curriculum.
4. The overall discipline of cadets whilst undertaking CCF training, although officers and adults in charge of training (including Regulars and others) will be responsible for the immediate discipline of cadets carrying out such training.

AIR SECTION FORMED

It was in the 1930s that the RAF or Air Sections first appeared. For the record, the Army, Cadet Force Association (ACFA) booklet 'The Cadet Story' 1860 - 1960 reported that in 1918 the Air Ministry proposed the setting up of special platoons of cadets to be instructed in RAF duties; was this perhaps the forerunner of the Air Training Corps (ATC)? As stated earlier, official records are few, but there is ample evidence of the existence of School Air Sections in the 1930's Combined Cadet Force

On page 10 of Volume I of the ATC Gazette of March 1941 it states that 'the Air Training Corps comes into being on February 1st and comprises the Air Defence Cadet Corps (ADCO) Squadrons, the University Air Squadrons and the Air Sections of the OTC.

In the Oundle's school magazine of 1938 the section on the OTC reports an 'RAF ' being set up to do RAF training through the medium of films and lectures given by the officers from No 11 FTS RAF Wittering, as part of a syllabus laid down the Air Ministry. Obviously there was a pre-war, officially supported and funded cadet organisation in schools solely devoted to RAF training.

The fullest account known of these early days of the RAF Sections is to be found in the publication 'A History of the First Hundred Years of Rugby School', in which it states the Air Section was formed in the Summer term of 1937 as part of an official plan to encourage schoolboys to take an interest in the work of the RAF.

ANNUAL CAMPS

On field days at annual camps, cadets were flown in Hind and Blenheim bombers. Perhaps those involved in providing cadet camps today would find it difficult to compete with the fun it must have been in 1937.

Each camp consisted of some 250 cadets from different CCF contingents and on each occasion the RAF produced 2 squadrons of Ansons (34 aircraft) for the whole week. The cadets were flown to a different aerodrome each day to demonstrations of the of the work of the various RAF Commands.

In 1948, the final parade was addressed by The Vicount Trenchard. Clearly the Service was prepared to go to considerable trouble to support and encourage membership of these Air Sections. As now there was a syllabus of training including Principles of Flight,

Navigation, Aircraft Recognition and Morse Code and, at the time, there were complaints that the syllabus was too academic.

SOMETHINGS HAVEN'T CHANGED

The Air Sections probably wore an Army OTC uniform but we know that Abingdon School Air Section wore an RAF armband, rather like a length of stable belt, with a crown and eagle.

It is clear, therefore, that there was, well before World War 2 RAF sponsored and RAF supported air cadet organization in the independent schools, which was running along similar lines to today's CCF(RAF).

Meanwhile outside the OTC schools, much was happening.

The formation of the Air Defence Cadet Corps (ADCC), in July 1938, in effect provided a foundation on which, 3 years later, the Air Training Corps was based. Some public schools, like Hele's, Exeter (now St Peters) formed ADCC units, which was given the number '13F'; others retained Air Sections. In 1941, Air Sections ADCC units joined together for the war years as ATC units.

OTHER CHANGES

Another change occurred on the outbreak of war. The name 'Officers training Corps' was abolished. The new title was Senior Training Corps' (STC) in the Universities and 'Junior training Corps' (JTC) in the schools.

After the war, the position of school cadets was rationalised. As a result, schools which had boys over the age of 17, with a minimum strength of 60 cadets, were invited to join the newly formed Combined Cadet Force, which started in 1948 with an initial CCF(RAF) strength of 3000.

AFFECTS OF THE POST WAR YEARS

The post-war years were not without their problems. The RAF's need for air-crew fell and many airfields regularly used by cadets were closed. The Flying Scholarship Scheme introduced in1950 introduced one of the most imaginative and far-sighted incentives that could be offered to a 17-year old. With annual camps in full swing, gliding courses and regular visits to parent stations, the Corps thrived. No record of this part of CCF(RAF) history, however short, would be complete without reference to that unique and well remembered device, the Primary Glider.

THE COMBINED CADET FORCE

The Volunteer Gliding Schools (VGS) had been using variety, of primary gliders for some years for slides and low hops prior to the 100 ft launch to qualify for the British Gliding Association 'A' Certificate. In 1952 Slingsby aviation started to produce 115 Type 38' Grasshopper'TX Mk1 primary gliders mainly for CCF (RAF) use. This was a very simple, robust structure consisting of a completely open fuselage and redundant wings and tail unit from earlier Type 7 Cadet Mk I gliders. Not every school was equipped.

An operating site had to be at least 150 yards long and 100 yards wide and a trained instructor had to be present. Oddly enough, the purpose of the Grasshopper was not to teach cadets to glide, but rather to develop a cadet's self discipline and leadership while introducing them to RAF procedures and 'inculcating air-mindedness' Whether it achieved its stated aims is not clear, but it was obviously great fun and was for all involved, not just the 'pilot', an excellent way to spend a summer's afternoon out of the classroom.

Launching a primary glider was indeed a team effort. Two teams of 6 cadets, each with a length of rubber bungee, would, on the word of command, walk forward each team moving left and right respectively from the line of flight, until the rubber was about twice its stretched length. All being well, the officer in charge would release the glider, no doubt his fingers crossed. There are no recorded serious injuries on the Grasshopper, but there were a few scares.

Following incidents with the Grasshopper it was established that structural defects had developed, consequently they were withdrawn from service.

VALUE OF CCF CONTINGENT TO SCHOOLS

Schools must provide leadership opportunities. The Corps has a vital role in this respect. Because the Corps is different from any other school activity it can provide you with other opportunities when you may find school endeavors unchallenging. Adventure Training takes up 40% of the syllabus which can lead the cadet into participating in the Duke of Edinburgh Award Scheme.

Time spent at annual camp, visiting service establishments are a tremendous experience for you.

What of the CCF today. The overall direction and policy for the ATC is set by the Tri-Service Inter Service Cadet Committee, the running of which falls to the Directorate of Reserve Forces and Cadets at the MOD.

THE COMBINED CADET FORCE

Purely RAF matters eg, syllabus content, camps and provision of flying resources are provided under the authority of AOC Air Cadets. The CCF RAF Sections across the country are managed by the CCF Branch at HQ Air Cadets.

CCF Cadets enjoy the same full range of activities provided for the ATC, but there is more emphasis on cadet responsibility, a fact reflected in the Staff Cadet ratio of 1:20 and the absence of Adult Warrant Officers and Civilian Instructors.

SELF TEST QUESTIONS

1. What changed its name to become the CCF.
2. Where are CCF contingents mostly based.
3. What constitutes the membership of a CCF contingent.
4. Who determines the policy controlling the CCF.
5. There are more than ??????? CCF/RAF contingents in the UK.
6. What is the minimum number of Cadets required to establish a CCF cadet contingent.
7. The CCF Air Cadets follow a similar training programme as who.
8. At what age does a CCF Cadet leave the CCF.
9. What is described as the core activities of the CCF Cadets.
10. What is the programme content of the CCF cadets 'Advanced Proficiency' training.
11. At what date were the earliest contingents known to have been formed.
12. Give examples of the various courses held during school holidays for officers and cadets organised by the:
    a. The Royal Navy and Marines.
    b, The Army,
    c. The Royal Air Force.
13. The CCF in a school are subject to the policy of the head Teacher. Describe the four areas of responsiblity they are answerable for.
14. When did the Air Ministry first propose setting up squadrons of cadets to be instructed in RAF duties.
15. What was the date that the Air Training Corps came into being.
16. At Annual Camps in 1937 Cadets were flown in what aircraft.
17. When was the year when Flying Scholarship was introduced.
18. What was the GRASSHOPPER used for.
19. Who sets the overall policy and direction of the Air Training Corps

Chapter 4

HISTORY OF THE AIR TRAINING CORPS

Like many youth organisations in the UK the early formation of the Air Training Corps was through the efforts of a few dedicated people, who could see the need to give young people the opportunity to experience the thrills of flying.

In late 1918 two men, one an ex Royal Flying Corps Flying Cadet Charlie Longman and the other an ex Air Mechanic Bob Weller both founded the Bournemouth Young Airmen's League. They were fortunate to have support of the then established Air League of the British Empire.

In 1929 it was decided to form a British Young Airmen's League and the aims of this were set out as below:-

"To create a national interest in aviation and to spread the gospel of "Airmindedness" among the younger generation.

The object of each squadron would be to imitate and practice the general routine of a civil aerodrome and the work carried out by squadrons of the Royal Air Force.

The members of each squadron to be classified so as to undertake various duties. By so doing each member would develop a feeling of importance and responsibility, and each squadron would become a useful unit.

Where possible gliding should be included. Members could be granted a distinguishing badge after passing certain "tests"

It was not until 1938 when the threat of an impending war was becoming more of a certainty, that the Air Defence Cadet Corps (ADCC) was formed under the guidance of the Air League of the British Empire.

The first squadron was formed at Leicester in July 1938.

The aim of the training was to "Train youths in all matters connected with aviation" and boys between 14 and 18 were allowed to join.

A squadron consisted of 100 boys, divided into flights of 25 and by the end of that year, only five months after, forty one new squadrons had been formed.

During 1939 more than 16,800 boys and 700 officers were members of the ADCC. The General Secretary of the ADCC was Air Commodore Chamier who devised the Motto "**Venture Adventure**" which we still use today.

HISTORY OF THE AIR TRAINING CORPS

The obvious advantage of having young men who had received some initial training in "all matters connected with aviation" was welcomed by the Royal Air Force and as a result a close working relationship developed.

Some of the more lucky cadets whose units were close to RAF stations carried out the first glider training.

By 1940 the ADCC was making such a contribution to the recruitment for the RAF that it was decided by the War Cabinet to establish an organisation on the widest basis to provide pre-entry training for candidates for aircrew and technical duties for both the RAF and the Fleet Air Arm.

FORMATION OF THE CORPS

As a result of this, the Air Training Corp was established. In **September 1940** there were 18,489 Cadets in the ADCC.

Throughout the war years the Air Training Corps became one of the most important pre-service training organisations providing the RAF with recruits who were "airminded" when they enlisted.

It was not an easy task for the many volunteer officers and instructors, who were all employed in their various jobs of "war work" during the day or night and then, as they do today, spent their spare time in training their cadets.

The Tiger Moth 7 as illustrated over page was familiar to cadets from the earliest days until replaced by the Chipmunk.

In the post war years there was a need to change the direction of the training and in 1947 by Royal Warrant the aims of the ATC were changed to include training in Citizenship, the promotion of sport and adventure activities.

In the same year exchange visits were started with Canadian cadets. Four lucky cadets accompanied the Royal Tour to South Africa.

1948 a major policy change was made to improve Glider Training by the introduction of the 2 seater Slingsby T21B called the Sedbergh enabling Cadets to receive instruction when flying.

1949 due to the fact that many cadets wanted to fly The Flying Scholarship was introduced taking 250 Cadets a year and training them to the standard of Private Pilot licence.

Throughout the following ten years a great deal of reorganisation of the training and administration took place.

As a result of this it established the future role of the Air Training Corps and many new ATC Wings were formed.

HISTORY OF THE AIR TRAINING CORPS

TIGER MOTH 7

The Territorial Army Volunteer Associations (now named Reserve Forces & Cadet Association) across the country took over the responsibility for the provision and maintenance of those ATC buildings not on RAF stations.

In **1953** His Royal Highness Prince Phillip, the Duke of Edinburgh became the Air Commodore in Chief. During this same year the new Training Syllabus was introduced.

In **1955** it was proposed that control and administration of the ATC would be passed from Home Command to a Commandant directly responsible to the Air Ministry.

It was also proposed that there should be a revision of training methods, the issue of battledress for cadets and better facilities for Air Experience Flights.

During **1957** the ATC were the first to have cadets awarded the Duke of Edinburgh Award Gold and Silver Awards. By 1957

In the same year it was decided that the corps would have its own fleet of 50 Chipmunk aircraft, established in 13 Air Experience Flights located at existing University Air SquadronsIn February 1959 the rank of Cadet Warrant Officer was introduced

The year **1958** was of special note as it saw the formation of Air Experience Flights with a fleet of 50 Chipmunk aircraft. At this time there were 27 Gliding Schools and 2 Gliding centres in existence.

In **1959** Flying Training Command took responsibility for the ATC, and in May

1960 the Headquarters Air Cadets was set up at White Waltham as a separate formation for organisation and direction of the ATC.

HISTORY OF THE AIR TRAINING CORPS

In the ten years 1951 to 1961 over 58,000 cadet entered the RAF, nearly 33,000 on Regular Engagements.
The new Training Syllabus was introduced in 1961.
In **1962** The ATC celebrated 21 years of "Venture Adventure" Prince Phillip, Duke of Edinburgh presented his Banner to the ATC at a ceremony held in the Royal Air Force Chapel, St Clement Danes Church, Holborn, London.

By **1963** the International air cadet exchange had grown to such an extent that it included the United Kingdom, Canada, Israel, Spain, Portugal, Greece, Turkey, Italy, France, Holland, Belgium, West Germany, Norway, Sweden, Denmark, Switzerland, Austria and Finland.

During the Easter and Summer Camp periods of 1964, ATC cadets went to RAF Stations in Germany for the first time.

ADVENTURE TRAINING INTRODUCED

1965 Adventure Training was officially recognised in **1965** as part of the training syllabus was carried out at the newly opened ATC Adventure Training Centre at Windermere in the Lake District.
Also in **1965**, ATC cadets took part in the Nijmegen March in Holland.

In **1967** a Review Committee - The Morris Committee - looked at the organisation of the ATC. They made many recommendations; creating ATC Regions to be controlled by Regional Commandants. Wings were redefined to comprise 20 squadrons.

The age of enrolment was lowered to 13 years 9 months.
Additional places were established to enable recruiting of more officers and instructors.

1950 Kirby Cadet Mk 3 Glider, taking off on winch launch.

HISTORY OF THE AIR TRAINING CORPS

The year **1968** saw the formation of 6 further Regions alongside the existing Scottish Region

The Headquarters Air Cadets moved from RAF White Waltham to RAF Station Brampton in Lincolnshire.

In April **1969** seven Regional Commanders assumed control and command of their new Regions.

The Air Training Corp's newspaper the Air Cadet News was established as a monthly newspaper.

1970 saw the first Inter Service Cadet Swimming Championship, between the Army Cadet Force, Sea Cadet Corps and the Air Training Corps.

In this year trials were started with the SLG (Self Launching Glider) fitted with an engine which was switched off on gaining the correct height.

1971 was the 30th birthday of the ATC, and in 1972 Air Navigation was introduced as an 'O' Level subject. The first ATC camps to be held in Malta were in 1973, they continued until Malta gained its independence and a change in the political climate in 1978.

Leading Cadet Stitt was the first cadet to fly solo the Slingsby T-53B on 15th August 1968.

1975 saw Headquarters Air Cadet on the move again and were established at RAF Station Newton in Nottinghamshire.

1976 Gibraltar was an Annual Camp venue for the first time.

1977 was the Queens Silver Jubilee Review of the Reserve Forces held at RAF Station, Finningley, South Yorkshire. The ATC took part in the Review and also put on a display for the occasion.

The Venture motor glider entered service at selected air cadet volunteer gliding schools.

HISTORY OF THE AIR TRAINING CORPS

In **1979** HRH The Duke of Edinburgh presented a new Banner to the ATC. In this year the first ATC camps were held in Cyprus.

POLICY CHANGE - GIRLS JOIN ATC

1980 saw a welcome change in recruiting policy when a scheme was introduced for girls to join the ATC.
The first award of the **Darce Sword** was made to the Best Cadet in the Corps.
Meteorology was introduced as an 'O' level subject.
1981 girl cadets were flying solo in gliders, gaining marksmanship badges and taking an active part in the DofE Award Scheme
1981 4th Feb was the 40th Anniversary of the ATC, HRH The Duke of Edinburgh, Air Commodore in Chief, presented a special award to the Corps to be known as the "Guinea Pig Prize" to be awarded in recognition of an outstanding individual performance.
Girls cadets joined 22 selected squadrons throughout the Corps.
Cadet Fiona BrownNo404 (Brough of Morpeth) Squadron being the first girl Cadet in the Corps to gain a Gold Award.
In **1982** following the success of the initial stages of the trial, the scheme for girls in the ATC was extended to one Squadron in each wing.
Proposals are put to the Air Council for the extension of the scheme.
The first woman to command an ATC Squadron No 2500 (St Neots) was Flight Lieutenant Janet Page WRAF(T).
FS James Smith of No 356 (Felixstowe) Squadron was the first recipient of the Kriegie Trophy as the best ATC cadet to attend Frimley Park Leadership Course.
In the same year, The Air Gunners Association presented the Corps with a trophy to be competed for in the pre-Bisley competition shoot.
RAF Station Wethersfield was the first USAF base to host a voluntary gliding school.
Flight Sergeant Simon Burrows of No 127 (Wakefield) Sqn and Cadet Dabiel Norman of No 1013 Sqn (Quantock) Sqn were awarded the Guinea Pig Prize who rescued a friend from the sea.
In 1982 FS Anthony Hambleton, the 1982 Dacre Sword winner was the first Air Cadet to fly in a tornado aircraft of TWCU at RAF Honington.
On 20th September the ASK 21 and ASW 19 Gliders came into service with the Air Cadet Gliding Organisation at ACCGS RAF Syerston.
Ten Vanguards (dual seat) joined the fleet as well as five Valiants (single seat) and two Janus Cs (dual seat).During 1983 Air Cadet

gliders took part in the National Championships at Lasham and Husbands Bosworth and at the Inter - Services Championships at Henlow.

1982 approval was given to replace the Sedberghs and Kirby Cadet Gliders and replace them with the ASK 21 Vanguard a tandem 2 seater high performance glider and the ASW 19 (Valiant) a single seater.

In **1984** the first award of the Dacre Brooch is made to a CWO Fiona Brown No 404 (Morpeth) Squadron by Mrs Dacre at a ceremony at Newcastle Airport. The Diamond Brooch is mounted on a blue sash bordered by gold braid. Below the brooch is the Corps motto. "Venture Adventure".

NEW GLIDER FOR ATC

On the 5th October at ACCGS, Lord Trefgarne, Under Secretary of State for the Armed Services, brought the Viking (Grob G103 Twin 11) glider into service.

Viking T Mk I The Grob 103 Viking entered service in 1984

They were the first of 100 new dual seat gliders to replace the Slingsby wooden gliders (12B and T31), delivered during 1984/5.

In May **1985** Her Majesty The Queen as Patron, presented the Royal Aero Club Diploma to the ATC. The award was made for:

> *"exceptional service in providing flying and gliding training
> and associated aviation skills to cadets 1941 to 1985".*

Two cadets from Cyprus No1(Akrotiri) Squadron were the first cadets to undertake a glider proficiency course on Venture gliders at ACCGS Syerston.

In **1986** the first Save and Prosper Scholarships were awarded to five cadets. The cadets spent a two weeks course at the RAF Gliding and Soaring Association at RAF Bicester.

HISTORY OF THE AIR TRAINING CORPS

The Gill Trophy was presented to No 2390 (Belfast Royal Academy) Squadron by Mrs Irene Gill, widow of the late Honorary Secretary of the Air Gunners Association at the Inter Service Cadet Rifle Meeting at Bisley in 1986 for the best aggregate score.

A new Adventure Training Centre was announced at Llanbedr, near Harlech, North Wales to be opened in the Spring of 1988.

FACTS

From 1983 to 1986 inclusive Air cadets provided some 26% of the annual RAF intake of officers, airmen and apprentices. In 1987, 76% of Direct Entry Pilots joining the Royal Air Force were ex-members of the Air Training Corps or Combined Cadet Force (RAF Sections).

1987 From the 1st January cadets could be enrolled into the Corps at the minimum age of 13 years and 3 months.

The Vigilant Grob B1098

1990 On the 1st March The Vigilant Grob B1098 entered service with the Air Cadets, it is a side-by-side 2-seat motor glider, with all round vision both forward and downward views.

1991 Golden Jubilee of the ATC, the 50th Anniversary of the founding of the Air Cadet movement.

Many events were held throughout the United Kingdom.

Chipmonk

HISTORY OF THE AIR TRAINING CORPS

1991 A significant landmark in ATC history came in 1991 with the Corps Golden Jubilee. The initial launch of the 50th Anniversary year took place on 31 January 1991 at the Southampton Hall of Aviation when the AOC Air Cadets, Air Commodore Skelley, received the Air League Challenge Cup from Mr Michael Cobham, chairman of the Air League. The cup was awarded to the Corps in recognition of the outstanding contribution made to British aviation over the past 50 years.

On the 3rd Feb, at St Clement Danes Church in the Strand, London, officers and cadets of the London and South East Region took part in the Corps Service of Thanksgiving, held in the presence of His Royal Highness The Duke of Edinburgh KG, KT, OM, GBE, AC, QSO, Air Commodore-in-Chief Air Training Corps.

In March two groups of adults and cadets set out on an Expedition to Nepal, they were from Herts/Bucks, Somerset, Bristol/Gloucester and No 3 Welsh Wing. Anniversary memorabilia was produced, including attractive plates and anniversary mugs.

1992. Initial Glider Training introduced to give young cadets an early chance of actually flying.

1999. A new Aircraft the GROB 115E (Tutor) was introduced for use at University Air Squadrons and Air Experience Flying.

HISTORY OF THE AIR TRAINING CORPS

SELF TEST QUESTIONS

1. Who and when formed the Bournemouth Young Airmen's League.
2. In 1929 a British Young Airman's League was formed. What were its aims.
3. When was the Air Defence Cadet Corps (ADCC) formed.
4. How many Cadets and officers were members in 1939.
5. Who devised the motto of th ADCC and what was that motto.
6. How many Cadets were there in the ADCC in 1940.
7. In what year was the new Training Syllabus introduced.
8. When did Air Experience Flights start.
9. From 1951 to 1961 how many Air Cadets joined the RAF.
10. When did the ATC first take part in Adventure Training.
11. When did ATC cadets go to RAF Stations in Germany.
12. When was Gibraltar an Annual Camp venue for the first time.
13. When did the Venture motor glider enter service.
14. When were Girls allowed to join the Air Training Corps.
15. Who was the first girl cadet to attain the D of E Gold Award.
16. Name the new Gliders that came into service during 1983.
17. What is the name of two new Glider that came into service in1984.
18. From the 1st January 1987 what was the minimum age for joining the ATC.

Chapter 5

DISCIPLINE, DRILL AND DRESS

When thinking about this section on Drill, Discipline and Dress it will come to mind that you may have seen Airmen of the Queen's Colour Squadron on television or you may have been lucky enough to have actually seen them `on parade'.

You cannot help being impressed by their smart turnout and the precision of their drill movements. They could not perform to the very high standards required unless they as individuals have strong personal discipline and are dedicated members of their "team".

An important part of your training involves teaching you to be a smartly `turned out', disciplined and a well organised individual.

Drill is a powerful aid towards teaching you these qualities. In a voluntary youth organisation it would seem to be a difficult task to instill discipline. However, it is not really a problem since, after all, you are a volunteer like everyone else in your squadron, who all rely on a much more important type of discipline - SELF DISCIPLINE.

You will be surprised how you can enjoy taking part in drill, especially if you have a good instructor who can make it interesting.

Once all of you have mastered the movements and are able to move smartly as "one body", then - and only then you will feel a real sense of pride, you will be alert and carry out orders instantly with precision.

As an airman you would be expected to carry out drills in an aircraft in exactly the same manner. No matter what job you have to do, if you are smart on parade you will develop the right attitudes towards improving your personal standards in all you do.

In the service environment, the immediate reaction to orders given in quick succession - as in drill, will often have to be applied to keep an efficient team together under a strain that would normally break it.

UNIFORM

Another aspect of your personal discipline is your uniform which is your personal responsibility.

The way you take care of it can be seen by your very appearance in it. Your reputation for `turnout' with your instructors will depend upon your attention to detail when wearing uniform, listen to their instructions and get it right first time.

DISCIPLINE, DRILL AND DRESS

You will now appreciate that there is more to drill than you might think, it is a team effort, more precise than the most highly trained Football team. The concentration of individual effort and the self discipline required by you will be hard to find in any other situation.

Once you and the others in your Squadron have become proficient enough at Drill you may appear in public or take part in parades that include marching through your home town often with a band playing you will be able to control the swing of your arms and the roll of your shoulders allowing you to feel the pride in your squadron and yourself - it takes some beating, and what is more you will enjoy every minute of it.

CARE of CLOTHING

You are fortunate to have your uniform issued to you free of charge. It must be appreciated that this costs a great deal of money to provide all cadets with uniforms and to carry stocks for exchanges. It follows that it must be treated with respect and taken care of.

If you are to be a credit to yourself and the ATC you must keep it clean, pressed and in good repair at all times.

You do need to learn how to correctly use an iron, do not leave it to others to clean and press for you.

This naturally applies just as much to you when in your civilian clothes, your turnout portrays how well you look after yourself and your standard of personal discipline.

All your clothes need hanging up properly on hangers, not thrown over a chair or dumped on the floor.

You will be expected to hand in a clean uniform when it comes to changing it, which can happen several times during your cadet service. Talk to your officers or instructor to find out the best and accepted method of cleaning it.

It is understood that young people grow quite rapidly at times, your Supplies Officer will have a system for exchanging uniforms. However, uniform supply is limited, thereforeit is your responsibility tomaintain the highest standards without defacing the uniform with iron marks or alterations.

HINTS FOR PRESSING UNIFORM

Do not let the hot iron come into direct contact with the material.. It makes it shiny or worse still, may burn it. You will then have to pay for a replacement. Use a damp not wet, non-fluffy cloth, (an old tea towel is ideal), place this on your trousers/skirt then place paper over this.

DISCIPLINE, DRILL AND DRESS

CARE and CLEANING of BOOTS

There are different ideas about how clean your boots should be. It is most likely that you will only have one pair of boots and they have to be worn for all your cadet activities. Ideally if you can manage it a pair of boots for Adventure Training and shoes for Squadron activities.

It is very difficult to wear them on an expedition one day and then have them fit for a "drill competition" the next!!

Most units have the common sense approach, they plan their activities so as their cadets can have time to smarten their boots for some special parade.

What is important is to make sure that they fit you comfortably and are kept in good repair, the uppers clean and well polished.

The laces must be straight across the eyelet holes, not crossing over them.

Should you get your boots wet, do not dry them in front of a fire or over heat.

Leather is a natural material and so must dry naturally. It helps if you stuff newspaper into them to absorb the wet/damp, replacing it after a couple of hours with dry paper.

Always have a spare pair of laces, with you. Only wear thick woolen socks with boots. Black socks are permitted for males, whilst females should wear Barely Black coloured tights.

If shoes are worn in uniform, they must be polished, laces tied neatly, and the shoes in good repair.

PERSONAL TURNOUT
MALES

Face clean and shaved if necessary

Hair not over the collar or ears, sideburns not below bottom of ears

FEMALES

Hair: If your hair is long enough to put up NEATLY, then do so. Try to keep your hair from 'falling' as it can be a problem on exercise or the ranges.

Do not wear fancy hair slides, bobbles or fancy scrunchies.

Earrings: ONE pair of plain studs.

It is advisable to remove them whilst on exercise, to prevent loss.

DISCIPLINE, DRILL AND DRESS

GENERAL ADVICE

Body Piercing
It is your personal choice whether you have body piercing. However, for your safety, these should be either removed whilst in uniform, or covered securely with a sticking plaster.
There is a real danger of these piercings being caught or becoming infected whilst undertaking most cadet activities.

Rings:
One signet ring is acceptable, but 'Rings on every finger' does not look right when in uniform. There is also a possibility they may slip off during an exercise or getting caught when weapon cleaning.

Neck Chains and Bracelets:
Should not be worn when in uniform, unless they are Medic Alert or similar.

When Compliments are paid:

NATIONAL ANTHEM
When on parade, stand to attention, only Officers and Warrant Officers salute, NCOs will if in charge of a party.
When not on parade, but in uniform, all ranks will salute.
When not on parade, and in plain clothes, all ranks will stand to attention.
If a hat is worn, it will be removed (Females do not remove hats).

STANDARDS GUIDONS AND COLOURS
As a squad on the march you will give an 'Eyes Left' or 'Right'.
As an individual, you halt; face passing Standards, Guidons or Colours.

PAYING COMPLIMENTS
Visiting Officers will always notice the standard of saluting in your Squadron; it will be their first impression of you and the Squadron. Make sure it is a good impression.

The Union Flag

DISCIPLINE, DRILL AND DRESS

INTRODUCTION TO DRILL

Throughout history, Drill has been the foundation upon which discipline; teamwork, pride and pageant have all taken equal part. In the days of the 'Brown Bess' musket, when in battle, the infantry formed a square in their three ranks in order to give effective firepower.

This action was carried out as a drill, taught and practiced on the barrack square. The discipline required to 'hold the line' was the difference between defeat and victory.

Drill parades were hard and rigorous, with harsh violence dished out by the instructors.

Times have changed, all services yet they still rely on drill to build team spirit and to train the individuals mind to respond to orders given in the quickest possible time.

When you are first introduced to Drill Commands, you may find that your reactions are slow and mistakes easily made. Fortunately your initial lessons are all completed at the 'Halt' i.e. stood still. It is difficult enough to stand still, especially when there is a fly walking down your nose - no matter, stand still!

Once you have mastered the initial movements and been taught how to march without your arms moving in the wrong order, you will suddenly find it all comes together, your squad starts to move as a team.

It will probably feel even better when you take part in a Civic or Cadet Sunday Parade. You will be with the rest of your Squadron, smartly turned out and marching behind a band.

It might sound odd to those of you who have not attended such Parades, but it gives you a real 'Buzz' and dare it be said, pride in your Squadron and the Air Training Corps. (Particularly if your family and friends are watching!)

REMEMBER: DO NOT WEAR YOUR UNIFORM
WITHOUT PERMISSION FROM YOUR SQUADRON
COMMANDER UNLESS YOU ARE ON CADET DUTIES

DISCIPLINE, DRILL AND DRESS

DRILL - INTRODUCTORY WORDS OF COMMAND

Used for Squad Drill

Good instructors give *INTRODUCTORY* words of command giving warning of what the next word of command is to be.

Many instructors do not do this; the result is the squad turning in different directions at the same time!

Before moving a squad in any direction, the instructor indicates what direction they intend to move them by using *INTRODUCTORY* words of command, before giving the actual command to execute the movement.

As a member of the squad, this does give you the time to work out the direction of your next move.

See the diagram on page 5- 12. Turn it sideways as if you were standing in the centre of the front rank of the 'squad', facing the same direction as the arrow pointing to 'ADVANCING'. The words of command you should be given to move the squad in any particular direction are as shown in the diagram.

TEACHING DRILL

The aims of Drill are:

1. To produce a Cadet who has self respect, is alert and obedient
2. To provide the basis for teamwork

Drill is exacting and strict attention to detail must be observed. You will need the following qualities to become an excellent Drill Instructor.

1. **PATIENCE.** Never lose your temper.
2. **ENTHUSIASM**. You must fire your squad with a will to achieve.
3. **CONSISTENCY.** Set yourself and the squad a high standard and do not deviate from it.
4. **HUMANITY**. Understand the squad's problems; praise readily,
5. **PERSONALITY.** As a drill instructor you must impress your squad - always have them under control, lead by example:
   1. A Always be impeccably turned out.
   2. When drilling a squad, stand to attention, always face them.
   3. When moving, march as you would wish your squad to march - no 'bimbling.'
   4. When demonstrating, be accurate; never exaggerate a drill movement. If the movement is with a rifle use that article and nothing else.

5. Never use bad language and sarcasm; it is the sign of a poor instructor.
6. Ensure that your words of command are clear, DO NOT do as some drill instructors, create your own 'drill language', it is bad practice.
7. Do not become over familiar or humiliate individual members of your squad.

COMPLIMENTS
Saluting - Origin and Information

The salute with the hand, the present arms and the salute with the sword were methods by which the person paying a compliment could show the person to whom the compliment was paid that no offence was meant and they were unarmed.

They were all gestures symbolic of loyalty and trust.

A salute is the normal greeting between comrades in arms. That a salute is properly and smartly given when you meet an officer is a basic matter of discipline.

That the salute is properly and smartly given is a matter of training. Failure by an officer to return a salute shows a lack of courtesy on their part.

DISCIPLINE, DRILL AND DRESS

THE QUEEN'S COMMISSION
All compliments derive their origin from the Sovereign, to whom the highest compliment, the Royal Salute, is paid.

PAYING COMPLIMENTS - Saluting
Saluting to the front - Common Faults
1. The body and head not remaining still and erect.
2. Allowing your right elbow to come forward.
3. Hand not flat and in correct position, finger tips not near to head at eye level.
4. Wrist bent - not in straight line with forearm.
5. Allowing left arm to creep forwards.
6. Left fist not clenched with thumb to front, arm not tight into side.

NOTE As an aid to good saluting, remember your right hand - with the palm of your hand flat, thumb on top, travels the 'longest way up and the shortest way down' when you are saluting correctly.

THE QUEENS COMMISSION
All officers in the Air Training Corps are holders of the Queen's Commission, and when compliments are paid by saluting it is in recognition of the Sovereign's Commission held in trust by that officer.

The actual Commission an officer receives is in fact a document on parchment paper signed and sealed by Her Majesty The Queen. Ask one of your officer to bring theirs along for you to see, it is a very special and interesting document.

DISCIPLINE, DRILL AND DRESS

DEFINITIONS USED IN DRILL

ALIGNMENT: Any straight line on which a body of cadets is or are to form.

CLOSE ORDER: Formation of a flight or squad in three ranks. (3 ranks)

```
x x x x x x x x - FRONT RANK
x x x x x x x x - CENTRE RANK
x x x x x x x x - REAR RANK
```

Each cadet in the centre and rear ranks covering the corresponding cadet in the front rank. Distance of 75cm (30 inches)

COLUMN OF THREES

```
                    x  x  x
                    x  x  x
                    x  x  x
                    x  x  x
                    x  x  x
```

A succession of cadets standing side by side in threes, covering the front files as in diagram above. Normal formation for marching on a road.

COVERING: As in both of the illustration above, one behind the other covering off the front files.

DIRECTING FLANK: Flank by which units march and dress, "By the Left/Right".

FILE: Any cadet in the front rank together with the cadet(s) immediately behind them.

FLIGHT: A sub-unit, two or more of which comprise a squadron. (approximately size of Army or Navy platoon)

FORMATION: A number of units grouped together under one commander.

FRONT: The direction in which units are facing or moving at any given time.

FRONTAGE: The extent of ground covered laterally by a body or bodies of cadets.

GUARD OF HONOR: A parade not exceeding 100 cadets formed to present formal ceremonial compliments to royal or residential persons.

`HALF GUARD': A parade not exceeding 50 cadets formed to present ceremonial compliments to other particular distinguished persons.

DISCIPLINE, DRILL AND DRESS

INCLINE: Half a turn, you move through 45°

FILE x x   **SINGLE FILE** x
    x x   x
    x x   x
Cadet formed up in pairs,   Single cadets formed up
covering off the front file.   Covering off the front
cadet.

MARKER: An NCO or cadet positioned to mark a point where the flank of a squad or unit is to rest/dress.

OPEN ORDER: Squad in three ranks with three paces between the ranks. (3 ranks). This affords space for inspections to be carried out.

OPEN ORDER: Squad in two ranks, with four paces between ranks. (2 ranks)

OUT FLANK: The opposite flank to the directing or inner flank.

PATROL: Small party of cadets commanded by an NCO, detailed to carry out some specific duty, such as guard, fire picquet etc.

PIVOT FLANK: The flank on which a unit pivots when changing direction.

PIVOT GUIDE: The guide on a pivot flank of a unit.

QUARTER GUARD: A small ceremonial guard, that may be mounted at the main entrance to a unit to pay compliments as required.
Not to be confused with a Guard of HONOR. Guard consists of I officer, I SNCO plus 6 other corporals and cadets. They form up in two ranks.

REVIEW: A ceremonial parade formed to honor a particular person.

RIGHT FILE: An odd numbered file.

SECTION: Subdivision of a flight - RAF Regiment formation.

SQUAD: Small body of cadets formed as working party etc.

SQUADRON: A unit of two or more flights (subunits), Approximately same size as Army/Navy company.

SUBUNIT: Smallest body of cadets under their own officer or NCO commander as part of unit.

DISCIPLINE, DRILL AND DRESS

SUPER-NUMERARY.	Extra ranks formed behind rear rank of unit, comprising of officers and SNCO's.
TO CANT:	To incline or tilt an object.
TO DRESS	To adjust and take up the correct alignment.
UNIT:	A group of two or more submits under a commander.
WHEELING:	A drill movement by which a body of cadets bring forward a flank on a fixed or moving pivot.
WING:	Formation consisting of two or more squadrons or units. (approx same size as Army Battalion or Navy Division).

WORDS OF COMMAND.

The information below is perhaps the most important for you to learn and practice, as it is only when you are able to correctly give yourself these words of command that you will become good at drill.

The commands given are for when you are "on the march" or "marking time". Like many skills it is only with practice that you will become perfect.

Words of command for Drill should always be given in two parts:-

1. **The Preliminary**
2. **The Executive**

The **PRELIMINARY** is to give you notice of the type of movement that is to follow, that is - provided you are paying attention, it gives you just those few seconds to think out what you have to do, so as when the **EXECUTIVE** word of command is given you respond immediately.

In the first example in the next page, the Drill Instructor, while you are on the move would tell you: *"TURNINGS/INCLINES ON THE MARCH"*, a warning order, followed - after a slight pause, by the **PRELIMINARY** command *"ABOUT"*, then the **EXECUTIVE** command *"TURN"*.

This will be the pattern during your early training in Drill, but once you become accustomed to the movements, the space or paces you are allowed between the PRELIMINARY and EXECUTIVE words of command will become shorter, and your wits will need to become sharper.

DISCIPLINE, DRILL AND DRESS

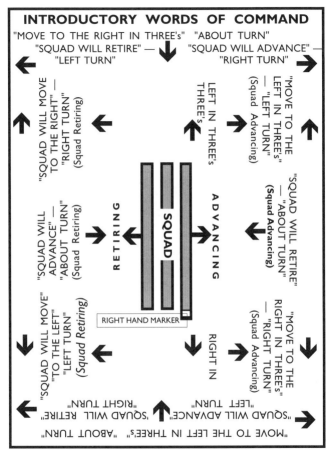

PHOTOCOPY AND ENLARGE THIS PAGE TO LEARN AND UNDERSTAND YOUR WORDS OF COMMAND.

DISCIPLINE, DRILL AND DRESS

COMMAND	TIME/PACE	WHEN EXECUTIVE COMMAND IS GIVEN
TURNINGS and INCLINES		
"About" - "TURN"	Slow & Quick	As the LEFT HEEL strikes the ground.
"Right" - "TURN"	Slow & Quick	As the LEFT HEEL strikes the ground.
"Right" - "INCLINE"	Slow & Quick	As the LEFT HEEL strikes the ground.
"Left" - "TURN"	Slow & Quick	As the RIGHT HEEL strikes the ground.
"Left" - "INCLINE"	Slow & Quick	As the RIGHT HEEL strikes the ground.
HALTING		
"HALT" (Marching)	Slow	As the RIGHT FOOT strikes the ground.
"HALT" (Marching)	Quick	As the LEFT HEEL strikes the ground.
"HALT" (Marching)	Double	As the LEFT FOOT strikes the ground.
"HALT" (Marking time)	Slow & Quick	As the LEFT FOOT strikes the ground.
COMPLIMENTS		
"Eyes" - "LEFT/RIGHT/ FRONT"	Quick	As the LEFT FOOT strikes the ground
"Eyes" - "LEFT/RIGHT/ FRONT"	Slow	As the RIGHT FOOT strikes the ground.
To "LEFT/RIGHT/ FRONT" "SALUTE"	Quick	As the LEFT FOOT strikes the ground.
To "LEFT/RIGHT/ FRONT" "SALUTE"	Slow	As the LEFT FOOT strikes the ground.
CHANGING THE TIME/PACE OF MARCHING		
"Break into double time" - "DOUBLE MARCH"	From quick Time	As the right heel strikes the ground
"Break into Quick time" - "QUICK MARCH"	From double Time	As RIGHT FOOT strikes the ground.
"Break into Quick time" - "QUICK MARCH"	From slow Time	As RIGHT FOOT strikes the ground.
"Slow - MARCH"	Slow	As RIGHT HEEL strikes the ground

DISCIPLINE, DRILL AND DRESS

COMMAND	TIME/PACE	WHEN EXECUTIVE COMMAND IS GIVEN
"Break into slow time"	-From Quick Time	As RIGHT HEEL
"SLOW MARCH"		strikes the ground.
"Step - "OUT/SHORT"	- Slow & Quick	As the LEFT HEEL strikes the ground.

MARCHING

"Change" -"STEP"	- Slow & Quick	As the RIGHT HEEL strikes the ground.
"Mark" - "TIME"	- Slow & Quick	As the LEFT HEEL (When Marching) strikes the ground.
"For" - "WARD"	- Slow & Quick	As the LEFT FOOT (When Marking Time) strikes the ground.

MOVING OFF WITH A PRECEDING UNIT

"Quick" - "MARCH"	- Quick	As their RIGHT HEELS strike the ground.
"Slow" - "MARCH"	- Slow	As their RIGHT FEET strike the ground.

USEFUL INFORMATION ON DRILL

Length of Paces in Marching.

Slow March	75cms (30inches)
Quick March	75cms (30inches)
March Sideways	30cms (12inches) " x Paces"

"Left" or "Right Close" -"MARCH"

Maximum number of five paces.

Double March	100cms (40inches)
Stepping Short	53cms (21inches)
Stepping Out	83cms (33inches)
Stepping Forward/Backward	75cms (30inches)

" X Paces" "Forward/Backward" "MARCH".

Maximum number of five paces.

PACES/TIME IN MARCHING

Slow March	60 Paces per minute.
Quick March	120 " " "
Double March	80 " " "
Sideways Marching and	120 " " "
Stepping Forward or Backward	

DISCIPLINE, DRILL AND DRESS

ADJUSTING ON PARADE

The term `Adjusting' on parade, is when you feel that your boot lace
has come undone, or your shirt is coming out of your trousers or even
worse is left to your imagination, but you must put it right before some
disaster happens.

So you ADJUST ON PARADE as explained below:-

Place your RIGHT FOOT 12 inches to the rear, make the required
adjustment and return to your previous position.

Should you be carrying a Rifle - GROUND ARMS first.

If you are stood AT EASE, always come to ATTENTION before
carrying out the ADJUSTMENT drill.

SIZING A SQUAD

This is a simple method of sorting out the different heights of cadets in a
flight or squadron so as they appear more uniform when seen as a
marching body.

This is especially important if you have some very small and very tall
Cadets in the flight or squadron as they would look most odd marching
next to each other.

You have all the cadets form a single rank with the tallest at one end and
the shortest at the other. The words of command are as follows:-

1. "Tallest on the RIGHT, shortest on the LEFT, in single rank" - "SIZE"
   (Cadets quickly sort themselves out to form the single rank)

2. "Squad" - "NUMBER" Starting with the RIGHT HAND cadet who
   shouts out "ONE", followed by the next who shouts "TWO" and this
   follows down the file until all have numbered themselves.

3. "Odd numbers, two paces forward" - "MARCH". Even numbers stand
   still.

4. "Number one stand fast" "Ranks RIGHT and LEFT" - "TURN". The
   front rank formed by the ODD NUMBERS turn to their RIGHT. The
   rear rank formed by the EVEN numbers turn to their LEFT.

5. "Form Squad" - "Quick" - "MARCH". The leading cadet of the REAR
   file wheels to the right followed by the remainder joining the end of the
   front file.

As this is taking place the first two cadets of the front file march to the
rear of number one, turn to the front, take up a position covering off
number one.

The remainder of the cadets continue to fill the Front, Centre and
Rear Ranks in that order, until the squad is formed.

DISCIPLINE, DRILL AND DRESS

INSPECTION OF A SQUAD/FLIGHT

To make room between the ranks all inspections are carried out at the Open Order.
Each Rank is stood to attention while being inspected, while those who are waiting or who have been inspected are Stood At Ease. The Words of Command that you will be given are as follows:-

1 "Squad"- "Squad" -"SHUN".

2 "Open Order" - "MARCH", "Right" - "DRESS", "Eyes" - "FRONT".

3 "Centre and Rear Ranks, Stand At" - "EASE".

4 "Centre Rank "SHUN", "Front Rank",
   "Stand at" - "EASE".

5 "Rear Rank "SHUN", "Centre Rank",
   "Stand At" - "EASE".

6 "Rear Rank, stand at" "EASE", "Flight - SHUN"

DISCIPLINE, DRILL AND DRESS

MARCHING AND DRESSING OFF

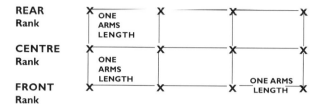

ABOVE DIAGRAM REPRESENTS A SQUAD CORRECTLY DRESSED AND COVERED OFF FROM LEFT TO RIGHT, AND FROM FRONT RANK - TO REAR

CHANGING DIRECTION - WHEELING ON THE MARCH

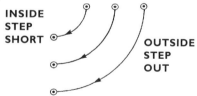

The term "Step Short" means reduce the length of your pace, "Step out" means slightly lengthen your pace.

By doing this while Wheeling you keep your Dressing in each file as it changes direction.

A common fault when giving the "Left or Right Wheel" is for the command to be given sharply, when in fact it should be drawn out - "WHEE-EEL", allowing the files to slowly change direction, keeping their dressing in threes.

DISCIPLINE, DRILL AND DRESS

DEVELOPING YOUR WORD OF COMMAND

The following information will help you develop good voice control. Practice whenever you can.

Explanation. Many drill instructors end up with sore throats after a prolonged drill practice. This may well be because they do not use their lungs correctly.

It is important to breathe in through your nose and take your breath 'right down to your stomach'. In other words, learn to breathe deeply. When giving a word of command, 'push' the air out.

Do not forget to stand to attention when giving commands. Standing with your feet apart or leaning backwards may result in straining your groin. KEEP YOUR WEIGHT FORWARD AND YOUR FEET TOGETHER.

Have your head up, looking directly at your squad; when giving the word of command AIM your voice straight over the squad.

Giving Words of Command.

Giving a Cautionary or preliminary word of Command you have to pitch your voice on the same note to ensure that it does not 'tail away' at the end. It must be short and sharp, "SQD". Then comes the Executive word of command, equally short and sharp, "SHUN". It is most important to develop the correct method of delivering commands; nothing is worse than a poor drill instructor. If you really cannot do it properly, leave it to someone who can.

Words of Command.

They must be pronounced CLEARLY. It is not just a sound. A quick tightening of the stomach muscles so that the word comes out quick, short and higher in pitch than the Cautionary produces the Executive word of command. Ensure that there is a pause between the Cautionary and the Executive. Failure to do this may result in the squad anticipating the word of command, thus the whole purpose of drill is lost - and chaos will reign!

Note: Use your mouth; the wider open it is, the louder the sound!

C	**Clear**
L	**Loud**
A	**As an order**
P	**With Pauses**

Remember the mnemonic CLAP when giving an order.

DISCIPLINE, DRILL AND DRESS

To summaries:
Power: Plenty of air into the lungs.
Pitch: Hold your head high and pitch the word of command high over the Squad.
Punch: Given quickly by tightening the stomach muscles.
Pronunciation: Make your words CLEAR, LOUD, AS AN ORDER.

Communication Drill

This Drill introduces an element of 'fun' into a Drill Lesson. It gives the individual Cadet the opportunity to use their voice as never before as they are competing with each other to make themselves heard above the rest of the Squad.

1. First demonstrate to the squad all words of command at the halt, including rifle drill if taught.
2. Then "conduct" the squad while they give elementary words of command; insisting on clarity and power from each cadet.
3. Divide the squad in to two ranks, place them about 25 meters apart, with 5 paces interval between each cadet.
4. Each cadet should now drill his/her opposite number 25 meters away without regard to those to the left or right of them.
5. After no more than ten minutes, change the ranks, so that the cadets in both ranks have a chance of controlling their opposite number.

Mutual Drill

Form the squad into three ranks and explain the introductory word of command and which are the DIRECTING FLANK.
Call out each member of the squad in turn to drill the squad and then call out another member of the squad to watch and be prepared to comment on his/her performance.
Note:
1. Be patient and make encouraging comments.
2. When correcting, be sure you address your remarks to the whole squad, they can all learn by one cadet's mistakes.

Testing you wits

'Ogrady' is a game practiced to sharpen your response to an order. If the instructor precedes an order with "OGRADY SAYS" then you carry it out, if not, any who move are 'knocked out' the last Cadet is the winner.

DISCIPLINE, DRILL AND DRESS

BADGES OF RANK & DISTINGUISHING BADGES

OFFICES

Cap Badge

Distinguishing Badge

Officer Cadet

Pilot Officer

Flying Officer

Beret Badge

Flight Lieutenant

Squadron Leader

Wing Commander

WARRANT OFFICERS & SNCO

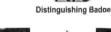

Distinguishing Badge

Senior NCO
Cap Badge

No 1 Dress   No 2 Dress
Sergeant (ATC)

No 1 Dress   No 2 Dress
Flight Sergeant (ATC)

Cap Badge

No 1 Dress   No 2 Dress
Warrant Officer (ATC)

No 1 Dress   No 2 Dress
Warrant Officer (ATC)
*(Ex RN/RAF Warrant Officer
or Army/RM Warrant Officer 1s only)*

Beret Badge

DISCIPLINE, DRILL AND DRESS

BADGES OF RANK & DISTINGUISHING BADGES

CIVILIAN

ATC
Lapel Badge   Civilian Instructor's
Lapel Badge

Chaplain's
Scarf Badge

Civilian Instructor's Arm Band

FLYING

Cadet Pilot

Cadet Pilot Navigator

Gliding Instructor

Glider Pilot

Blue Wings

Silver Wings

Gold Wings

DISCIPLINE, DRILL AND DRESS

BADGES OF RANK & DISTINGUISHING BADGES

CADETS

Cap Badge

18 Yrs+
Cadet Warrant Officer

18 Yrs+
Cadet Flight Sergeant

18 Yrs+
Cadet Sergeant

Cadet Warrant Officer

Cadet Flight Sergeant

Sqn Identification Badge

Cadet Sergeant

Cadet Corporal

Distinguishing Badge

Cadet Sergeant

Cadet Corporal

First Class Cadet

Staff Cadet

Senior Cadet

Leading Cadet

First Class Cadet

MARKSMAN

Squadron Marksman

Wing Marksman

Regional Marksman

Corps Marksman

Cadet 100

5-22

DISCIPLINE, DRILL AND DRESS

BADGES OF RANK & DISTINGUISHING BADGES

SPECIALIST

Junior Leaders
(CS95 only)

Adult First Aid

Youth First Aid

Leadership

Nijmegen

Communicator

Junior
Leader

Gold DEA   Silver DEA   Bronze DEA

BAND

Drummer   Bandsman   Trumpeter

Drum Major

Instrumentalist
(Gold if attended Music Camp)

Piper

Pipe Major

DISCIPLINE, DRILL AND DRESS

SELF TEST QUESTIONS

1. What is Saluting in recognition of.
2. What is a squad in "Close Order".
4. What would you be doing correctly "the longest way up and shortest down".
5. What is a Directing Flank use for.
6. If a squad of 20 cadet are marching on a road, what formation would they be in.
7. How do you dry out your leather boots.
8. Up to how many cadets would be in a Guard of Honor.
9. The pocket of your uniform must not be what...
10. How should your Beret band be on your forehead.
11. On what foot is the HALT given.
12. Marking Time, when is the HALT given.
13. What is a Quarter Guard.
14. What does the drill term "To Dress" mean.
15. What do you understand by an "INTRODUCTORY" word of command.
16. What sort of socks should you wear with boots.
17. When do you "Step Short" and "Step Out"
18. At Close Order what is the distance between ranks.
19. Marking Time, the HALT is given when the knee is ...
20. What and who are Supernumeraries.
21. Why do you have Preliminary and Executive words of command.
22. What is the difference between an "Incline" and a "Turn".
23. How many pace can you "Sideways March".
24. How many paces per minute is the Quick March.
25. What do you understand by "Adjusting" on parade.
26. How do you "SIZE" a squad and why.
27. Before a squad/flight is inspected, what has to be done before it started.

DISCIPLINE, DRILL AND DRESS

DID YOU KNOW ???

**** The services policy regarding tattoos is as follows:

"It is services policy that a person with tattoo marks which, because of size, position or nature would be detrimental to the Service, is ineligible for enlistment, re-enlistment or continued service in any of the armed services." Tattooing is to be discouraged, and unacceptable tattoos as outlined below may result in applications being made for discharge under Queens Regulations.

Any tattoo(s), excessive in size or number, offensive or obscene, which is visible when wearing parade uniform (not including shirt sleeve order or sports clothing). The visible area comprises the head, neck and hands.

Tattoos - Guidance. The principles to be followed in each individual case are:

a. Offensive, Racist or Obscene. A Tattoo(s) which is/are offensive, obscene or racist will be a bar to enlistment or re-enlistment regardless of where they are on the body.

b. Visible Area. Is defined as:

  (1) **Head and Neck.** Any tattoos which is/are visible above the collar-line of a conventional round collar 'T' shirt will be a bar to enlistment or re-enlistment.

  (2) **Hands.** Any tattoo(s) which is/are visible, on either side of the hands, below what might be described as the 'watch strap' or 'bracelet' line may be a bar to enlistment or re-enlistment subject to exceptional circumstances.

c. **Arms and Legs**. Non-offensive tattoos visible on the arms or legs will not normally be a barrier to enlistment.

****** YOU KNOW NOW - DON'T GET TATTOOED *****

Chapter 6

CAREER DEVELOPMENTS

The world of work becomes more competitive each year; there is also a growing industry in new technology presenting challenges and opportunities.
Your time in the Cadet Force will have provided you with some useful life skills.

FURTHER EDUCATION

You may have left school without many useful qualifications, or need further qualifications to follow your chosen career. Colleges of Further Education offer career studies and leisure courses in formats to fit in with most people's lives. Many thousands of people of all ages study through the Open University, an excellent way to take your own time in gaining qualifications, perhaps even a degree.

THE FACTS OF LIFE

Contributing a percentage of your wages to pay for housekeeping should not include all washing, ironing, cleaning and cooking. Take the opportunity to learn how to do all these strange things - you may need them when you set up on your own.

LEAVING HOME

During your Cadet career, you were away from home on weekends and Annual Camps. Although this may give you an advantage over those who have never been away without their parents, it is still a very emotional time. You may be only too pleased to leave 'home' and feel a sense of relief at finally escaping, but If you have been fortunate in having a caring home environment, where despite disagreements you share common interests and count your parent(s) or those who have guided you through childhood as friends, it is more difficult to leave without real heartache and bouts of homesickness.
Write, phone, text, email, visit - let your family and friends know your safe, share in your successes and support you when things are not so good.

DECISION MAKING - USE S.W.O.T.

S.W.O.T. means **S**trengths, **W**eaknesses, **O**pportunities, **T**hreats.
Doing a SWOT list is an excellent aid to decision-making, particularly
career choices. It is simple to create the form but more difficult to
complete, as you must be honest with yourself.

Take a sheet of paper and draw four columns. Place the headings along
the top of the page along with the subject of your SWOT list. You
may well find that one of the difficulties in completing the form is that
your Threats can also be seen as Opportunities; your Weaknesses,
Threats or Opportunities. That is the idea of this list, to make you
think where you need to improve and to highlight your Strengths.
When you have completed your lists, number each point in order of
importance and make your decisions using all the information you have on
your form.

THE WORLD OF WORK

When you have made your choice, whether it is further education or
the workplace, you will still need to complete application forms and
write letters to prospective employers.

From the moment you apply for the application form your aim is to
convince the employer that you are the person for the job. The
following list is provided as a prompt.

1. Photocopy your application form, or use sheets of paper to draft
    out what you want to say.
2. When you have completed your application form - take a
    photocopy to remind you of what you have written, very useful if
    you are fortunate enough to gain an interview. It may also be useful
    for completing other application forms.
3. Some advertisements ask for applications "in your own writing". This
    may be because the vacancy requires some written work.
4. Put a covering letter with your application saying what job you are
    applying for.
5. Where an advertisement states "Letter of application and CV" use
    the Specimen Letter provided in this section as a guide.
7. Make sure that the completed letter is neat, well set out and with no
    spelling mistakes. Use good quality paper, and where appropriate,
    matching envelope.
8. You can, if you would like a job at a particular firm/business, write
    and enquire about possible vacancies. Address your letter to the

appropriate person and ensure you have their correct name, job title and address.

9. CURRICULUM VITAE means the course of your life' is normally abbreviated to CV. when writing be honest about experience and qualifications. Remember to update it regularly your Careers Advisor will have given/can give you useful formats for this document.

10. Keep your CV short, factual and a maximum of two A4 pages, if possible.

11. Personal References and Testimonials: Chose someone who knows you well, your Squadron Commander, any adult outside the family circle.You will be asked for the name of your previous employer if applicable. Do not forget to ask these people before you give their names.

YOU HAVE AN INTERVIEW

Congratulations! All your hard work has had the desired result. Now, prepare properly for the final stage - your interview.

THE AIM OF AN INTERVIEW

The prospective employer has sifted through all the application forms and short-listed several suitable candidates. Obviously, they will need to meet you, ask questions, and expand on the information you have given them.

WHAT YOU NEED TO KNOW ABOUT EMPLOYERS

1. What sort of training will they give you, is it formal and part of your contract of Employment?

2. Do they allow time off for block release or Further Education as part of your training, and encourage staff to attend?

3. How easy or difficult is it going to be to get to and from work, how long does it take, how much will it cost.

4. If you are a member of the Territorial Army, or Cadet Force, will they grant you leave for Annual Camp or courses.

5. Are there any outside activities, sports etc. that the company encourages?

6. How do they promote people - is it internal or internal and external applications

7. Make clear notes of what questions you want answered at the interview; remember to take the notes with you.

CAREER DEVELOPMENTS

YOUR IMAGE

If you want the job, you have got to make the right impression on the person(s) interviewing you.

- Ensure your appearance is smart but comfortable.
- Be on time, five minutes before due time if possible.
- Take your Record of Achievements, Certificates etc. and put them in a folder.
- On entering the interview room, make eye contact, shake hands with the Interviewers and make a greeting (good morning/ afternoon etc.).
- Sit comfortably, and do not slouch.
- Think through your answer, and then speak. Always try and answer as fully as possible, don't 'woffle'.
- Make eye contact with your interviewer(s) when answering their questions
- If you do not understand the question, say so.
- If you are asked if you have any questions, those that have arisen from the interview should come first, then produce your question list, and ask!

Questions that you might be asked at an Interview

1. Tell me/us about yourself
2. Why do you want to work for this company
3. What makes you think you would be suitable for this job
4. What personal qualities do you have to offer us
5. Where do you see yourself in 5 years from now
6. What subject did you enjoy most and why (taken from your CV)
7. Have you had any experience of work
8. Why did you leave your last employment
9. Would you be interested in attending training courses.
10. Would you be prepared to go to day release
11. Would working overtime be any problem for you.
12. Would you be prepared/like to move between departments
13. Are you prepared to move from the area if necessary
14. Can you work on your own
15. Do you play any sports if so who for.
16. What other hobbies and interests do you have
17. Do you use a computer at home
18. Would you like to ask any questions
19. What has been the best/lowest point in your life so far.

AFTER INTERVIEW

If you were successful, congratulations, if not, wait a few days then, phone the company and ask for feedback. They may give you some constructive criticism to help you with your next interview - if it is for the same company, you will be remembered positively.

YOUR JOB

Being a member of the Air Training Corps will help you fit in with their disciplines of working life. Apply the principles of being a good Cadet to being a good employee, and remember, all experience is useful even if it does not appear so at the time.

SPECIMEN LETTER

Mr J.M.Jones (Initials & name of the person)   Your home
The Job Title. Director. Manager. Partner etc. address
The Name of the Firm.   here on the right
Number & Name of Street,   Telephone/ Email
 Name of Town/City.   to contact you
County & Post Code.   Day/Date/Month/Year

Dear Sir/Madam or the persons surname Mr/Mrs if you already know them.

The first sentence saying what job it is you are applying for.

Details of your age, school attended, say what subjects you have studied and to what standard.

Any part-time jobs you have had, training schemes taken part in.

A paragraph about yourself, school duties, clubs or organisations you belong to and any responsibilities you have had.

Your hobbies or interests, sports activities.or involvement in the ATC, Duke of Edinburgh Award or any other achievements that would be of interest to a potential employer.

Tell them that you would like to work for them and that you would like to be considered for an interview.

A sentence at the end saying when you would be available to attend for an interview if you were chosen as a potential employee.

You finish it off

Yours faithfully,

Sign your name - then under it

PRINT YOUR NAME - NEATLY - IN BLOCK CAPITAL LETTERS.

THE ROYAL AIR FORCES ASSOCIATION FLYING SCHOLARSHIP SCHEME

Introduction

The RAF ASSOCIATION Flying Scholarship scheme provides the winning candidate a course of up to 35 hours flying training, and up to 12 hours for the four runners up, in light aircraft primarily to encourage young people of high calibre to obtain a National Private Pilots Licence. The scheme is open to male and female members of the Air Training Corps.

These scholarships are provided as a thank you to members of the Air Training Corps for all the support they give to the RAF Association each year in helping to raise funds for the Wings Appeal.

Training is given at selected clubs throughout the UK and covers all/ part of the tuition needed for the award-holder to obtain or go towards the completion of a National Private Pilots Licence (NPPL) up to a maximum of 35 hours flying.

This is not open to those who already hold an NPPL or PPL with a single Engine Piston-engined (SEP) aircraft rating.

Eligibility

1. A candidate must have been a member of the Air Training Corps for at least 12 months immediately prior to applying.
   Nationality Requirements
2. A candidate must have been a Commonwealth citizen or a citizen of the Republic of Ireland since birth or have been born in a country or territory, which is (or then was) within the Commonwealth or Republic of Ireland.
3. Each parent of a candidate must have born in a country or territory which is (or then was) within the Commonwealth or Republic of Ireland and each parent must be (or was at death) a commonwealth citizen or a citizen of the Republic of Ireland and is, or has been, one or the other at all times since birth.

4. The term 'Commonwealth citizen' Includes:
> a British citizen a British Dependent Territory citizen
> a British overseas citizen
> a British subject under British Nationality Act 1981
> a citizen of an independent Commonwealth country

5. A waiver of the nationality requirements above may be granted under exceptional circumstances by application to the Royal Air Forces Association.

Residence Requirements

6. Candidates, whether or not they are of UK origin, should normally have resided in the UK for a minimum of 5 years immediately preceding their application. In certain circumstances, particularly where an applicant is of UK origin, a shorter period of residence may be accepted and a waiver of part of the residence requirement may be granted provided that evidence of assimilation into the UK can be demonstrated.

Educational Qualifications

7. A candidate must, at the time of application, hold GCSE awards at Grade C or higher in English Language, Mathematics and 3 other subjects, only one of which may be non-academic (eg art, music), or the equivalent of such passes.

Age Limits

8. A candidate must be at least 17 years of age and under 20 years of age at the First of January of the year of application.

9. Flying training will not commence before the age of 17 and will not be undertaken without the written consent of a parent or guardian where the candidate is under the age of 18.

General Requirements

10. A candidate must be medically fit and able to obtain a UK NPPL medical declaration of health from his/hers doctor.

11. A candidate must be prepared to undergo a Flying Scholarship aptitude test.

12. Winning candidates must be able to attend a course of flying for a continous period of 45 days.
    Due to weather conditions it is assumed that the training will normally take before the end of October.

13. Winning candidates will be expected to attend the RAF Association Annual Conference at either Blackpool or Bournemouth, to be presented with their scholarships personally by the RAF Chief of Staff or their representative.

Selection Procedure

Method of Application

14. Applicants are to be nominated by a RAF Association Branch or Squadron Commander and applications must be submitted by 31st January for consideration in that year. However, applications from unsuccessful candidates will not be considered until at least 12 months have elapsed from the date of the previous application. Application forms can be obtained from the RAF Association Area HQ or the RAF Association CHQ, or from the web site **www.rafa.org.uk.**
Application forms should be submitted by a RAF Association Branch or Air Training Corps Squadrons to the
>RAF Association Central HQ,
>117½ Loughborough Road,
>Leicester,
>LE4 5ND

Short-listed candidates will be informed by mid March of the year of application.

Selection Procedure

15. Short listed candidates will be invited to the RAF Officers and Aircrew Selection Centre (OASC), RAF Cranwell, Lincs. for a board interview that includes flying scholarship aptitude tests and an interview. Candidates will then be debriefed and advised in writing whether or not they have been successful.
The decision of the selection board is final.

Expenses

16. Second class rail fare will be paid from a candidate's place of residence to RAF OASC. Meals and accommodation will be provided for the duration of the tests.
The maximum allowances will be notified separately.
Similar arrangements apply to award winning candidates attending the RAF Association Annual Conference venues.

17. Practical arrangements for the implementation of flying scholarship awards are made by the RAF Association in conjunction with the Air League Educational Trust.

18. Candidates will be expected to pay for their own transport costs to the flying school.

19. Flying Scholarships are valid only until the end of March of the year following the award.
However, training normally takes place during the spring or summer of that year with a view to completion of training by the end of the year.

20. Flying scholarships are valid only until the end of March the following year from the award. An award not completed or taken up within this period cannot be carried over to the following year, unless it is due to circumstances beyond the candidate's control (eg sudden illness or exceptional weather conditions).

21. A candidate who fails to meet the required standard and cannot complete the course will not be given a second chance.

Notes:
The Royal Air Forces Association reserves the right to vary the terms and conditions of the scheme outlined above.

The Royal Air Forces Association, 117½ Loughborough Road, Leicester, LE4 5ND

Charity Registration No. 226686

Cadet Vocational Qualification Office (CVQO)

Based at the Cadet Training Centre in Camberley, Surrey, CVQO is a registered Charity responsible for managing vocational qualifications for members of the Combined Cadet Forces, Sea Cadet Corps, Army Cadet Force and Air Training Corps.

The qualifications on offer have been carefully selected to show employers and educators the wide range of skills that young people and adults learn in the Cadet Forces. These skills include leadership, teambuilding, problem-solving, communication, health and physical fitness.

By offering qualifications designed to develop and improve these important practical skills, CVQO aims to provide members of the Cadet Forces with greater opportunities in both the classroom and the workplace.

"By providing a trusted standard of excellence, CVQO encourages and rewards achievement in both vocational and academic education."

Lieutenant Colonel Edward Woods, Director, CVQO

CVQO is accredited by Edexcel, City & Guilds and the Institute of Leadership and Management (ILM) to deliver a wide range of qualifications including the BTEC First Diploma in Public Services and the BTEC First Diploma in Music for Cadets, and up to level 5 Graduateship Awards for Adult Instructors.

BTEC First Diploma in Public Service

This internationally respected qualification is equivalent to 4 GCSEs at A*-C level (4 Standard Grades at levels 1-3 in Scotland). The course mixes theory and practical elements with an emphasis on leadership, teamwork, communications, problem solving and fitness.

The syllabus has been designed to improve valuable life skills including CV preparation, interviewing techniques, communication, first aid, adventure training, health and nutrition.

Cadets must be at least 16 years old to enrol.

In addition to existing Cadet activities, Cadets are required to complete the course syllabus which includes supervised adventure training activities and occasional weekend training.

CAREER DEVELOPMENTS

The BTEC Award is accredited by Edexcel.
The BTEC Programme is FREE for Cadets.
To enrol, contact your local Cadet headquarters.

"When I applied to university, the admission's tutors were very interested in the fact that I had earned a qualification completely in my own time outside of school and I feel it helped set me apart from the other applicants."
Joanna Woods, former Air Cadet from Sussex.

BTEC First Diploma in Music

"The qualifications offered by CVQO focus on communication, leadership and teamwork; all important skills that Universities look for in potential students." Dr. Alan Pearson, Principal of St Hild and St Bede, Durham University

Since September 2005, Cadets over 16 with an interest in music are able to earn a vocational qualification equivalent to 4 GCSEs at A*-C level (4 standard grades at levels 1-3 in Scotland).

The BTEC First Diploma in Music curriculum has been designed to develop a basic understanding of the music industry and combines technical skills with theory and practical elements. The BTEC Award is accredited by Edexcel.

Upon successful completion, Cadets will have demonstrated an understanding of all aspects of the music business including music selection, composition, performance, marketing, legal issues and budget forecasting. Cadets are expected to be able to play a musical instrument prior to enrolling on the course.

The BTEC Programme is FREE for Air Cadets.
To enrol, ask to your Squadron Commander or log onto
www.vqaward.org

Duke of Westminster Award

The Duke of Westminster Award is an annual prize which has been created by CVQO to recognise outstanding Cadets.
To be considered for the Duke of Westminster Award, Cadets must possess a wide range of skills and have demonstrated these attributes through a consistently high level of commitment and throughout his/her Cadet career.

CAREER DEVELOPMENTS

Cadets are nominated by their wing headquarters and must be enrolled in CVQO's BTEC Program to be considered for the award. Once nominated, Cadets must write a letter to CVQO explaining why they should be consider from these letters, a short list is produced and the finalists are interviewed by members of CVQO management team. Nominees are judged on academic achievement, contribution to society, communication skills, and contribution to Cadets.

The winning Cadet is presented with a certificate along with a cash prize to be used towards further training.

Adult Qualifications

For those of you who stay on in the ATC as adults there is the added advantage of continuing your vocational training. Whether you are teaching nutrition in the classroom or survival skills in the forest, Adult Instructors are inspiring today's youth to become tomorrow's leaders. It is the aim of CVQO to reward the efforts of those individuals, by providing them with the opportunity to earn a respected vocational qualification that recognises their achievements within the Cadet Forces and will also be beneficial in their civilian career.

With a wide range of awards on offer, CVQO has the ideal qualifications to help Adult Instructors get ahead both personally and professionally.

No funding is available at this time for Adult Qualifications and participating adults are responsible for all costs. For more information on each qualification please visit **www.vgaward.org**

"What I find particularly appealing about this innovative scheme is that young people, the future of this country, are being encouraged to achieve. Furthermore, it is entirely complementary to the education system"

Major General, Duke of Westminster,

Assistant Chief of the Defence Staff (Reserves and Cadets).

CVQ CHOICES

With seven different awards on offer, CVQO has the ideal qualification to suit your needs. So don't delay, enrol today and begin reaping the benefits! For a list of Adult Qualifications on offer, log onto
www.CVQO.co.uk/adult.php

Learning & Development

This qualification is offered to those adults who attend the KC-VI CCF Advanced course, the JOSC course or the Officer Initial Course. The courses obtained under Learning and Development are:
I-10 and L 11 - Enables Learning through presentation, demonstration and instruction.
A 1 _ Assesses candidates through a range of methods.
A2 - Assesses candidates through observation V 1 - Internal Verifier.

First Line Management

These qualifications are only suitable for newly recruited ACF and SCC adults and for whom are about to attend their Initial Training or Instructional Methods course.
Introductor Certificates in First Line Management

Licentiateship in Youth Leadership Training

This qualification is suitable for all adults who are involved with cadets and hold the relevant rank required for the qualification, Licentiateship in Youth Leadership and Training.

Graduateship in Youth Management and Training

This qualification is suitable for all adults who are involved with the cadets and hold the relevant rank required for the qualification Graduateship in Youth Management and Training

For dates and details of all courses contact the CVQO office, Frimley Park, Surrey Tel: 01276 - 60171 1

Information and details of CVQ have been published with the kind per-mission of the CVQ Office, Frimley Park, Surrey.

NVQ ADULT QUALIFICATIONS
Qualifications on Offer

Qualifications	NVQ	Awarding	Body
Learning and Development			
L10 & L11 - Enables Teaching Through Instruction,	Part Level 3		Edexcel
Presentation and Demonstration			
A1 - Assessment Using a Range of Methods	Level 3		Edexcel
A2 - Assessment through Observation	Level 3		Edexcel
V1 - Verification Award. Demonstrates Ability to	Level 4		Edexcel
Conduct Quality Assurance of Assessment Process			
First Line Management			
Introductory Certificate in First Line Management	Level 3		ILM
Licentiateship			
Licentiateship in Youth Leadership & Training	Level 4		City & Guilds
Graduateship			
Graduateship in Youth Management & Training	Level 5		City & Guilds

MAKE YOUR FUTURE COUNT
CVQO

YOUR
OPPORTUNITY
TO
STEP FORWARD
AND
STAND OUT

CAREER DEVELOPMENTS

Qualifications on Offer

Awarding Body	Award	Level	Comparable to
City & Guilds	Membership in Strategic Youth Management	7	Master's Degree
City & Guilds	Graduateship in Youth Management and Training	6	Honours Degree
City & Guilds	Licentiateship in Youth Leadership and Training	4	Diploma
ILM	Award in First Line Management	3	A level
Edexcel	L10 and L11 Enables Learning through Presentation, Demonstration and Instruction	Part 3	AS level
Edexcel	A1 Assessment using a Range of Methods	3	A level
Edexcel	A2 Assessment through Observation	3	A level
Edexcel	V1 Verification award demonstrates the ability to Conduct Quality Assurance of the Assessment Process	4	Diploma
ILM	Corporate Membership	-	-

CAREER DEVELOPMENTS

Self Test Questions

1. How does being a cadet help you in your career.
2. What is meant by 'job satisfaction.
3. What is a good reason why you should change a job.
4. Why is experience costly.
5. In making a decision what options should you consider.
6. Employers sometimes ask for applications in writing - why.
7. Why do you first write a letter in pencil.
8. What is Cranwell and where is it located.
9. What do you understand by the presentation of a letter
10. What is a CV.
11. Name five main headings to consider for a CV
12. What is the aim of an interview.
13. What should you know about a prospective employer.
14. How must you prepare for an interview.
15. What is the image you should present to an interviewer.
16. Could you take notes/questions to ask at an interview.
17. Give six questions you might ask yourself if you are 'rating' or 'assessing' a person
18. Why might you have to undergo a medical examination before employment.
19. What age do you have to be to join the Royal Air Force.
20. How can your friends/family help you to prepare for an interview.

REMEMBER -
"YOU NEVER GET A SECOND CHANCE TO MAKE A FIRST IMPRESSION"

CVQO

APPROACHING 16 OR OVER?
HAVE YOU COMPLETED:

JNCO or SNCO or other Cdt Leadership
Courses or CSLA ☑

D of E Phys Rec or Sporting Event ☑

2 AT Activities (including Gliding & Flying)
Training ☑

Ldg Cdt or D of E Exped & First Aid ☑

D of E Exped or 1st Class Cdt or
AT Exercises ☑

THEN YOU HAVE **78%**
TOWARDS A DIPLOMA!

ADD TO THAT...
1 Workbook
and
1 Project

RESULT:
1 BTEC
First Diploma
in Public Services

100%

COST:
FREE!

WHAT ARE YOU WAITING FOR?

It's worth 4 GCSEs grades A*- C or 4 Standard Grades levels 1 - 3
Contact your VQ Officer to find out more.

 City & Guilds Approved Centre   edexcel   ilm Accredited Centre

Cadet and Adult Qualifications

www.cvqo.org
01276 601718

CVQO Ltd. Registered Charity No. 1135234 Registered in England & Wales No. 5730992 Registered in Scotland No. SC 039201

6-18

Chapter 7
EXPEDITION TRAINING

Expedition training can be the most exciting and fun subject of your cadet training. It is also the most important, bringing other skills you have been taught in to practical use. The skills and knowledge you gain in expedition and adventurous training will benefit you throughout your life. Not forgetting that it is an important part of the Duke of Edinburgh's Award Scheme.

THE COUNTRY CODE
Expeditions may take you over Military Training Areas, privately owned property, or land where the public has rights of access. The Country Code applies wherever you are. You have a personal responsibility to ensure that you protect the natural beauty of the countryside and the wildlife living there. The message is, **abuse it and lose it.**

THE PRAYER OF THE TREE

You who pass by and would raise your hand against me, hearken ere you harm me.

I am the heat of your camp fire on a cold night, the friendly shade screening you from the summer sun.

My fruits are refreshing draughts quenching your thirst as you journey on.

I am the beam that holds your house, the board of your table, the bed on which you lie, the timber that builds your boat.

I am the handle of your hoe, the door of your homestead, the wood of your cradle, the shell of your last resting place.

I am the gift of God and the friend of man.

You who pass by, listen to my prayer, harm me not.

Anon

EXPEDITION TRAINING

The COUNTRY CODE is a series of ten reminders based on common sense – and common failings. Thoughtless disposal of litter is perhaps the most unsightly and costly problem our countryside faces. For instance, did you know that cows love shiny ring pulls from drink cans; they eat them along with the grass and they can perforate their stomachs. Next time you are in the country, have a look at the rubbish others leave behind – pretty isn't it?

"LEAVE NOTHING BUT YOUR FOOTPRINTS"

RESPECT THE PEOPLE AND LIFE OF THE COUNTRYSIDE

PROTECT ALL WILD LIFE

GO CAREFULLY ON COUNTRY ROADS

SECURELY FASTEN ALL GATES

EXPEDITION TRAINING

THE COUNTRY CODE

GUARD AGAINST RISK OF FIRE

USE GATES AND STILES

KEEP DOGS UNDER PROPER CONTROL

LEAVE NO LITTER

KEEP TO THE FOOTPATHS

SAFEGUARD WATER SUPPLIES

EXPEDITION TRAINING

DISCIPLINES OF PERSONAL HEALTH AND HYGIENE
HOW TO WALK – BOOTS AND FEET

You are issued with one pair of feet, with some of the most delicate bones in your body; so it makes sense to try and look after them! Some of you may already have problems with your feet through wearing badly fitting shoes.

BOOTS

It is most important to make sure that your boots are comfortable, giving your ankles the support and protection they require. They are expensive, and even if you can afford two pairs – one polished up for parades, the other kept for 'heavy work', unfortunately your feet will grow and trying to walk in boots at the age of 16 bought when you where 14, is a very painful experience and will do untold damage to your feet.

Good quality, well fitting boots or shoes are an investment, not only will they look after your feet, preventing problems later on, they SHOULD last longer.

FITTING BOOTS

1. When you go to buy new boots, take a thick pair of socks or two pairs of normal socks to wear when trying on your boots.
2. Make sure you can move your toes and that when standing still your toes do not touch the toe of the boot.
3. A method of testing the fitting is to be able to get a finger down between your heel and the back of the boot. If you can do this and your toes just touch the toe of the boot, they should fit you comfortably.
4. Fully lace up the boots to check that the uppers have enough room for your foot and that they are comfortable.

CARE OF BOOTS

1. Keep your boots 'well fed', leather will dry and crack if you do not put polish on them regularly.
2. If your boots get wet, do not dry them too close to heat, they will go hard and crack. Stuff them with newspaper; changing it often, this draws out the damp.
3. Always clean mud off your boots, it dries the polish out of the leather causing cracking and lack of water resistance.

EXPEDITION TRAINING

CARE OF YOUR FEET
SOCKS
To give you and your feet the best chance of comfort, it is important to have natural fibre socks. Make sure that you have at least two pairs of thick Wool, Cotton or a mix of the two is ideal. Natural fibre lets your feet 'breathe'. Keep your socks in good repair; 'holey' socks cause blisters. If you use the terry 'tube' socks, they are better worn inside out as there is less chance of friction.

FEET
When walking with a backpack, the extra weight you carry on your back is equivalent to more than three times the same weight on each foot. Your balance is more critcal and you will adjust to a different 'gait' When walking the weight of your body is transferred to the ball of your foot rather than the heel. Your normal "civilian pedestrian" feet will need some extra help to cope.

Make sure your boots are "broken in" before expedition work.

Wear thick 'boot socks'

Prepare your feet – if you have corns etc. see a chiropodist - if you don't wish to be a casualty

Keep your feet clean, dust them every morning (or more often if necessary) with a foot powder. Do not use too much powder, it will 'clump' and be uncomfortable.

Wash your feet regularly, rub them dry and check that your toe nails are not sharp.

Change your socks from one foot to the other, (stops the sock from forming too closely to your foot).

NEVER SOAK YOUR FEET WHEN ON THE MARCH, a quick dip, quick dry and then walk on IS beneficial.

TREATMENT OF BLISTERS
Prevention is better than cure, if when you check your feet you find a reddened patch of skin, this is a blister waiting to happen.

To prevent further pressure, apply a plaster or a strip of hypoallergenic tape to the affected area.

EXPEDITION TRAINING

If you already have a blister and wish to open it, either use a sterile lance or sterilize a needle by holding it in the flame of a match and letting it cool before use.

To lance the blister, prick the skin at the side then gently press the liquid out until the blister is flat. Apply a plaster or a sterile dressing secured by two strips of plaster applied like a cross. It is important to keep the area clean to guard against infection.

WET FEET

Should you get your feet wet, if at all possible dry them and your boots, putting on fresh socks. "Walking to dry them" will make your skin tender and you will end up a casualty.

are YOUR FEET always happy ?

CRAMP

If you have been walking for a long period, or perhaps your boots are laced up too tightly, you may get a sudden very painful spasm in your leg muscles. Loosening off your boots and massaging the affected area is the best treatment. The cramp should go in a few minutes.

APART FROM YOUR FEET....

THIRST

After the first few hours of walking, particularly in hot weather, you may find that you develop a great thirst, not necessarily because your body has need of fluid, but by your mouth feeling dry. An alternative to drinking large quantities of water is to chew a blade of grass or suck a prune.

A further alternative is to carry a piece of raw onion in your mouth; it also helps prevent your lips from cracking. (Petroleum jelly does the same job for your lips).

When on an organised Cadet or Duke of Edinburgh's Award expedition, care is always taken to ensure that there is an adequate supply of water available. Remember you should drink 3/4 litres of water each day. However, should you have been without water for a long period, sip slowly to prevent your stomach going into cramps. Never swallow snow or ice, let it melt first, preferably by boiling it. Do not assume that spring water is fit to drink, who knows what is in the water further upstream? Remember to sterilise your water bottle before you use it, by using a sterilising tablet.

ALCOHOL

As a Cadet you are not supposed to drink alcohol. Alcohol slows reaction, impairs thinking and in cold weather can make you more susceptible to hypothermia. Alcohol slows down the heart rate, and therefore slows the 'heating system' to the body.

PERSONAL MEDICATION

If you have a medical condition that requires you to take medication, **ENSURE THAT YOU HAVE ENOUGH WITH YOU, MAKE SURE YOU PACK IT WHERE YOU CAN FIND IT!**

PERSONAL HYGIENE

This might be seen as a low priority when you are on expedition or camping, yet the reverse is true. Sweat stays on the skin surface and if not removed can lose you friends and cause sores particularly between the legs, under the arms, around the waist and feet. It takes self-discipline to keep clean, particularly so if there is only cold water to wash in.

Clean your teeth regularly; a build up of old food and drink makes your mouth feel dry.

Weather and time permitting, wash out dirty socks and underwear, this will prevent them festering in your kit.

Wash Kit

Keep your soap in a soapbox; it prevents it from going soggy and becoming un-usable, keep your wash kit in a plastic bag to keep it clean and dry. Try to dry your towel, it will stop it smelling - hang it out in the fresh air.

CLOTHING AND EQUIPMENT

You are never certain what sort of weather you may be faced with in the UK, in less than an hour it can change from bright warm sun to cold, damp or rain. This makes it difficult to be dressed in the right gear. You need to remember that whatever you chose to wear needs to:

Keep water out – keep your body heat in"

JACKET/ANORAK

If your jacket lets water in, your clothing underneath will get damp or wet. Wet clothing will not insulate your body; in fact it will cool you quicker, increasing your chances of becoming a casualty through hypothermia.

Cheaper waterproofs are effective - they keep water out. The down side is that because the fabric cannot 'breathe' your body heat cannot escape and you may get very hot and damp from the inside.

Modern 'breathable' waterproofs are available. They are lightweight, keep you dry and are expensive! It is suggested that if you really enjoy walking or expeditions and plan to continue after you have completed your Duke of Edinburgh's Award, then save up for one of these jackets.

A less expensive alternative is to have a decent warm jacket (non – waterproof), and buy a waterproof CAGOULE. Most have a ventilated yoke at the back and they pack neatly to sit on the top of your kit for easy access.

SHIRTS AND UNDERWEAR

Many experienced walkers wear woollen vests and tops because it has the best insulating and breathing properties. Some people find that wool next to the skin is most uncomfortable. Whatever you wear, apply the 'ONION SKIN PRINCIPLE'. This means wearing several thin layers of clothing (two minimum), to trap the warmth in. It is better to wear two thin layers rather than two thick – it holds more air in. Always keep an extra 'layer' in your kit, as you may well need it.

EXPEDITION TRAINING

HATS

If the sun is blazing down, wear a hat; it will protect you from uncomfortable sunburn and prevent possible sunstroke.

If the weather is cold and damp, wear a hat; it will prevent you losing valuable body heat. BALACLAVAS are a good choice as they can be pulled down over your ears and face if it is very cold or windy.

PERSONAL KIT LIST

Expeditions are either in uniform or civvies. Whatever the kit, wear your jacket. (Your County may well have cagoules to loan out for expedition work).

The following lists are an example of what you will need to carry with you.

To be carried on you:

Map, compass, Pathfinder Protractor/Romer, Whistle on lanyard, Matches in a waterproof container, Plasters, Pencil and notebook. Unless told otherwise a mobile phone in working order.

To be carried in your backpack:

Personal cleaning kit, towel, spare underclothes and socks, Mess tins with knife fork and spoon, pan scrub for cleaning your mess tins, reserve food such as Kendal mint cake, chocolate, raisins.

Remember – you carry what you take so think about weight.

Mug – metal preferred as you can heat it up, but plastic will do. A water bottle with a secure top. Groundsheet and a good length of strong string. A small torch, sleeping bag liner and a survival bag or blanket.

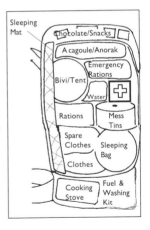

The following can be put into a kit bag to be delivered to camp site – if that is how the expedition is being organised, otherwise you will have to carry them yourself.

Sleeping bag, spare change of clothing, spare boots or shoes if available. Trainers, wool pullover. *NOT TO FORGET YOUR BUNGEES*

EXPEDITION TRAINING

PACKING YOUR BACKPACK

The type and capacity of backpack you are able to use can make all the difference to the way it is packed. If it does not have a frame, you will need to be careful not to overload it as you may end up with hard and odd shaped items sticking into your back whilst carrying it.

The emphasis is packing INTO the backpack, not hanging boots or other items on the outside until you look like a Christmas tree on the move. Look carefully at the **LOAD CARRYING** and the **DISTRIBUTION** of the load as illustrated in the diagrams. Stove fuel should be packed in a well-sealed polythene bag stored well away from your rations. All clothing and your sleeping bag should also be kept in polythene bags. It is a good idea to use a strong polythene bag as a liner for your kit bag; it will keep the contents dry.

It is worthwhile taking some time to practice packing your backpack correctly and then wear/carry it to ensure that it is comfortable.

As a rough 'rule of thumb' you should not carry more than one quarter of your body weight.

LOAD CARRYING — The RIGHT and Wrong methods

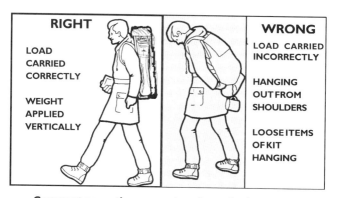

RIGHT

LOAD CARRIED CORRECTLY

WEIGHT APPLIED VERTICALLY

WRONG

LOAD CARRIED INCORRECTLY

HANGING OUT FROM SHOULDERS

LOOSE ITEMS OF KIT HANGING

Carry not more than a quarter of your body weight

EXPEDITION TRAINING

LAYOUT OF A CAMP SITE

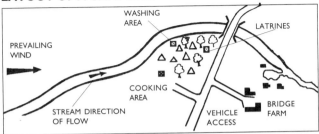

WASHING AREA

LATRINES

PREVAILING WIND

COOKING AREA

STREAM DIRECTION OF FLOW

VEHICLE ACCESS

BRIDGE

FARM

Your Officer or Adult Instructor will have gained permission for you to camp on the land and for you to have the authority and training time. If you are camping out with some friends for a few days, remember it is very important to gain permission from the landowners first.
The ideal campsite is one offering shelter from the prevailing wind, on well-drained fairly level area, facing East to hopefully catch the early morning sun. It should be as far away as possible from any houses, be close to a clean water supply and be in the open.

IS IT SAFE?

1. Is the site below the level of a river, lake, dam or reservoir, whose banks could burst or overflow in the event of a severe storm, or in a dried-up stream which 'comes to raging life' in a storm.
2. Is the site under overhanging rocks or cliffs, or any other form of danger, for example under a bridge or viaduct.
3. Ensure that the ground does not slope down from the bivi area to where the cooking area is set out, and that the tents are not close enough to be a fire risk.

CAMP LAYOUT

1. Can the tents/bivi's be correctly pitched in the area and sheltered from the wind and not under trees
2. If a squadron or flight camp, a COOKING AREA sited where there is no risk of causing fire, properly set out for the purpose to be conveniently close to the bivis, but again, not too close in case of fire.

EXPEDITION TRAINING

3. Toilet/washing area defined, sited down wind and away from the tent site and cooking area. Latrines must be given some privacy.
4. Some access for a vehicle.

LATRINES

One of our normal everyday occurrences is the use of a toilet. Normally you sit in solitary comfort, door shut and perhaps a magazine to read. You will not find it quite so civilized in the field! There are a few important things to remember.

Hygiene: In spite of being "in the field" you have to take more care about using the toilet facilities and cleaning your hands. There is a greater possibility of infection: to have digestive problems in the field is no picnic.

CONSTRUCTION OF A FIELD LATRINE

On military land it is normal to see portable toilet units servicing frequently used camp areas. Some Counties have chemical toilets for field use. However, should these items not be available, knowing how to construct a field latrine is a useful skill. It will need a spade or shovel as digging a hole in the ground is essential as any exposed excrement attracts flies. Try to lift any grass over the chosen site carefully; it can be replaced before leaving .

You will need to dig a hole not less than 44cm (one foot six inches) deep and 22cm (nine inches) wide. The earth taken from the hole should be piled up ready to be used by each individual to cover excrement and finally to fill the hole before leaving the site. If time permits, a 'seat' can be made for the latrine, see diagram.

Before leaving, the ground used for the toilet must be clearly marked with a sign stating that it is 'soiled ground'.

Privacy when using a latrine is an important factor, therefore some sort of screen or concealment is desirable. Your Instructors will no doubt introduce some sort of control.

EXPEDITION TRAINING

One method is to provide a container for the toilet paper that is left in a prominent position. Each user must remember **to return it after use.** The message – when the toilet is "engaged" the container is **not there**. Simple, but effective.

Note: it is important to put the toilet roll in a plastic bag to keep it dry.

PREPARING FOOD IN THE FIELD

Your experience of cooking may be limited to zapping a pre-prepared meal in the microwave, cooking in the field is a little different.

Traditionally, one of the first tasks on reaching a campsite is to "brew-up" for the whole group.

During cold weather, particularly if you have been physically active or walking, it is important to have hot drinks regularly, and when you do have a meal, to ensure that it is hot, to sustain you.

COOKERS

You may use butane gas cookers, or 'hexi cookers' that use small blocks of solid fuel in a folding tin container. The most effective way of using a hexi cooker is to scrape a hole in the ground deep enough to shield your mess tins when they are on the cooker. This prevents any wind blowing your fuel out and keeps the food from chilling.

Important note: Make sure that you never use your hexi/butane/ other cooker where it could cause a fire, for instance on dry leaf mould in wooded areas.

MESS TIN COOKING

Mess tin cooking is usually carried out with two of you "teaming up" as a cooker is efficient enough to produce hot food for two.

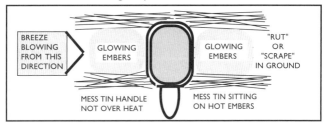

EXPEDITION TRAINING

If you are lucky to be issued with tinned rations, there are two important points for you to remember.

1. Make sure there are two holes made in the top of the tin before you heat it, otherwise the tin could 'blow' and scald you badly.
2. If you have aluminum mess tins, do not use the water your tins have 'cooked in' to make a hot drink. It can be used for washing yourself or your tins.

Solid fuel cookers make a sticky black mess on the bottom of your mess tins, an easy way to remove most of it is to rub it hard along grass, then use a pan scrub to remove the rest. Remember to clean the inside, wipe out with grass, and then wash out.

FOOD-RATIONS

The need for a balanced diet becomes more important as the distance you travel increases and the 'going' gets harder.

If a journey is to take several days you will have to plan your menus giving variety and a balanced diet.

The amount of food you require daily will depend upon the type of country you are moving over and how much you are carrying.

If it is mountainous then your body will use more energy for you to replace by more energy producing food. Extremes of hot or cold weather have the same effect.

Food has to be carried, too much will add unnecessary weight to your load; too little and you will go hungry and that will cause problems.

The use of dehydrated foods *(Pouched Foods)* are very useful, especially as emergency rations.

If you can take dehydrated food you select the items that give you the most carbohydrates (sugar, starches and fats).

Note; additional water will be required if using dehydrated rather than pre-prepared 'ready' meals.

Only take food you like and enjoy. Keep all your meals simple to prepare and eat foods hot as often as you can.

'All in' stews are very good as you only need one mess tin to cook it in and it will be hot which is important.

EXPEDITION TRAINING

FOOD HYGIENE

When on an expedition or exercise the very last thing you will think about will be food hygiene.

Food Poisoning - through using dirty mess tins or using fresh rations that have not ben properly cooked can really spoil your fun - and everyone elses!

1. While you are eating your hot food put a mess tin of water on to boil.
2. Ensure you clean Mess Tins and KFS *properly* use very hot water.
3. Carefully wrap cooked food if you intend to eat it later.
4. NEVER EVER RE-HEAT RICE.
5. Take all your rubbish, tins, plastic with you - **leave nothing but your footprints**

COMPOSITE RATIONS

As a Cadet you may have Service issue Composite Rations (**COMPO**) issued on field training. These rations have been developed over many years to give the soldier a high quality balanced diet.

CONTENT OF COMPO RATIONS

Compo is issued in a 24 hour Ration Pack ('rat pack'), which is produced in different menu selections. Compo rations are slowly being replaced by a pouched system. Pouched rations can be eaten hot or cold. If heating, follow the instructions on the pack ensure the food is hot. If a pouch is punctured and food is visible it should not be eaten.

BOIL IN THE BAG

Ensure that you carry extra water - or have access to extra water for these meals as they require more to cook correctly.

Cook your food in your mess tin to ensure it is thoroughly heated, thus preventing possible food poisoning

TO HEAT CANS

You can cook compo rations 'in the can' by piercing **TWO** holes in the lid of the can, stand the can in your mess tin and fill with water until the can is half submerged. Bring to the boil and boil for TEN minutes. Handle carefully when opening a hot can. This is a quick and easy method of cooking the food, but it does not taste quite as good as when heated out of the tin.

WATER PURIFICATION TABLETS

These are part of your ration pack and it is important that you know how to use them. Normally, drinking water is provided on Cadet organised training, but there may be an occasion where this does not happen. For Drinking Water, add one tablet to a litre of water, leave for TEN MINUTES before use. Leave for at least **THIRTY MINUTES** if using to make up your Lemon or Orange drinks. You must remember your **liquid intake** must be 3 to 4 litres per day. Once you are thirsty, it is too late.

WINDPROOF/WATERPROOF MATCHES

These matches MUST be kept for lighting your Hexamine blocks in bad weather conditions. Don't use them for any other reason or you will be in difficulty if rain or bad weather sets it and you have:
**NO WINDPROOF/WATERPROOF MATCHES ......
    NO HOT FOOD – NO HOT DRINK – NO WARMTH
Don't forget you will be assessed on you outdoor cooking for your award.**

USEFUL MEASURE TO NOTE

If you fill your small mess tin to the bottom rivet that holds the handle hinge, you will have HALF a PINT of water in the tin.

HILL WALKING SKILLS

Any walk over a reasonable period of time requires you to have a rhythm in the way you walk. This is especially so when HILL WALKING and carrying a loaded backpack. It is best to start out at a steady pace, one that you feel capable of keeping up for a few hours. If you are finding it difficult to talk or sing whilst walking, you are walking too fast – slow down. A slow plodding pace will get you to your next stop point as quickly as walking fast and having to take regular breaks. The other bonus is that you will not feel hot, sticky and overheated. Wise walkers conserve their energy and enjoy their walk.

EXPEDITION TRAINING

CLIMBING A HILL

Climbing directly up a hill puts strain on your calf muscles and Achilles tendons. Walking in a "zigzag" fashion across the slope your feet will be in full contact with the ground, with less chance of slipping. It may be slightly further to walk, but far less tiring.

WRONG **RIGHT**

KEEPING YOUR BALANCE

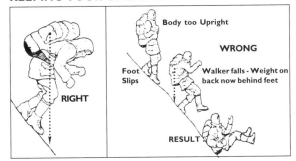

RIGHT

Body too Upright

WRONG

Foot Slips

Walker falls - Weight on back now behind feet

RESULT

Descending a slope safely carrying a full backpack requires some skill. Running or attempting to slide down is not recommended. Your balance plays a great part, the main thing is to bend both knees and lean forward. By adopting this stance your legs act as springs and absorb the shaking up your body would have had. Descend by traversing across the slope, keep your hand on the uphill side and near to the ground for support should you slip. Keep off any slopes with loose stones or scree. The golden rule is if a slope frightens you too much – find another way down.

EXPEDITION TRAINING

CROSSING RIVERS or STREAMS

In the first place never attempt to cross a river on your own.
Such hazards are best avoided unless there is no safer alternative.
When crossing a stream or shallow river an Instructor must always be
present. Never attempt to cross a river or stream in full flood. Water
is a powerful element and it is easy to underestimate its force. There
may also be hidden dangers such as stones, weed etc. that will cause
you to fall. Remember, you will end up with wet boots and probably
wet feet. The best plan is to find a good crossing point, a bridge or
ford. Do not attempt to build a raft unless one of your qualified
instructors are with you and checks it for safety before use.

STOPPING FOR A REST

On any walk taking several hours you must stop and rest at regular
intervals. The time between each stop will depend on the 'going' –
difficult or easy. When resting lay down and raise your feet higher
than your head. Don't halt for more than five minutes or your muscles
will stiffen up.

CARE OF THE ENVIRONMENT

Trees are a valuable natural resource, which take many years to
mature. Many of the wild animals, birds and insects rely on trees for
their food and protection.
In Britain we cannot grow sufficient trees to meet our needs and
import many million pounds worth of timber each year.
We must take care in preserving what we have, follow the Country
Code. Do not break branches off trees, or carve in to the trunks.
Remember the Prayer of the Tree at the beginning of this Chapter.

IMPROVISED SHELTER

There will be occasions when you do not have a tent to shelter in.
The British wervicemen have the reputation of being able to improvise,
"Any fool can rough it, but a trained serviceman will make themselves
comfortable under any conditions". As a Cadet, you should try and
follow their lead. See the illustrations on the next page to give a few
ideas on how to put up improvised shelters.

EXPEDITION TRAINING

(a) A shelter with two ponchos constructed on the same principle as a BIVI for two.

(b) A poncho shelter made against a fallen tree trunk for one person. The groundsheet must be on the side of the trunk away from the prevailing wind.

(c) Another example of a poncho type of shelter for one person. The rope must be strong enough and the open side of the poncho away from the prevailing wind.

IMPOVISED SHELTERS

IMPROVISED TENT

Using a string/rope between two supports, (perhaps suitable trees), tie poncho over the string, pegging the bottom edges to the ground. This type of "tent" can also be put up against a fence or wall using one half of the tent as shown in the picture as the triangle A – B – C. To make a Basha for two you need two ponchos string or bungees (at least 6), meat skewers or tent pegs are useful (8 or 12 are needed). A length of strong string is always useful to have in your kit. Tent

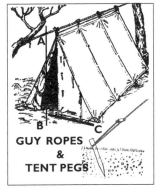

GUY ROPES & TENT PEGS

pegs must NOT be driven into the ground with the head of an axe, use the proper mallet. The pegs should be driven in to the ground at an angle (see diagram) and not so far in the ground that they cannot be seen.

EXPEDITION TRAINING

ADVENTUROUS TRAINING & PHYSICAL ACTIVITIES

Having a responsible attitude towards all activities you take part in goes a long way to ensuring your safety and the safety of others. This means careful planning and preparation. The Rescue teams often report that "The party was totally unprepared for the expedition", or "They had not been trained in map reading", even worse, the Coroner at an Inquest reported "They had no idea that the deceased was suffering from Hypothermia".

Your Officers and Adult Instructors have the responsibility of ensuring that all adventurous training and physical activities are correctly planned; this includes suitably qualified persons to instruct or guide you through. Part of the planning is briefing you the Cadet in all aspects of the activity. This will include the kit you require, who will be in charge of the training/activity, who the designated First Aid Person is, where they will be sited.

You may also be given 'no go' areas, make sure you know where they are.

Your responsibility to yourself is to make sure you take the correct kit and follow instructions given.

Your responsibility to all the other Cadets is to be alert. Watch out for others, if you are working in hot weather, heat exhaustion can occur quickly. In cold or wet and windy weather, hypothermia can happen to the best of us. Your Instructors will be watching out, but it is almost impossible to see everything.

If you see another Cadet about to do something that will put him/herself or others at risk, don't be slow in trying to stop them. It is not 'sneaky' it is being responsible.

Perhaps most important of all, enjoy the experience – give it your best.

EXPEDITION TRAINING

THE ACTIVITIES THAT ARE CONSIDERED AS ADVENTUROUS & PHYSICAL ARE AS FOLLOWS:

Mountaineering – including Hill Walking, Rock Climbing, Abseiling, Skiing, Caving, Canoeing, Off Shore Sailing, Rafting, Swimming, Gliding or Hang Gliding, Paracending, Sub - Aqua Diving and all activities involving the hazard of water.

OFFICIAL PERMISSION
On no account should you organise activities without the knowledge and assistance of your Officers or Instructors.

For your safety's sake,
REMEMBER – SHOULD THERE BE AN ACCIDENT YOU

ARE ONLY COVERED BY INSURANCE IF THE ACTIVITY

IS OFFICIALLY PLANNED AND ORGANISED.

PREVENTION OF ACCIDENTS ON OUTDOOR ACTIVITIES - PLANNING

Your Instructors will expect you to work through and be involved withthe planning process as part of your training.

Plan your route beforehand, ensure all members of the group are fully briefed and all have copies of the Route Card, map refs and check points and RVs, campsites and your Estimated Time of Arrival all supported by **accurate map references.**

If you are walking in areas where there are rescue posts or mountain rescue posts, know their locations and procedures including the map references of telephone boxes. Decide on a **Lost Drill** e.g. "Go West till you strike the main road" or "Keep walking down – stream".

EXPEDITION TRAINING

BEFORE YOU GO

1. As an individual, always carry a map, compass, protractor, pencil, whistle, small first aid kit and a torch In your jacket or in pockets
2. Have emergency rations such as chocolate, glucose tablets, dried fruit etc. DON'T eat them unless in an emergency.
3. Always carry warm clothing, but reduce non – essentials like two sweaters when one will do.

BEFORE YOU SET OUT

1. Don't overdress, leave off the pullover – carry it on top of your pack until the harder part of the walk is over.
2. Report to the local Rescue Post giving them a copy of your Route Card and expected time back.
3. Check the weather conditions and the forecasts for the duration of your walk

OUT ON THE HILLS

1. Always stay together; unless there is an injured person, in which case half of the party should stay with the casualty, while the other half goes for help.
2. Walk at the pace of the slowest person.
3. If you go out as a group, never travel in groups of less than five.
4. Remember to observe the Country Code.
5. Carry at least one polythene survival sack or sleeping bag per two persons.
6. Stick to the route agreed.
7. Make one decision among the group on the direction to take. If a compass bearing is used, have others check it, then trust your compass.
8. Do not assume that your mobile phone will work.
   If the weather deteriorates –
   DON'T PRESS ON; TURN BACK.
9. If fog descends, **carefully** find a sheltered place, ensure you keep as warm and dry as possible, have a hot drink. Use your whistle to make the distress call if necessary.
10. Don't throw stones; these can dislodge bigger ones and could cause an accident.

EXPEDITION TRAINING

IF YOU DO GET LOST:

1. **DO NOT SPLIT UP**
2. **DO NOT PANIC**
3. **DO NOT FORGET TO USE YOUR MAP, COMPASS AND COMMON SENSE**
4. **REMEMBER THE INTERNATIONAL DISTRESS CALL – SIX BLASTS ON YOUR WHISTLE OR SIX TORCH FLASHES PER MINUTE.**

SAFETY ON THE HIGHWAYS

By day or night, when moving as an individual on foot you must:

1. Use a footpath; if there is not one, walk on the side of the road facing the nearest traffic (normally the right hand side), keep as close to the side as possible.
2. Cross motorways by bridges or underpasses, railways by bridges or level crossings.
3. When dark, keep an extra sharp lookout and wear a high visibility jacket/tabard or if not available, light coloured clothing which will show up in the lights of a vehicle.

Note: Walking on the highways at any time as a group should be organised and led by an Instructor.

EMERGENCY PROCEDURES

Emergency Messages

The Police are responsible for calling out the rescue services. The information they will require is as follows:

A. The exact location of the injured person(s) with a six-figure grid reference and a description/landmarks of the area for a helicopter pilot to identify.
B. The number of injured persons and their names.
C. The nature of their injuries.
D. The time of the accident.
E. Mobile Phone number(s) held by members of the group.

EXPEDITION TRAINING

Those going for help must remember the area and landscape with any particular reference point to help find the site on return with a rescue party. (Write the information down).

Waiting for help to arrive

1. Those looking after the injured should set up shelters and carry out emergency first aid with particular reference to the prevention of hypothermia/exposure.
2. It will be necessary to mark the site with light coloured clothing or bandages on sticks where they can easily attract attention.
3. There are International **Ground to Air Signals** that can be used to communicate with rescue aircraft; these are shown on the next page.
4. In addition to these signals, **A RED FLARE, A RED SQUARE OF CLOTH** or a **FIRE** are also recognised **International Alarm Signals.**
5. Setting out clothing or items of kit, or a person lying down taking up the shape of the letter can make the shape of each signal. Get help any way you can.
6. Be alert; watch out for the rescue party to guide them in by the quickest route.
7. Make yourselves as comfortable as possible; 'brew up', eat HOT food, keep together, keep warm, keep up the morale.

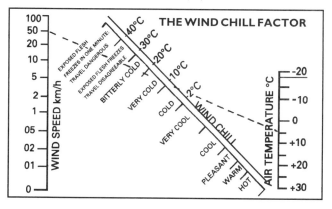

GROUND TO AIR SIGNALS

		REQUEST ASSISTANCE
letter	signal	
		WE ARE PROCEEDING IN THIS DIRECTION
letter	signal	
		MEDICAL ASSISTANCE REQUIRED
letter	signal	
		NO WE DO NOT NEED ANYTHING
letter	signal	

EXPEDITION TRAINING

WIND CHILL FACTOR

Insufficient attention is paid to the combined effect of air temperature and wind speed has on the human body. This combined effect is the **Wind Chill Factor.** The air temperature may be quite warm, but it only needs a wind blowing at 24 k.p.h. (15 m.p.h.) to cause body cooling, particularly to the head, face and hands.

Wind speeds above 24 k.p.h. cool the body slower, but can cause the body to burn up more energy; there is also the hazard of being blown over whilst walking. The diagram on previous page 7-24 is reproduced from the book *Mountain craft and Leadership by Alec Langmuir* and illustrates graphically how important it is to be aware of the Wind Chill Factor. As an example it shows:

The air temperature at +5 degrees C, at a wind speed of 50 k.p.h.

(31 m.p.h.) it crosses the Wind Chill Line at "Very Cold".

Always wear or carry windproof clothing

PRECAUTIONS & ADVICE

Before setting out on a hill walk or expedition, you would be well advised to check out the wind speeds and ensure that you take adequate steps to prevent rapid chilling.

Try and keep warm and dry, wet clothing combined with Wind Chill can cause Hypothermia

Wear a hat and gloves

Eat the right food, keep energy levels high

Do not get too tired

Never underestimate or ignore the Wind Chill Factor.

Check First Aid Chapter for the treatment of Extremes of Temperature (heat and cold).

EXPEDITION TRAINING

SUMMARY

Accidents don't just happen; they are CAUSED.

Most accidents occurring on outdoor adventurous activities no matter where they take place are due to one or more of the following reasons:

1. Not involving senior more experienced members of your squadron and not gaining permission to carry out the activity.
2. Insufficient detailed preparation, planning and training. RECCE not done properly, no rehearsals. Menu not planned for the activity or area to be traveled.
3. Not having the right clothing, e.g. wearing jeans and unsuitable footwear for hill walking.
4. Carelessness or casual attitude by those taking part.
5. Overestimation of the strength and stamina of those taking part.
6. Not enough practical experience – especially in map reading and camp craft.
7. Not paying sufficient attention to detail, failing to notice the signs of deteriorating weather conditions.
8. Not turning back when common sense says 'turn back'.
9. Not 'looking out' for other group members, not noticing the effects of heat or cold
10. Failure to work as a team, getting into a panic.
11. Not accepting advice from experienced people while en-route.
12. Failing to provide accurate route cards, RV points, timings etc.

GO FLY - A SURVIVAL KITE

A Pocket Sized piece of kit to rescue those lost on an expedition or lost as darkness falls, may, if kitted out with a Survival Kite be brought to safety sooner.

The size of a cigarette pack, the kite inflated by mouth to become a two square metre metalic aerofoil beacon for scearch parties, It will take to the air in winds as low as just 4mph. Its flight is so stable it remains airbourne while survivors sleep.

Kite reflects radar signals and its visability can be further enhanced by adding a small "light stick", the brightly glowing chemical indicator.

Other uses, it can be worn as a vest under outer garments directing heat back to the body or wrapped around a broken limb and then inflated, used as a splint.

EXPEDITION TRAINING

KNOTS AND THEIR USES

A lot depends on knowing how to tie just the right knot or hitch for a particular job.

While learning to tie knots it is no use using a thin string or twine made up of loose strands. You need a piece of rope or cord not less than a quarter of an inch thick and several feet long.

An important point to remember is that it is not a good idea to ever cut a rope just to shorten it, as you will find that no sooner had you cut it, than you needed a longer rope for some other purpose.

As mentioned in the Expedition Training, it is always useful to have a length of string or rope with you, but there is not much point in having a rope if you don't know how to tie a useful knot in it.

Like most skills it is only through practice that you will become proficient, this is especially so with knots.

The occasion you need to use a knot will more than likely be in an emergency situation, you must realise that this will mean instant re-action with no time to think of what to do. This is when your ability to tie the — "right knot at the right time" — could prevent a disaster.

A ROPE

The main part of a rope is called the "standing part" - see illustration. When the end is bent back toward the standing part, the loop formed is called a "bight", regardless of whether it crosses the rope or only lies parallel with it.

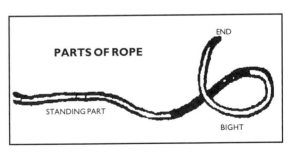

PARTS OF ROPE

END

STANDING PART

BIGHT

EXPEDITION TRAINING

KNOTS AND THEIR USES.

THUMB KNOT and FIGURE OF EIGHT KNOT
Both used to make a 'stop' on a rope: to prevent a rope from fraying at the end.

REEF KNOT.
For joining two dry ropes of the same size. The most generally useful knot. Always used in First Aid

SINGLE SHEET BEND.
For joining two ropes of different size.

DOUBLE SHEET BEND.
For joining two wet ropes of different size.

HAWSER BEND.
For joining larger ropes or cables.

DRAW HITCH.
For fastening a 'head rope' (e.g., a boat's painter) so that it can be quickly released.

EXPEDITION TRAINING

CLOVE HITCH
This is the most useful knot that you will ever learn. It can be made under strain, will not slip on itself nor along a pole, and can easily be cast loose.

TIMBER HITCH
is useful for hauling, the more it is pulled the firmer it holds.

TWO HALF HITCHES. Two turns of a rope, which, when drawn together, holds securely. It is the quickest and simplest way to make a rope fast to a post.

ROUND TURN and TWO HALF HITCHES. The quickest way to make a rope fast under strain. One of the most useful and easily made knots .

FISHERMANS BEND.
For fastening ends of ropes to spars, poles, etc., or to other ropes.

BOWLINE ON THE BIGHT
To form a loop that will not slip. One loop is made larger than the other. This is the sling for lowering a person from a building.
It enables the person to be supported, with the longer loop under the knees and the short loop under the armpits.

THE SPANISH WINDLASS

This is not a knot, but is closely related to them. You may come across a situation where knowing how to use a Spanish Windlass could be helpful.

The windlass as you will see from the diagram, gives you great pulling power on a rope, by means of a lever using it to wind the rope round a post or stake, one end of which is in the ground.

The rope is wound round the post and a bar or piece of wood with the rope hitched over it.

The power given could be used to haul a boat out of the river or to move a vehicle, one end of the rope is fastened to the object to be moved, and the other is made fast on to a tree or some other suitable anchor. The stake or post must be strong and sound, likewise the material used for the lever as there is considerable pressure on both when in use.

Check your rope for any damage and be sure it is strong enough for the job.

Arrange your rope as in the diagram, pulling the lever round the stake.

The stake needs to be held firmly by driving it into the ground making the hole big enough for it to turn. It may be necessary to "overhaul" your windlass as too much rope may be wound round it, it will depend upon the size of the

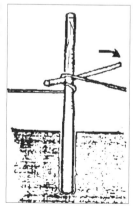

stake used for the windlass and the distance you have to haul the object.

Warning - it can be dangerous if you do not use strong enough material, or if it snaps or if you let go of the lever.

Check your rope and Windlass frequently, secure the load you are pulling with other rope to prevent it running away in the event of an accident.

EXPEDITION TRAINING

LASHINGS

Lashings are used for fastening poles or spars together they should be finished with a reef knot when both ends of the rope or yarn are available, or with a clove hitch if only one end is available.

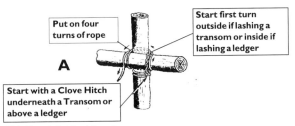

Put on four turns of rope

Start first turn outside if lashing a transom or inside if lashing a ledger

A

Start with a Clove Hitch underneath a Transom or above a ledger

(A) Straight lashing to spars.

For lengthening a spar or for repairing a broken spar. The lashing is made fast to the spar with a clove hitch, and is then passed round and round the spars; the end is made fast by another clove hitch or by passing the end under the last few turns and then tightening them up.

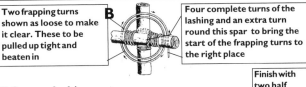

Two frapping turns shown as loose to make it clear. These to be pulled up tight and beaten in

B

Four complete turns of the lashing and an extra turn round this spar to bring the start of the frapping turns to the right place

B) Square lashing.

For lashing one spar to another at right angles. The lashing is started with a clove hitch, consists of at least four complete turns round the spars and two or more frapping turns, and is finished with two half-hitches round the most convenient spar.

Finish with two half hitches. Outside on a Transom inside - on a Ledger

EXPEDITION TRAINING

SHEAR LEGS LASHING

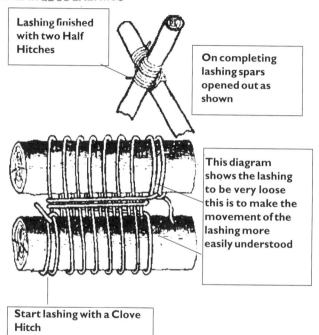

Lashing finished with two Half Hitches

On completing lashing spars opened out as shown

This diagram shows the lashing to be very loose this is to make the movement of the lashing more easily understood

Start lashing with a Clove Hitch

Shear legs lashing

For lashing spars at adjustable angles. The spars are placed side by side; a clove hitch is made round one spar and the rope is taken loosely six or eight times round both spars above the clove hitch without riding.

Two frapping turns are made round the lashing, and the end of the rope is made fast to the other spar by two half hitches just above the lashing.

EXPEDITION TRAINING

SPLICING

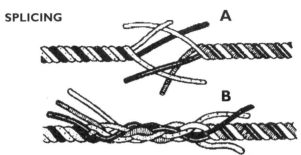

Diagram 'A' shows strands ready for splicing. Diagram 'B' shows the splice after each of the 6 strands have been passed through twice. From here, the strands are reduced in diameter by half and worked through once, then by half again, and through once to finish. Work from right to left, 'over and under'.

Splices are permanent and strong, and do not increase the thickness of the rope by much.

a. Short splice.   **For joining two ropes.**
b. Back splice.   **For ending off a rope permanently.**

WHIPPING

Whipping is used to prevent the end of a rope unravelling and is best done with sail twine; it is less permanent than the backsplice but does not greatly increase the thickness of the rope.

Rope 'Whipped' at end to prevent fraying

KNOWING HOW TO TIE THE RIGHT KNOT, IS A SKILL YOU WILL USE THROUGHOUT YOUR LIFE. PRACTICE AND MORE PRACTICE MAKES PERFECT

EXPEDITION TRAINING

EXPEDITION TRAINING ABBREVIATIONS

AALA .... Adventure Activities Licensing Authority
ACAT .... Air Cadets Adventure Training
ACTI .... Air Cadets Training Instruction
ACATI .... Air Cadets Adventure Training Instruction
ACATTP ..... Air Cadets Adventure Training Technical Panel
ACO .... Air Cadet Organization
ACP .... Air Cadet Publication
AJSMEL(S) ... Advanced Joint Service Mountain Expedition Leader
                  (Summer)
AT .... Adventure Training
ATC .... Air Training Corps
BCU .... British Canoe Union
BELA .... Basic Expedition Leader Award
BET .... Basic Expedition Training
BMC .... British Military Contingent
BMG .... British Mountain Guide
BST .... British Sports Trust
CI .... Chief Instructor
CIC .... Cave Instructor Certificate
CTE .... Competence Through Experience
COS AC ..... Chief of Staff Air Cadets
DCI .... Defence Council Instruction
DLA .... Defence Land Agent
DEO .... Defence Estates Office
DofE .... Duke of Edinburgh's
GRA .... Generic Risk Assessment
HQAC .... Headquarters Air Cadets
H&S .... Health and Safety
HSE .... Health and Safety Executive
JSAT .... Joint Service Adventure Training
JSCI 1 .... Joint Service Canoe Instructor Level 1
JSCI 2 .... Joint Service Canoe Instructor Level 2
JSCI 3(IK) .... Joint Service Canoe Instructor Level 3 (Inland Kayak)
JSMEL(S) ..... Joint Service Mountain Expedition Leader (Summer)
JSMEL(W) ... Joint Service Mountain Expedition Leader (Winter)
JSRCI .... Joint Service Rock Climbing Instructor
JSRCL .... Joint Service Rock Climbing Leader
KNBLO .... Royal Dutch League for Physical Culture
LCMLA .... Local Cave and Mine Leader Assessment

EXPEDITION TRAINING

LTAR .... Land Training Areas and Ranges
MIA .... Mountain Instructor Award
MIC .... Mountain Instructor Certificate
ML(S) .... Mountain Leader (Summer)
MLT .... Mountain Leader Training
MLTUK .... Mountain Leader Training United Kingdom
MLTS .... Mountain Leader Training Scotland
ML(W) .... Mountain Leader (Winter)
MOD .... Ministry of Defence

SELF TEST QUESTIONS

1. What are the ten Country Code Rules.
2. What sort of socks should you wear on an expedition
3. The weight you carry on your back is equal to ....times the weight on your feet.
4. What do you dust your feet with.
5. How do you open a blister and what with.
6. If you are very thirsty, should you eat snow.
7. What do you carry on the outside of your ruck sack.
8. When looking for a camp site, what do you have to have from the owners.
9. What do you check out for safety when choosing a camp site
10. Is it a good idea to put up a tent under trees.
11. If you have to use water from a stream, what do you first do with it.
12. Where would you site the latrine and washing area, and why.
13. In a camp for several days you construct a latrine, how is it done and what are the important sizes.
14. When sighting a latrine what do you do about providing privacy, and how important is it.
15. How is privacy maintained for those using a Portaloo or field toilet.
16. What is the advantage of digging a small hole to put your cooker into.
17. What should you always leave behind at a camp site.
18. Why can't you go off on your own expedition as a Cadet,
19. Five of you are on an expedition, one is injured, how many would normally go for help.
20. When planning a route what must you produce and give someone a copy of .

21. The weather is getting bad on an expedition, do you go on or turn back

22. What is the distress call/signal with: a. Whistle. b. Torch, and the Emergency Ground to Air Signals.

23. What do you understand by the Wind Chill Factor.

24. What added danger is there if you get wet on a cold and windy day.

25. You use ONE Water Purification Tablet to how much water.

26. Before heating tins in a mess tin of boiling water, what must you do.

27. Describe three types of improvised shelters.

28. How would you sterilize a water bottle.

29. How do you 'end-off' a rope.

30. What happens if you walk for some distance with boots full of water.

31. How can you test a pair of boots are about the right size.

32. In cold weather without anything covering your head, how much body heat can you lose.

33. With pouched rations what is the best way to ensure you get a hot cooked meal.

34. What do you always take away from your camp site.

35. What do you leave at your 'base camp' before departing on an Expedition.

FINALLY -

When you draw a tent from the stores to use on expedition, what state do you expect it to be in ?

Answer: dry, clean, good repair and complete with guy ropes, pegs and mallet all properly packed.

How do you ensure that your tent is as described above?
Answer: Ensure that all stores returned are clean, dry and complete as issued.
Report defects/damage to the Equipment Officer.
Your ability to carry out these check efficiently, when you are tired is all part of your training.

Chapter 8

Fieldcraft

Introduction

The principal skill to be successful at escape and evasion is to be expert at applying Fieldcraft in any given situation. It is a subject most enjoyed as it is usually fun and gets you and your `mates' to turn out in strength, especially if it says on the programme that it's going to be an *Escape and Evasion* exercise, if it's at night - so much the better.

We are not suggesting that all cadets still like playing `cowboys and Indians', but perhaps Fieldcraft could be described as organised cowboys and Indians!.

If you live in a city/town you are at some disadvantage to see Fieldcraft in action, however, if you are able to get into the countryside or live in or near it, you will be aware that the wild life `get a living' off the land by being experts in the use of their skills of; stealth, patience, speed and fitness, stamina, planning and cunning and being natural experts at camouflage and concealment.

Natural Skills

Fieldcraft is their prime skill in catching their food and in many ways to be good at Fieldcraft you could do no better than to study wildlife at every opportunity.

Observe how a cat stalks its quarry, how the Sparrow Hawk, hovers patiently, observing the right moment to drop in on the Field Mouse, how the Fox who uses the hedgerows to move from one field to another, see how well a Rabbit is camouflage against the ground, all of these examples are types of Individual Fieldcraft skills exercised for the purpose of either *defence or attack*.

In your case, having knowledge of Fieldcraft brings together and practices some of the skills required to evade capture or to act effectively as a sentry.

Individual Skills

Once you have an understanding of the need to imitate those skills that wild life practice to survive in the field, then you will be on the way to attaining an acceptable standard of Individual Fieldcraft.

FIELDCRAFT

Even when you are mentally and physically fit, you will need a lot of practice and patience, to develop the natural ability to react in defence of your survival, both as an individual and as a member of a group. Be good at fieldcraft and survive - you seldom get a second chance.

Method of Judging Distance

WHY JUDGE DISTANCE; if you can judge distance you will know the approximate area in which to look when given an order. If your sights are not correctly adjusted on the range, your shots will probably miss the target.

Use a Unit of Measure

100 metres is a good unit, The Range is marked out at 100 metre intervals.
A Full Size Football pitch is about 100 metres long.

DO NOT USE THE UNIT OF

MEASURE METHODOVER

400 METRES IF YOUCAN'T

SEE ALL THE GROUND

BETWEENYOU AND THE

TARGET AREA/LOCATION

APPEARANCE METHOD

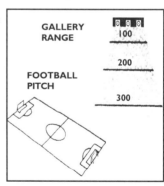

USE COMMON OBJECTS FOR APPEARANCE METHOD

FIELDCRAFT

AIDS TO JUDGING DISTANCE

When you know what 100 metres looks like, practice fitting your Unit of Measure between you and a target.

APPEARANCE METHOD

By noting what a person looks like at a set distance, you can then use the Appearance Method. Common objects may also be used for this method

FIELDCRAFT

Things seem closer

Further away

REMEMBER

Things seem closer .. In bright light, if they are bigger than their surroundings, if there is dead ground between you and them, if they are higher up than you.

Further away ... With sun in your eyes, in bad light. When smaller than surroundings. Looking across a valley, down a street or along a path in a wood, if you are lying down.

KEY RANGES

If the range to one object is known, estimate the distance from it to the target.

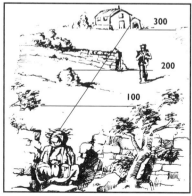

BRACKETING

Calculate mid-distance between nearest possible and furthest possible distance of target.

Nearest	- 100
Farthest	- 300
Mid-distance	- 200

HALVING

Estimate the distance halfway to the target then double it:

$100 \times 2 = 200$

FIELDCRAFT

PERSONAL CAMOUFLAGE AND CONCEALMENT

The enemy is looking for you so - don't make it easy.
Merge with your surroundings

TOO MUCH   **JUST RIGHT**   **TOO LITTLE**

LOSE YOUR SHAPE
Make sure nothing shines.
Blend in with your
surroundings - if
they vary, so
must you

AVOID SKYLINES

Stand back from
merge into the shadows -
don't lean out
You WILL BE SEEN

FIELDCRAFT

Don't use isolated cover - it stands out

SOMETHING IS SEEN BECAUSE OF ITS:-

Shape

Shadow } **IS FAMILIAR OR STANDS OUT**

Silhouette

Surface

Spacing } **IS DIFFERENT FROM ITS SURROUNDINGS**

Movement

SEEING IS ....NOTICING DETAILS

EASY TO SEE   **DIFFICULT TO FIND**

SHAPE .... Disguise you shape - including equipment and weapons.

FIELDCRAFT

SHADOW .... Keep in the shadows

SILHOUETTE .... Don't skyline

SURFACE..... Don't differ from your surroundings.

FIELDCRAFT

SPACING... Keep spread out - but not equally spaced.

MOVEMENT .... Move carefully - slowly when concealed - sudden movement will attract attention.

Look through cover - if possible - not round it .
You **MUST SEE** without being **SEEN.**

FIELDCRAFT

TARGET RECOGNITION
The correct target must be located and fired at

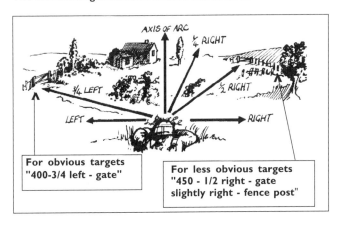

For obvious targets
"400-3/4 left - gate"

For less obvious targets
"450 - 1/2 right - gate
slightly right - fence post"

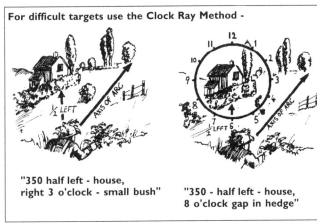

For difficult targets use the Clock Ray Method -

"350 half left - house,
right 3 o'clock - small bush"

"350 - half left - house,
8 o'clock gap in hedge"

FIELDCRAFT

MOVE QUIETLY AT ALL TIMES
Keep your weapons out of the mud.
MOVEMENT AT NIGHT
Movements used during daylight are not suitable at night-they have to be adapted.
THE GHOST WALK
Lift legs high, sweeping them slowly outwards. Feel gently with toes for safe place for each foot, put weight down gently.; Keep knees bent. Use the left hand to feel the air in front of you from

head height down to the ground checking for obstructions, trip wires, booby traps or alarms etc.

THE CAT WALK
Crawl on hands and knees. Search ground ahead for twigs, move knee to where hand has searched.

THE KITTEN CRAWL
It is quiet- but slow. It is very tiring. Lie on your front, search ahead for twigs, move them to one side.

Lift your body on your forearms and toes, press forward and lower yourself on to the ground.

NIGHT NOISES
At night you hear more than you see.

Stop and listen.
Keep close to the ground,
turn your head slowly and use a
cupped hand behind the
ear. Freeze if you hear a
noise.

FIELDCRAFT

MOVING AT NIGHT - REMEMBER

Keep quiet .... have no loose equipment. Move carefully ... use the Ghost walk, Cat walk or Kitten crawl.

Clear your route by hand, search carefully in front of you ... dry vegetation will make a noise.

Use available cover ... flares, thermal imaging and night observation devices will turn night into day.

Keep to the low ground ... you split your party at night at your peril.

LISTENING AT NIGHT

If the enemy is about - keep an ear close to the ground. The closer you are to the ground, the more chance you have of seeing the enemy on 'skyline'. Keep your mouth open this opens your ear canal and aids your hearing.

FIELDCRAFT

NIGHT VISION

We can see in the dark - but REMEMBER our eyes take 30 minutes to get used to the dark.
We see less than in daylight. We see shapes - not detail.
We see skylines and silhouettes. We may see movement.

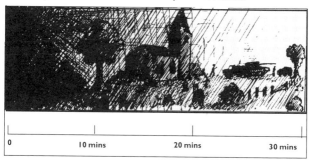

| 0 | 10 mins | 20 mins | 30 mins |

YOUR EYESIGHT

Your eyes have two sets of cells, one set for daylight (CONES) in the centre of your eyes, the other set for darkness (RODS), which are around the CONES.

The night cells work when the day cells are affected by falling darkness.

With constant practice night observation can be improved. If you have a cold, headache or are tired it can reduce your night vision.

You will find that there is a limit to the time you can concentrate effectively on any given point or your vision becomes blurred.

Most service units use Thermal Imaging (night sights) that "turn darkness into daylight" in as much that they pick out an object giving out heat (body heat).

The SUSAT sights on the SA80 MK2 Rifle (an optical sight) has advantages similar to that of binoculars for night observation.

FIELDCRAFT

BRIGHT LIGHT RUINS YOUR NIGHT VISION

If caught in the light of flares take cover at once in open ground.

If in a wood - FREEZE. If you see a flare, quickly close one eye to protect your night vision, use the other eye to look about you taking advantage of the light, but do not move suddenly as this will give you away.

DUTIES OF A SENTRY

Sentries are the eyes and ears of the squadron. If they do their job well, their squadron will be safe and secure.

When you are a Sentry make sure:-

That you know and understand your orders. That you know what to do if your post is approached by a person or vehicle.

That you ask questions if you do not understand anything.

What ground to watch. Direction of the enemy.

Signal for defensive fire.

Names of prominent landmarks.

Where neighbouring posts are situated.

Information about patrols that maybe in the area, or coming through your post.

FIELDCRAFT

SENTRIES AT NIGHT IN THE FIELD

At night sentries work in pairs.
Sentries must know:-

1. What to do if anyone approaches their post.
2. What ground to watch.
3. The Password.
4. Sentries close to the enemy must know :-

   Direction of the enemy.

   Name of land marks.

   Where neighbouring posts are.

   Signal for defensive fire.

   About patrols that may come in or out through their post or near them.

FIELDCRAFT

HOW TO CHALLENGE.

When you see movements which you think may not be your own forces - alert your Patrol Commander.

Say '**HALT**' **HANDS UP**.

'**Advance one and be recognised**'.

'**Halt**'.

Give the challenge half of the password - quietly, so that only the first man can hear it.

ACTION - Allow friendly forces through, know how many and count them through - one at a time.

Section opens fire at enemy troops.

NOTE Be aware of a common trick which is for the enemy to approach a sentry, listen and learn the first half of a **PASS WORD** then fade away.

An inexperienced sentry may allow this to happen. The same enemy then approaches another sentry and challenges them before they can challenge them.

Again the inexperienced sentry might then give the reply then allow the enemy into their position.

So be careful and never allow anyone into your position unless you can positively identify them, when in doubt call for help.

USE YOUR SENSES.

What are your senses, how can they help in Fieldcraft? On a patrol or on duty as a sentry you will use your EYES and EARS, and your TOUCH when feeling your way through woods or difficult cover. Your sense of TASTE may not be used, but your sense of SMELL — depending upon the SMELL — may remind you of taste. SMELL can give you away and the enemy. Body smell or the smell of cooking, or anything else drifts on the air and can give away your position.

FIELDCRAFT

CHOOSING A ROUTE.

If you have to advance across country, check that you know where to make for. Then decide on the best route.

REMEMBER

Routes must be planned ahead.

You must move in bounds or stages from one observation point to another.

You must check your direction - are you keeping on course.

Always use a compass

Must not be seen but should be able to observe without restriction.

If you have to take a risk choose a route which offers the risks early in your approach rather than later on, since you will have less chance of being seen.

The best route will - have places to observe the area - without being seen yourself.

Don't go blindly on towards and into an unknown area.

Give good positions and cover for sentries.

You must be able to take offensive action if necessary.

Let you move without being seen.

Not to have impassable obstacles such as marsh land or open ground or ravines.

FIELDCRAFT

PACING

Pacing is necessary because you must always know how exactly far you have gone when counting a number of your own 'paces'.

You should know your 'Pacing Scale', over different types of ground conditions, I.E. Tarmac roads or tracks, grassland, woodlands etc.

To find your PACING SCALE, put two markers out 100m apart. Walk the distance between them as you would on a patrol, counting the paces as you go.

If it has taken you 120 paces to cover the 100m, then that is your PACING SCALE.

It follows, to use this scale if you were on a patrol and had to go a distance of 300m, you would have to count out 360 paces.

Under some conditions you can use a specific length of string, tying knots at every 120 paces. Having used the length of string, un-tie the knots and repeat the process on the next 'leg' of your route.

It is always advisable to have a CHECK PACER, remembering to check that your PACING SCALE is the same by day and night.

NAVIGATION

This is the art of moving from one place to another and consists of three important stages that MUST be carried out if you are to be successful, they are as follows:-

1. **PLANNING**
2. **KEEPING DIRECTION**
3. **GOOD PACING**

PLANNING -You must plan your route in advance, using maps, air photos, sketches and information from previous patrols or recces.

KEEPING DIRECTION - Always take several compasses and as many 'pacers'. Always get someone else to check your navigation, at both the planning stage and while you are executing the movement. It is often hard to keep direction, especially at night, in fog or in close country.

When it is necessary to make a detour to avoid an obstacle or seek cover, it is easy for leaders to miss the correct lines of advance.

AIDS TO KEEPING DIRECTION.

Some of the aids to keeping direction are:-

a. The compass, map and air photographs.

b. A rough sketch copied from a map or air photograph.

c. Keeping two prominent objects in view.

FIELDCRAFT

d. Using a series of easily recognisable landmarks, each visible from the previous one.

e. The stars and also the sun and moon if their natural movement in the sky is understood.

f. Memorizing the route from a map or air photograph. Helpful details are the direction of streams, distances between recognisable features coupled with pacing, and the course of contours.

g. Trees in exposed country tend to grow away from the direction of the prevailing wind. Moss may grow on the leeward side of tree trunks.

h. Remembering the back view, patrols and others who may have to find their way back should look behind them from time to time and pick up landmarks to remember for the return journey.

j. Leaving directions marks on the outward journey, these may be pegs, small heaps of stones.

k. If the route is being walked by day by those who are to guide along it by night, they must take note of skylines and objects or features which they will be able to recognize in the dark.

SELECTING OF LINES OF ADVANCE.
Remember the keyword - **'G R O U N D'**

G	Ground from the map. The type of ground; Open/close country, Rolling/flat.
R	Ridges, water courses and watersheds (highest) mark on map or talc.
O	Observation – good view points.
U	Undergrowth - study woods, scrub, trees, villages.
N	Non Passable obstacles, such as rivers, ravines, marsh land.
D	Defilade covered lines of advance and areas which offer cover can now be selected.

"TIME SPENT IN RECONNAISSANCE ...
... IS SELDOM WASTED"

FIELDCRAFT

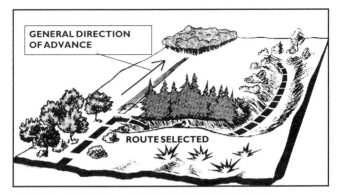

OBSERVATION — SEARCHING GROUND

The skill of searching ground is based upon learning to `scan' an area using an accepted system.

It will test your concentration and exercise your knowledge of `why things are seen' and the principles of Camouflage and Concealment.

In the diagram we have - for the purpose of illustrating to you — drawn lines across the landscape.

In practice you would choose prominent features, landmarks, roads etc., and draw your imaginary lines across the landscape through these reference points.

FIELDCRAFT

SCANNING

As seen in the illustration on the previous page, the landscape is divided into **FOREGROUND, MIDDLE DISTANCE** and **DISTANCE**. You can further divide this by indicating a centre line (again based on reference points), calling left of the line **"LEFT OF ARC"**, and right of the line **"RIGHT OF ARC"** as shown in the illustration.

Having divided the landscape, the correct method is to scan each area horizontally (left to right or right to left).

View the area in short overlapping movements in a very precise manner, especially any features that are at an angle from your position.

Searching

While scanning you may see something move or that requires further investigation. There may be an area where you may come under observation from, it would be as well to check that out early.

Weather conditions can give you a clue when searching, frost on bushes, foot marks will show up clearly, if the weather is hot camouflaged positions can be given away when leaves or grass dry off changing colour.

Search across hedges and rows of trees , NOT along them. At all times consider WHY THINGS ARE SEEN.

PYROTECHNICS — Blank Ammunition & Thunder Flashes, Flares and Smoke.

As an Air Cadet you *may be involved* in exercises with the RAF Regiment or other Cadet Forces (including the CCF) where Blank Ammunition, Thunder Flashes, Flares and Smoke generators are used. You **must be made aware** of the Safety Standards required when taking part in training where pyrotechnics are to be used.

All pyrotechnics by their very nature contain explosive materials. Without exception they are all very dangerous, especially if used in a confined space or explode within a few feet of you.

Loss of sight and hearing, badly burned hands and faces are serious injuries sustained by individuals from pyrotechnics.

You will be told when pyrotechnics are in use and instructed as to the correct Safety Precautions to be observed by all ranks taking part in the exercise.

NO CADETS WILL BE PERSONALLY INVOLVED IN THE OPERATION OF THUNDER FLASHES, SMOKE GENERATORS OF ANY TYPE OR FLARES OF ANY DESCRIPTION.

FIELDCRAFT

SELF TEST QUESTIONS

1. To be good at Fieldcraft you need to have what.
2. For what reason do you use: Unit of Measure. Key Ranges. Bracketing.
3. Give an example of "Unit of Measure".
4. When carrying out Personal Cam what do you have to remember.
5. What is "Isolated cover", would you use it.
6. Why are things seen, what must you remember about "smell".
7. What is important about Shape, Shadow, Silhouette.
8. Silence when moving at night, how do you prevent any noise from your kit you are wearing/carrying.
9. Explain the use of 'the clock ray method'.
10. Give a method of moving at night.
11. How long does it take for your eyes to get used to the dark.
12. When a FLARE "goes up", what do you do.
13. When do sentries work in pairs.
14. What are the Duties of a Sentry.
15. What is the correct CHALLENGE a sentry should give, when and how should it be given.
16. What helps you to listen at night.
17. A Sentry close to the enemy must know — What.
18. Give the three important points to consider when "choosing a route".
19. How do you work out your own PACING SCALE.
20. Give six methods used to help you Keep your Direction.
21. How do you split up an area you are going to SCAN and SEARCH.
22. In daylight, you must not fire a blank at anyone less than, how many metres away, and at night what is the rule.
23. What is the Key Word "GROUND" used for, and what does it indicate.

SAFETY WARNING FIRING BLANK AMMUNITION
With all field training when blank ammunition is in use,
NEVER aim directly at any cadets or adults,
**DO NOT AIM AT ALL IF THEY ARE LESS
THAN 50 METRES AWAY FROM YOU.**

Chapter 9

The Duke of Edinburgh's Award Scheme

The Duke of Edinburgh's Award Scheme is a voluntary, non-competitive programme of practical, cultural and adventurous activities for young people aged 14-25.

The Award programme consists of three levels, Bronze, Silver and Gold. Each have differing criteria for entry and the level of achievement necessary to complete each award.

Air Cadets who meet the age criteria can join the award scheme. Each award is broken down into 4 areas (5 for gold) which participants must complete successfully to receive their award. These are:-

Service
Helping others in the local community.

Expeditions
Training for, and planning of a journey.

Skills
Demonstrate ability in almost any hobby, skill or interest

Physical Recreation
Sport, dance and fitness.

Residential Project(Gold Award only)
A purposeful enterprise with young people not previously known to the participant.

The Award is widely recognised by employers as it helps demonstrate that award holders are keen to take on new challenges, have a higher level of self confidence than their counterparts, have leadership qualities with the added experience of teamwork.

THE DUKE OF EDINBURGH'S AWARD

You will have to buy your **Entrance Pack** which will include your Record Book. This is your first commitment to the scheme - your personal stake in it.

Help will be given to you along the way, but **it has to be your effort.** As you progress, you will be expected to choose, design and develop your own programme from the many options available.

ADVANTAGES

The scheme adds an extra dimension, excitement and purpose to your Cadet career and beyond to your 25th birthday.

The award will bring you into close contact with many other young people and you will no doubt develop lasting friendships.

The self confidence, awareness, determination and enthusiasm displayed by successful participants has given Award holders holders a deserved good reputation, giving you a distinct advantage when embarkingon you career. Potential employers recognise the scheme and its objectives and see it as evidence that you have **STICKABILITY.**

YOUR OPPORTUNITY

As a Cadet you have the advantage to take part in the scheme, whilst continuing with your cadet career.

This has been made possible by many of the subjects within your ATC Training Syllabus fitting in with the requirements of the scheme.

It must be stressed, that it is **not compulsory** or mandatory for you to only count ATC related activities towards your DofE award, nor is the list of activities mentioned in the chart the only ones accepted, there are a great many more that your Award Leader will be able to tell you about.

However, any aspect of ATC activity can, with some help and imagination on the part of your instructors, working with the Award Leader, be brought into a DofE Award programme; this is most likely to be the case in respect of the Expedition option in the Silver and Gold Awards.

Your Award Leader will have several leaflets and books that you will be able to read. It is advisable that you do just that before making up your mind to take up the challenge.

All that we can tell you, is that if you do join the Award Scheme, and see it through all the way, you will never regret it.

THE DUKE OF EDINBURGH'S AWARD

DOE - Bronze Award

Cadets must be at least 14 years old to start the Bronze award and can expect it to take a minimum of six months to complete. To complete the Bronze award, cadets must complete a service, skill, physical recreation and plan and prepare for a 2 day venture.

Based on an average of 1 hour per week, a cadet must actively take part in a service, skill and physical recreation for 3 months. These can of course run alongside each other and do not have to be concurrently.

For details of the conditions for each part of the Bronze award, consult your Handbook.

The minimum age for completing the Bronze award is 14 and a half years. On completion, cadets will be presented with their award by their Commanding Officer as well as a badge to wear on the uniforms.

DOE - Silver Award

Cadets must be at least 15 years old to start the Silver award and can expect it to take a minimum of six months to complete. This time frame is extended for cadets starting the award scheme at this level (Direct Entrant), to 1 year.

To complete the Silver award, cadets must complete a service over 6 months, a skill and physical recreation for a total of nine months (cadets can choose to do either for 6 months and the other for 3 months) and plan & prepare for a 3 day venture, while Direct Entrants must undertake an additional 6 months in either the service or the longer of the skills or physical recreation.

For details of the conditions for each part of the Silver award see the Award Hand Book

The minimum age for completing the Silver award is 15 and a half years or 16 years for Direct Entrants. On completion, cadets will be presented with their award by their Commanding Officer as well as a badge to wear on their uniforms.

THE DUKE OF EDINBURGH'S AWARD

DOE - Gold Award

The Gold award is the highest level in the Duke of Edinburgh Award scheme. Cadets must be at least 16 years old to start the award and can expect it to take a minimum of one year to complete.
This timeframe is extended for cadets starting the award scheme at this level (Direct Entrant), to one and a half years.

To complete the Gold award, cadets must complete a service over 12 months, a skill and physical recreation for a total of eighteen months (cadets can choose to do either for12 months and the other for 6 months) and plan and prepare for a 4 day venture, while Direct Entrants must undertake an additional 6 months in either the service or the longer of the skills or physical recreation.

In addition, Gold participants must also complete the residential element of the award. This involves undertaking a shared activity in a residential setting away from home for 5 days and 4 nights, with people who are not already known to them.
To help cadets complete this section, the annual summer camps are the ideal opportunity, as many camps take two or more squadrons. This means that the participant will be working with people they have never come across before.
There are other avenues available if the cadet or his award leader can arrange it. Other possibilities include youth hostels or sailing ships.
For details of the conditions for each part of the Gold award, see ACP 19
The minimum age for completing the Gold award is 17 years or 17 and a half years for Direct Entrants. On completion, cadets will be invited to either London or Edinburgh to be presented with their award by a key figure, quite possibly HRH Prince Phillip.
The cadet will also be presented with a Gold Award badge to wear on their uniforms, usually by their Commanding Officer.

THE DUKE OF EDINBURGH'S AWARD

SKILLS SECTION NOTES
Suggestion:

This requires you to take up an approved activity from the Duke of Edinburgh's Award Handbook.

You will need to talk to your Award Leader, to help you decide what you are to do. You will be required to take a keen interest in this and study it in some depth, during which time you will become quite an expert in your own right.

Note: Should you wish to take up a skill not listed, then it can be submitted by your Dof E Officer through the proper channels for approval. You must wait for approval before proceeding. This applies to all levels of the Award Scheme.

As examples, some of the activities are: Skill at Arms & Shooting, Drill, Drumming, Bugling, Forces Insignia, Bands, Marksmanship, Signalling, Model Aircraft and many topics from your ATC Syllabus etc.

An assessor, who will be a recognised expert in the activity will be appointed to see you through the skill.

You will be given an "ideas list" of things you could do to progress in the activity, and you will agree with your assessor how far you can progress in the time allowed (3 or 6 months depending on choice). If you are new to the Skill you will probably start at the beginning.

If you have already had some experience in the Skill, you will start from a point where you will be extending your knowledge. At the end of the period you will be assessed on how well you have done.

PHYSICAL RECREATION NOTES
Suggestion:

To choose an activity from the list in the Duke of Edinburgh's Award Handbook and participate for a minimum period. Again you will discuss this with your Award Leader. If there are standards set by the governing body of the activity, you will be expected to try for these.

Note: The Award requires regular participation over 3 or 6 months, which significantly exceeds the minimum period required by the rules. You will need to consider this when choosing your Physical Recreation.

CHART SHOWS HOW ATC ACTIVITIES FIT IN WITH THE D of E AWARD SCHEME

	SERVICE	EXPEDITION (On Foot)	SKILLS	PHYSICAL RECREATION	RESIDENTIAL PROJECT
BRONZE	Service courses organised at Sqn level. Group I - Community Service Group 2 - Service requiring specialised training. Group 3 - Service requiring specific qualifications. See DofE Handbook for details.	Expedition organised at Squadron level or possibly completed on Wing Adventure Training Course.	Aeronautics: Leading Cadet - Bronze Senior Cadet - Silver Staff Cadet - Gold Air Rifle Shooting Ceremonial Drill (ATC) Gliding (ACGS Staff Cdts) Marksmanship: (.22 Rifle Shooting).	Physical Achievement Tests organised at Squadron level or other qualifying physical recreation activity. (See Award Handbook for details)	No requirement at this level of the Award
SILVER	Youth Service - Uniformed Orgs Gp 3. Hold rank of Cadet Corporal (minimum) period of 6 months & take part in Org & Training of the Squadron.	Same applies as above	In all cases training muss be continuous for the minimum qualifying period for each award level. Details of Skills Training required at different levels of the Award can be found in ACP 19. "Duke of Edinburgh's Award in the ATC" or the Award Scheme Skills Programmes Index.	Same applies as above	No requirement at this level of the Award
GOLD	Youth Service - Uniformed Org Gp 3. Hold rank of Cadet Sgt (minimum) or be a Staff Cadet for 12 months & take part in the Org & Trg of the squadron.	As above plus: Optional completion by Open Gold Expedition. (Details of which are published quarterly in the Award Journal)	Same applies as above	Same applies as above	Attendance at ATC Annual Camp or Trg Course lasting at least 5 days (4 nights) NOTE: Camp Commandant or Offr i/c must be informed of need for assessment requirements BEFORE the event.

THE DUKE OF EDINBURGH'S AWARD
THE PROCESS TO BE FOLLOWED FOR THE SECTIONS OF THE AWARD
SERVICE SECTION

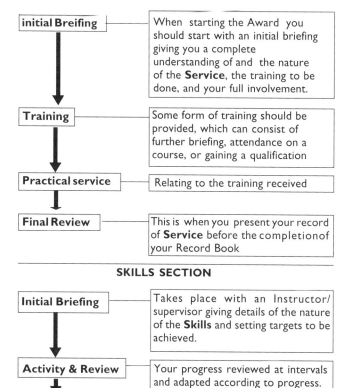

initial Breifing — When starting the Award you should start with an initial briefing giving you a complete understanding of and the nature of the **Service**, the training to be done, and your full involvement.

Training — Some form of training should be provided, which can consist of further briefing, attendance on a course, or gaining a qualification

Practical service — Relating to the training received

Final Review — This is when you present your record of **Service** before the completionof your Record Book

SKILLS SECTION

Initial Briefing — Takes place with an Instructor/ supervisor giving details of the nature of the **Skills** and setting targets to be achieved.

Activity & Review — Your progress reviewed at intervals and adapted according to progress.

Final Review — This is when you present your record of **Skills** before completion of your Record Book

THE DUKE OF EDINBURGH'S AWARD

EXPEDITION SECTION

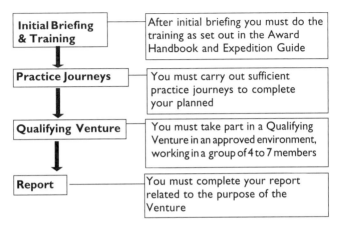

Initial Briefing & Training	After initial briefing you must do the training as set out in the Award Handbook and Expedition Guide
Practice Journeys	You must carry out sufficient practice journeys to complete your planned
Qualifying Venture	You must take part in a Qualifying Venture in an approved environment, working in a group of 4 to 7 members
Report	You must complete your report related to the purpose of the Venture

PHYSICAL RECREATION SECTION

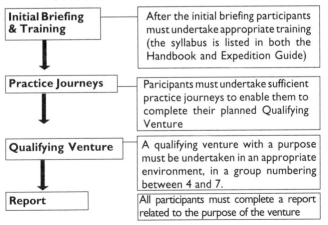

Initial Briefing & Training	After the initial briefing participants must undertake appropriate training (the syllabus is listed in both the Handbook and Expedition Guide)
Practice Journeys	Paricipants must undertake sufficient practice journeys to enable them to complete their planned Qualifying Venture
Qualifying Venture	A qualifying venture with a purpose must be undertaken in an appropriate environment, in a group numbering between 4 and 7.
Report	All participants must complete a report related to the purpose of the venture

THE DUKE OF EDINBURGH'S AWARD

SPORTS AND PHYSICAL FITNESS

As a Cadet and young person it is important to be as physically fit as you can. It will assist you in your Cadet career, keep you mentally alert and increase your stamina.

Sport and fitness is part of your training, give it as much effort as any other training you do. Participate in Squadron, Wing and Regional or National sporting events it is part of your commitment to the Cadets. You may not attain a winner's medal, but any Cadet who is prepared to try is a winner.

TEAM SPIRIT

Individual sports', swimming for example, requires encouragement, self-discipline and constant practice. An individual swimmer relies on team spirit to succeed; the coach, fellow swimmers, family support are all involved in the success of an individual.

Taking part in sport or physical training as part of a team is the same. Sometimes a team has to help an individual to shine in order to win the game – TEAM SPIRIT!

A SPORTS PERSON IS ONE WHO:-

PLAYS THE GAME FOR THE GAMES SAKE.

PLAYS FOR THE TEAM AND NOT FOR THEM SELVES.
IS A GOOD WINNER AND GOOD LOSER;
I.e.; MODEST IN VICTORY AND GENEROUS
IN DEFEAT.

ACCEPTS ALL DECISIONS IN A PROPER SPIRIT.

IS CHIVALROUS TOWARDS A DEFEATED OPPONENT.

IS UNSELFISH AND ALWAYS READY TO HELP
OTHERS TO BECOME PROFICIENT.

AS A SPECTATOR APPLAUDS GOOD PLAY ON
BOTH SIDES.

NEVER CHALLENGES UMPIRES, JUDGES OR REFEREES
- NO MATTER WHAT THE DECISION.

THE DUKE OF EDINBURGH'S AWARD

ALWAYS LOOK FOR OPPORTUNITIES TO PLAY ENERGETIC GAMES - ESPECIALLY AT CAMP

If you work hard at your exercises - play games hard and enter into sport with a will and the right spirit — you will not have any fitness problems.
The RAF Sports Control Board governs all sporting activities in the RAF. Many years ago a definition of a **SPORTS PERSON** was drawn up. (See the previous page)
It is just as relevant today, and as difficult to follow, but keep it in mind whenever taking part in sports.

YOUR HEALTH

Unless you are fit and have the stamina to carry out the different types of training throughout your Cadet career, your Instructors will have to make a decision NOT to allow you to take part in some of the activities or exercises because of the risk of you becoming a casualty through being unfit.

Food

Many of us are 'Food Junkies', eating too much sugar, fat and starch - or just eating too much! If you decide to increase your stamina and get your muscles working for you rather than against you, it may well be that your desire to 'binge' disappears!

Medical

Those of you with medical conditions should always check with their Doctor to ensure that they can take part in sports and physical activities. It is perhaps even more important for you to keep fit. As a passing note, some of our top athletes have Diabetes and look what they have attained.
N.B. Make sure that your Adult Instructors and Officers are aware of your medical condition.

THE DUKE OF EDINBURGH'S AWARD

EXERCISE DISCIPLINE

You do not need to join a Health Club or build a 'Home Gym' in your bedroom, just practice some of the simple exercises you know already – DAILY. Sit – Ups, Press Ups, Running on the Spot, Arm Swinging etc. Do not forget the two-mile speed walk or run twice a week.

Use the Duke of Edinburgh's Award Fitness Tests as the measure of your ability.

The Fitness Feeling

Once you have attained a good level of fitness you will feel great! Alert and ready to take part in other activities. All you need now is the SELF DISCIPLINE to keep it up.

A WORD OF CAUTION

Remember that you are ONLY INSURED WHEN TAKING PART IN OFFICIALLY RECOGNISED CADET EVENTS AND ACTIVITIES, SUPERVISED BY QUALIFIED COACHES AND/OR INSTRUCTORS.

For example, if you have challenged another Squadron to a game of football, you must get it made 'official', that way if anyone is injured or property damaged, it will be covered by insurance.

RAFTING - COULD THIS COUNT AS PART OF AN EXPEDITION?

If you need any help or information for your Duke of Edinburgh's Award, get in touch with your Wing D of E Award Officer

---

THE DUKE OF EDINBURGH'S AWARD

PHYSICAL ACHIEVEMENT TESTS

These may be used to qualify in the physical Recreation Sction of the D of E Award.

Points required to qualify:

> **First Class** - 12 points. **Leading** - 18 points.
>
> **Senior** - 24 points. **Staff** - 30 points.

NOTE: For the Award you are required to undertake all SEVEN events and select SIX to count. A reasonable rest is allowed between each event. Tests may be spread over TWO days.

SCORING MALE CADETS					
Points Scored					
Events	**1**	**2**	**3**	**4**	**5**
Speed Test Time (secs)	28	26	25	24	23
Ball Speed Bounce Catches 30secs	30	35	40	45	50
Trunk Curl Test Number in minute	20	28	34	40	45
Bailey Bridge Number in 30 secs	12	17	19	21	22
Push-Up hand/foot version No in 1min	15	23	27	34	50
or Push-Up hand/knee moderated version. Number in minute	25	37	44	58	68
Single Leg Squat Thrust. No in 30 secs	40	60	70	76	82
Run Time (mins & secs)	4.20	4.00	3.40	3.20	3.10

NOTE: Score may be counted for either Push-Ups hand/foot version, or Push-ups hand/knee moderated version but not both.

THE DUKE OF EDINBURGH'S AWARD

SCORING FOR FEMALE CADETS
Points Scored

Events	1	2	3	4	5
Speed Test Time (secs)	32	28	27	26	25
Ball Speed Bounce Catches 30secs	20	26	32	36	38
Trunk Curl Test Number in minute	10	20	28	32	36
Bailey Bridge Number in 30 secs	12	16	18	20	22
Push-Up hand/foot version No in 1min or Push-Up hand/knee moderated	8	14	18	24	30
version. Number in minute	14	24	28	40	45
Single Leg Squat Thrust. No in 30 secs	35	50	65	70	80
Run Time (mins & secs)	4.50	4.30	4.10	3.50	3.40

Note: Scores may be counted for either Push-ups hand/foot version or Push-Up hand knee moderated version, **but not both.**

Physical Achievement Programme

Points required for Star Awards.
The MINIMUM number of points for you to qualify at each level of this subject are set out in the chart below.

Training Level	Participation	Performance	Additional Pts	Pass Qual
First Class	6	3	3	12
Leading	10	4	4	18
Senior	12	6	6	24
Staff	12	6	12	30

Note: Points are awarded for *participation* on a basis of 1 point for each half-hour of training. No more than two participation points may be gained in any one week.
Additional points may be gained by either further participation or by improved performance

THE DUKE OF EDINBURGH'S AWARD
DESCRIPTION AND CONDITIONS OF TESTS

Speed Test: Cross **TEN** times between two lines marked on ground or floor NINE metres apart. Each line crossed or touched by one foot.

Stamina Run

Twenty laps of a regular circuit 12 metres by 8 metres, each corner marked by a small object. The score is determined by the time in which this exercise is completed.

Ball Speed Bounce

Using a Netball or a size 5 Football, stand behind a line 2 metres from a wall. Hold the ball with two hands against the chest. Ball must be

thrown with two hands so as to rebound from the wall into the hands behind the restraining line.

Count each successfully caught ball in 30 seconds. It is recommended that a brick or similar solid surface is used for this event to ensure a satisfactory rebound.

Push-Ups

Hand/Foot version: Lie face down on the floor, hands under shoulders, palms flat on the floor.

Straighten arms without locking, to lift body, leaving only palms and toes on floor.

Bend elbows until nose only touches the floor or return to starting position.

Repeat push-ups. Scoring ceases if body sags. The score is the number of push-ups completed in one minute. or alternatively:-

Hand/knee moderated version:

Lie face down on the floor, hands under shoulders, palms flat on the floor with lower legs bent upwards from the knees.

THE DUKE OF EDINBURGH'S AWARD

Straighten arms, without locking, to lift body, leaving only the palms and knees on floor, so that knees, hips and shoulders are in a straight line.  This straight line should be maintained and the hands should not be allowed to move back towards the knees. Bend elbows until nose touches the floor or return to starting position.

Repeat push-up. The score is the number of push-ups completed in one minute. Girls may find it easier to lie face down on the floor, hands under shoulders, palms flat on the floor with legs bent upwards from the knees on the floor.

Bailey Bridge

Start in the front support position (body in a straight line supported by hands and toes only) with shoulders near to and facing a chair, stool or box on which is placed a small object, bean bag, keys, a stone etc.,.

The seat of the chair should be 45cm from the floor.

Take the object from the chair seat with one hand, place it on the floor, pick up the object with the other hand and replace it on the chair seat.

Continue the cycle, using alternate hands. Count the number of times the object is successfully placed on the chair in 30 seconds

SINGLE LEG SQUAT THRUST
Starting Position:

Set up two lines 50cm apart. Crouch with both hands placed flat on the floor and with the toes touching the front line.

Take one leg back so that the foot is on the floor behind the rear line.

The test:

Change legs so that each foot is alternately thrust over the rear line, with the hips remaining high.

The score is the number of single leg squat thrusts, ie when each foot crosses the line, completed in the thirty seconds.

TRUNK CURL TEST

(To be performed on a towel, mat or suitable equivalent).

Lie on the back with legs bent. A 90 degree angle should be maintained between the upper and lower legs. Place hands on cheeks. Ankles should not be held. Sit, curling trunk and head until both elbows touch upper legs and then return to the starting position. Although the feet may leave the floor, the right angle between the upper and lower legs must be maintained. The score is the number of curls completed in one minute.

Get all your D of E Award CLOTHING & KIT from CADET DIRECT

THE DUKE OF EDINBURGH'S AWARD

SELF TEST QUESTIONS

1. What four sections are common to all Awards.
2. What is the age you can enter the Bronze, Silver and Gold Awards?
3. At what level of your training are you most likely to qualify for the Bronze Award.
4. Give two examples of where a Senior Cadet Instructors Cadre might fit into an Award.
5. What is the upper age limit for gaining an Award.
6. How many kilometers are suggested for Bronze, Silver and Gold Expeditions on foot.
7. Before going on an Expedition what do you leave behind.
8. What is the minimum period of time you must undertake for a particular Skill at Silver level?
9. In the Physical Recreation section what is the minimum period of time you must take to qualify?
10. What is the important proviso which enables you to count Annual Camp as your Residential Project (apart from the time requirement)?
11. During Expeditions the minimum recommended calorie intake per day is 1000, 2000, 3000 or 4000?
12. Can Drill be taken as a Skill in the Award?
13. What do you have to buy to start your Award.
14. Do you all enter as a team in your squadron for the Award?
15. Who is the Award Officer in your Squadron/Wing ?
16. Are you permitted to do an expedition other than on foot?
17. Can Skill at Arms be counted as a Skill towards the Award?
18. How many in the team doing a Qualifying Venture?
19. Who sets the targets to be achieved in Physical Recreation?
20. Who completes an account of the Expedition?
21. Name fourteen recognised 'skills'.
22. At what level of the Award do you do a Residential Project?
23. Name two alternative types of Expedition you can undertake over the age of 16?

FIRST AID, HEALTH & SAFETY

Chapter 10

Introduction

First Aid is the immediate help given to someone who is ill or injured. Think for a moment, if you were ill or injured wouldn't you want someone to stop help and you? First aid skills are easy to learn and with regular practice and knowledge it can be of benefit through-out your whole life, to you, your family members and friends. Please note that first aid is not an exact science and often casualties do not respond in a way you hope they will and of course the outcomes of a casualty are not always successful, so don't be afraid to talk things through with someone if you have been affected by giving first aid treatment. As a junior cadet, you have access to gaining the nationally recognised Youth First Aid qualification which is valid for three years, approved by HQ Air Cadets, a special centre of St John Ambulance. A senior cadet aged over 14 can undertake the adult first aid qualification Activity First Aid, progressing from aged 16 years to the Health & Safety Executive recognised First Aid at Work certificate. Remember DO NO HARM.

Assessing the Situation (AMEGR)

As a first aider when you come across a situation you must act quickly, but calmly to

Assess the situation. After finding out what happened you must remove any hazards or dangers to

Make the Area Safe, ensure you do not become a casualty. Then approach the casualty to see if they are conscious and decide to give the appropriate

Emergency Aid treatment. Once you have got the facts,

Get Help, lastly

Report what has happened to your squadron staff, they may be able to help you. You may need to *clear up* the squadron area, *stock up* your first aid kit, then *brew up* after all your hard work and efforts!

Telephoning for Help

After assessing the situation and casualty/ies you can dial **999** or **112** for the emergency services. State which service you require; police, fire, ambulance, mine, mountain, cave and fell rescue (via the police).
If you are unsure of your location, do not panic, your call can be traced. Stay on the line until the control officer clears the line.

FIRST AID, HEALTH & SAFETY

You will need to tell the emergency services:
1. Your telephone number
2. The exact location of the incident
3. Type of incident eg. Traffic accident, two cars, three people.
4. The number, gender and approximate age of the casualties and any other information you may know about their condition such as "Man, late fifties, suspected heart attack"

Details of any hazards such as gas, toxic substances, relevant weather conditions such as ice or fog.

If you have to leave a casualty alone minimise the risk to the casualty by carrying out *Emergency Aid*. If you have a helper, ask them to do this and tell them to come back and tell you help is on its way.

The Primary Survey (DRAB)

Remembering this sequence is really important to enable you to look for life-threatening conditions quickly.
It can be used on casualties over the age of 1.

D – DANGER

Are there any risks to you, the casualty or by-standers. If so, remove it if safe to do so or you may need to enlist help to move the casualty. Top tip – never move a casualty unnecessarily.

R – RESPONSE

Check the casualty, are they visibly conscious? Does the casualty respond to your voice or gently stimulation, if yes, check for other conditions and treat as necessary. If no, carry on with the primary survey. **Summon help if needed by shouting.**

A – AIRWAY

Open the casualty's airway by gently tilting the head back and lifting the chin.

B – BREATHING

Check for breathing by placing your ear by their mouth and nose to listen, look and feel for no more than 10 seconds. What kind of breathing is it? Noisy, easy or difficult. Are they breathing normally?
If they are breathing you will need to place the unconscious casualty into the recovery position.
Are you alone or do you have a helper? Either go or send for help at this point. You must have carried out your DRAB checks before sending for help – the emergency services will need to know this information.
Any casualty unconscious for more than 3 minutes will need to go to hospital, urgently.

FIRST AID, HEALTH & SAFETY

In an unconscious casualty, the greatest danger is that food, vomit, blood, water, other substance or the tongue may block the **AIRWAY** and prevent the casualty from breathing.

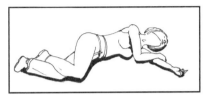

OPEN THE AIRWAY, LIFT THE CHIN UPWARDS WITH THE INDEX FINGER AND MIDDLE FINGERS OF ONE HAND, WHILST PRESSING THE FOREHEAD BACK WITH THE PALM OF THE OTHER HAND.

How to place in Recovery Position (from laid on their back).

1. Kneel beside the casualty. Remove bulky objects such as phones, keys, spectacles.
2. Ensure the casualty has straight legs.
3. Place arm at right angles, palm facing upwards.
4. Bring arm farthest away across the chest, holding the back of the hand against the side of the cheek nearest to you.
5. With your other hand grasp the far leg, on the far side just under the knee and pull it up, keeping the foot flat on the floor.
6. Keep the hand against the cheek, pull on the far leg towards you and onto their side.
7. Adjust the bent leg nearest to you at right angles. Tilt the head back gently to keep the airway open. If left in the recovery position for longer than 30 minutes, then turn onto the other side.
8. If you suspect spinal injury, try to keep the spine straight, inline with the head.

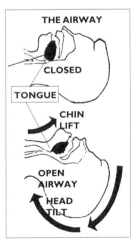

THE AIRWAY

CLOSED

TONGUE

CHIN LIFT

OPEN AIRWAY

HEAD TILT

10-3

FIRST AID, HEALTH & SAFETY

CHAIN OF SURVIVAL

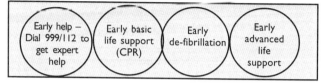

Early help –
Dial 999/112 to
get expert
help

Early basic
life support
(CPR)

Early
de-fibrillation

Early
advanced
life
support

A Secondary Survey (Head to Toe)

Once you have provided the initial treatment for the casualty, you will
need to look for other clues to find out what is wrong with the
person. It involves taking a history and physically examining a casualty
and scene around them. Do they have any medication on them? Do
you know if they have any allergies? When did they last eat? To carry
out a head-to-toe survey you will need both hands to examine the
casualty, to compare and contrast opposite sides of the body and
limbs. Look carefully at the situation they are in and at the casualty.
Ask the casualty and on-lookers questions and listen carefully to their
answers. Your senses may prove helpful in looking for clues, such as
unusual smells. Communication is key and you will need to inform your
casualty about what you are doing and also gaining their permission.
Some casualties may be very sensitive about you touching them. Do
things that only the casualty will let you. DO NO HARM.

Head to Toe (Secondary) Survey

1. Start at the head, run your hands over the scalp & look for
   bleeding, swelling or indentation. In all cases, try not to move the
   head or neck.
2. Check both ears for fluid.
3. Check eyes, the pupils should be equal in size.
4. Check the nose for any fluid such as blood.
5. Check the rate & depth of breathing, note any unusual odour.
6. Check the mouth. DO NOT remove dentures unless they are
   causing an obstruction. Look for wounds.
7. Look at the face for wounds, any irregularity or symmetry.
8. Note the colour and temperature of the skin.
9. Loosen tight clothing at neck; look for swelling or wounds.
10. Look for a medic alert or talisman, worn at the neck or wrist.
11. Feeling down the chest for swelling, irregularities or wounds. If they
    are conscious ask them to take a breath to assess for equal
    movements and to listen for any lung sounds.

12. Check the collar bones for deformities.
13. Check each arm in turn for irregularities, wounds, needle marks etc. Ask them to bend and straighten fingers and elbows.
14. Check both hands & fingers for injury.
15. If there is a problem with movement or loss of feeling in the arms do not examine the spine, otherwise place your hands under the hollow of the back to check for swelling, tenderness or irregularity.
16. Look at the abdomen for bruising, wounds, tenderness or rigidity.
17. Place your hands on either side of the hips & gently rock the pelvis, noting any differences in motion. Make a note of any incontinence or bleeding from the private areas.
18. Check and examine each leg in turn for wounds, swelling or stiffness at the joints. Ask the casualty to bend & straighten in turn.
19. Examine each foot and ankle for swelling, irregularity and movement.

Following a secondary survey, treat any problems you find, and note down any abnormalities you may have found to pass on to the emergency services.

Cardio Pulmonary Resuscitation (CPR)

The circulatory system pumps blood around the body. When the heart stops we can artificially pump blood around the body by performing chest compressions. Combining chest compressions with rescue breaths is known as CPR. It is important firstly to ensure professional medical help is on its way to ensure the best outcomes of the casualty and then carry out CPR to buy time until help arrives. After carrying out the *Primary Survey* and checking for normal breathing, you may find agonal breathing – which is described as short irregular gasps, sometimes referred to as the death rattle (the last breath of the casualty). This is not normal and this casualty requires CPR.

Adult Procedure

1. Kneel beside the casualty.
2. Aim for the centre of the chest and place the heel of one hand on the chest. Now place the other hand on top of this and inter lock your fingers and keep them off the casualty's body.
3. Keep your arms straight and directly over your wrists, do not bend your elbows.
4. Press straight down 4 – 5 cm (one-and-a-half to two inches), keeping your elbows straight. Release the pressure fully but don't take your hands off the chest.

FIRST AID, HEALTH & SAFETY

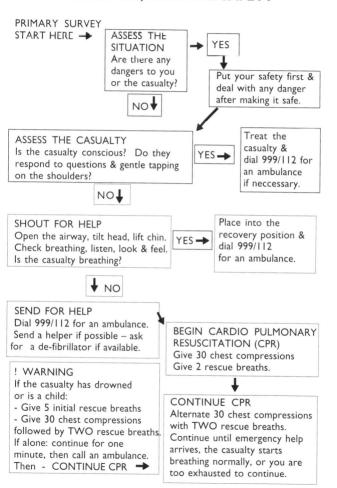

PRIMARY SURVEY
START HERE →

ASSESS THE SITUATION
Are there any dangers to you or the casualty?

→ YES

↓

Put your safety first & deal with any danger after making it safe.

NO ↓

ASSESS THE CASUALTY
Is the casualty conscious? Do they respond to questions & gentle tapping on the shoulders?

YES →

Treat the casualty & dial 999/112 for an ambulance if neccessary.

NO ↓

SHOUT FOR HELP
Open the airway, tilt head, lift chin. Check breathing, listen, look & feel. Is the casualty breathing?

YES →

Place into the recovery position & dial 999/112 for an ambulance.

↓ NO

SEND FOR HELP
Dial 999/112 for an ambulance. Send a helper if possible – ask for a de-fibrillator if available.

BEGIN CARDIO PULMONARY RESUSCITATION (CPR)
Give 30 chest compressions
Give 2 rescue breaths.

↓

! WARNING
If the casualty has drowned or is a child:
- Give 5 initial rescue breaths
- Give 30 chest compressions followed by TWO rescue breaths.
If alone: continue for one minute, then call an ambulance.
Then - CONTINUE CPR →

CONTINUE CPR
Alternate 30 chest compressions with TWO rescue breaths. Continue until emergency help arrives, the casualty starts breathing normally, or you are too exhausted to continue.

5. Give 30 chest compressions at a rate of 100 compressions per minute (not quite two per second).
6. Give 2 rescue breaths.
7. Continue giving 30 chest compressions and 2 rescue breaths until:
   - Professional help takes over
   - The casualty starts breathing normally
   - You become exhausted

Rescue Breaths Adult Procedure

1. Ensure the airway is open by gently tilting the head back and lifting the chin.
2. Keep supporting the casualty's chin with the index and middle fingertips of one hand.
3. With your other hand, pinch the nostrils with your thumb and forefinger.
4. Take a breath and place your mouth over the casualty's making a good seal (you can use a face shield if you have one).
5. Breathe steadily into the casualty's mouth for about one second whilst looking out of the corner of your eye, watching the chest rise.
6. Keep your hands in position, remove your mouth from theirs, let their chest fall.
7. Make no more than two attempts to achieve two effective rescue breaths, before repeating chest compressions.
   - If you do not wish to give rescue breaths or are unable, then give chest compressions only.
   - If it is a drowning casualty give five initial rescue breaths before you start chest compressions. If alone, call an ambulance after one minute of CPR.
   - If breathing is absent or agonal, call 999 or 112 – if there is a bystander, ask them to do this for you. Get a de-fibrillator if there is one available.
   - If there is another rescuer present change over every two minutes with minimum disruption.
   - CPR is an important part in the chain of survival for a casualty whose heart has stopped.

FIRST AID, HEALTH & SAFETY

BLEEDING

First aid priorities

- Assess the casualty's condition
- Reassure and comfort the casualty.
- Think about hygiene – wear disposable non-latex gloves if possible.
- Control blood loss by applying pressure and elevating the injured part (or if it's a minor wound, clean with water first)
- Minimise shock
- Get medical help if necessary

To control severe bleeding - remember EXPEL

Expose the site of injury

e**X**amine the injured part for any foreign particles or objects

Pressure upon the wound (get the casualty to do it if possible)

Elevate injured limb (above the level of the heart will reduce blood loss)

Lay the casualty down in the most appropriate position (unless it's bleeding in the head – raise the head, if it's bleeding in the chest sitting is best)

"If the face is pale – raise the tail". (Generally).

APPLYING A DRESSING

- Wear disposable gloves
- Place pad over area to be dressed, retain hold of short end of bandage
- Wind remainder and secure
- I blood comes through that first dressing you will need to put another on top
- If blood comes through both dressings – remove them, start again, applying a bit firmer pressure
- Check for circulation beyond the bandage (feel warmth of skin, check circulation at ends of fingers, press nail bed briefly until pale then release the pressure – if the colour doesn't return, the bandage may be too tight – remember to ask the casualty if it is too tight!)

FIRST AID, HEALTH & SAFETY

APPLYING A DRESSING

If an object is embedded
- Wear disposable gloves
- Do not remove the object
- Press on either side of the embedded object
- Build up padding on either side of the object and secure
- Support the injured part in an elevated position

Whilst waiting for help. carrying out your secondary survey, in all casualties you will need to monitor the vital signs and record them if possible. These are **B**reathing, levels of **R**esponse and **P**ulse.
Remember BRP!

BURNS AND SCALDS

First Aid Priorities
- To stop the burning and relieve pain
- To maintain an open airway
- To treat associated injuries
- To minimise the risk of infection
- Get urgent removal to hospital

The priorities are to quickly cool the burn or scald and treat the casualty for shock, the casualty will need hospital treatment.

Remember to:

STOP (the casualty from panicking),

DROP (the casualty onto the ground),

WRAP (in a blanket or jacket) and

ROLL the casualty to extinguish any flame.

To assess the severity of burns use the following as a guide:

Size of burn (1% is classed as the size of the casualty's palm)

Cause (flame, chemical, steam, hot liquids, electrical, sunburn, friction etc)

Age of casualty (the very young and old are more vunerable)

Location on the body (some areas are more sensitive than others)

Depth (there are three depths; superficial, partial-thickness & full-thickness)

Recognition (dependent on cause)
Pain, blistering, reddened skin, signs of shock, intense stinging pain, tenderness, skin pale and waxy, peeling skin, charred skin, singed hair etc.

FIRST AID, HEALTH & SAFETY

Treatment (Burns and Scalds)
1. Do not touch the burned area
2. Apply cold running water for at least 10 minutes (20 for a chemical)
3. Remove any jewellery or other constrictions
4. Cover with a sterile dressing – cling film or a polythene bag make good temporary dressings
5. Treat for shock (lay casualty down, maintain normal body temperature, reassure)
6. Get medical help if necessary

Bone, Muscle and Joint Injuries
These are caused by sudden impact. The type of injury is determined often by the mechanism or mechanics of injury (how something has happened, the forces applied). It can be difficult sometimes to determine exactly what the injury is, if in doubt – ship them out.
When you are in any doubt always treat as a suspected fracture.

Fractures – Recognition
A history or fall or recent blow, snapping sound, difficulty in moving limb, severe pain, tenderness, distortion or swelling, bruising, signs of shock if injury is severe.

Treatment
1. Tell the casualty to keep still & not to move

2. Wear gloves if possible

3. Cover any wounds and secure

4. Steady and support the injured limb and stabilise with any props or materials you have handy

5. Get medical help

If you are in a remote situation and help is a long time in arriving you will need to use plenty of bandages (if available) to immobilise the limb. Use padding between joints for comfort. Tie off bandages on the uninjured side.

FIRST AID, HEALTH & SAFETY

A. Closed Fracture. Skin not broken.

B. Open Fracture. Bone has broken surface of skin. Dangerous; external loss of blood and serious risk of infection.

C. Complicated Fracture. When internal nerve or organ is also injured and when fracture is connected with a dislocated joint.

D. Symptoms and Signs. Casualty heard it break. Pain at site of injury. Swelling, bruising later. Deformity, bone grating and shock.

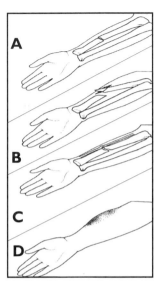

Sprains and Strains – Recognition

Pain, tenderness, difficulty in moving the limb, swelling or distortion, bruising.

Treatment

1. Any doubt, treat as a fracture
2. Use the RICE procedure (as explained below)

RICE Procedure

Rest the injured area

Ice – apply ice wrapped in material or cold compress to the area for 10 minutes.

Compression – apply soft even pressure with a stretchy bandage

Elevate – the limb (check the bandage every 10 minutes that it is not too tight)

10-11

FIRST AID, HEALTH & SAFETY

Shock
Disruption to the circulatory system caused by illness or injury which prevent blood being pumped to the vital organs such as the brain, heart, lungs and kidneys can cause a potentially fatal medical condition known as shock.

Recognition
Pale, ashen, cold clammy skin, rapid pulse, becoming weaker as time progresses. As the casualty becomes worse you may see; rapid shallow breathing, nausea, vomiting, casualty feels weak or giddy, dizzy, restlessness. The casualty may be aggressive due to the brain being short of oxygen – in this case they are literally fighting for their life. You may see yawning or gasping for air, again due to low blood oxygen in the body's tissues. Decreasing consciousness.

Treatment
1. Treat any cause
2. If injuries allow, lay them down, keep the head low (no pillows) and raise the legs gently (this improves blood flow to the brain)
3. Give plenty of reassurance, loosen tight clothing (if appropriate) at waist and neck
4. If appropriate insulate underneath the casualty by using a blanket, cover them also. Remember to maintain normal body temperature.
5. Dial 999 or 112 for an ambulance – if you have had to treat someone in this position, they will need to be transported in this   position
6. Monitor the vital signs BRP (breathing, levels of response and pulse)
7. If the casualty goes unconscious, carry out your DRAB then place into the recovery position

DO NOT – move a casualty unnecessarily, leave them alone unless to get help, give a sweet drink, allow them to smoke or eat. If the casualty complains of thirst, moisten their lips.

Head Injuries
These should be taken as serious conditions. Medical advice should always be sought. There are three main types of head injury:
1. Concussion – where a temporary loss of consciousness is followed by complete recovery after a blow to the head.
2. Compression – a build up of pressure on the brain, which is usually corrected by surgery. This can develop up-to several days after the impact.
3. Skull-fracture – where impact is strong enough to fracture (break) one of the bones of the skull. Your role is simple: Maintain an airway, monitor levels of consciousness, get medical help.

FIRST AID, HEALTH & SAFETY

Extremes of Temperature
Hypo-thermia
This develops when the body temperature falls below 35 degrees celsius (95 degrees Fahrenheit). This can be caused by prolonged exposure to cold temperatures out-doors. Made worse with a wet casualty. Moving air will have a greater cooling effect so a high "wind-chill factor" can increase the risk of a person developing hypo-thermia (see page 7-24 Wind Chill Factor).

Recognition
Shivering, pale, dry cold skin, apathy, disorientated, or irrational behaviour, lethargy or impaired consciousness. Slow and shallow breathing, slow weakening pulse.

Treatment
First Aid Priorities
- To prevent the casualty from losing more body heat
- To re-warm the casualty slowly
- To obtain medical help if necessary

Action
1. Quickly replace any wet clothes, with warm, dry garments
2. If a warm bath is available then do this, the water should be warm but not too hot – about 40 degrees Celsius
3. Put casualty to bed, give warm drinks, soup or high energy chocolate to help re-warm them
4. Cover the head for additional warmth
5. Stay with the casualty until colour and warmth return

FROSTBITE
Recognition
Initially pins and needles, pallor followed by numbness, hardening or stiffening of skin, colour change to the skin of the affected area.

Treatment
1. Move the casualty to a warm place
2. Warm the affected area (usually the extremities) in your lap or the casualty's armpits, AVOID rubbing
3. Place affected area in warm water, apply a light dressing
4. Raise or support the affected limb and take the casualty to hospital.

FIRST AID, HEALTH & SAFETY

Effects of Heat
You may come across sunburn, prickly heat, heat exhaustion and heat stroke,

Sunburn – over exposure to the sun or sunlamp, made worse at high altitude or where water or snow is present. This is often superficial, in severe cases can appear lobster-red and blistered and the casualty may also suffer from heat stroke.
Treatment – move the casualty out of the sun, relive pain and discomfort. Cool with cold water, use calamine or after-sun preparation.

Prickly heat
This can be a highly irritating, prickly red rash, tiny red spots or blisters occurring in hot weather. Due to sweat glands being blocked by bacteria and dead skin cells. Sweat is trapped and cannot evaporate.
Treatment – move the casualty to a cool area, cool the skin by sponging with cold water.

Heat Exhaustion
Caused by loss of salt and water from the body through excessive sweating. The casualty sweats profusely, due to prolonged activity, dehydration develops leading to heat exhaustion. There may be headache, dizziness and confusion, loss of appetite and nausea, sweating with pale, clammy skin, cramps in the arms, legs or abdominal area, rapid, weakening pulse and breathing.
Treatment – move to a cool place, lay casualty down, raise the legs, give plenty of water to drink (with a weak salt solution – 1 tea spoon per litre), even if they recover quickly, ensure they get urgent medical help.

Heatstroke
Caused by the "thermostat" in the brain not working properly. The body becomes dangerously overheated often due to a high fever or prolonged exposure to heat. This condition can develop quickly, often with no warning. It may also follow heat exhaustion. There may be headache, dizziness, and discomfort, restlessness and confusion, hot, flushed and dry skin, rapid deterioration in the levels of response, a full bounding pulse and the body temperature may be over 40 degrees celsius.

FIRST AID, HEALTH & SAFETY

Treatment – Lower the casualty's temperature after removing outer clothes by wrapping them in a cold, wet sheet and keep the sheet wet until their temperature falls to 38 degrees. You can fan the casualty or sponge them alternatively. Once the body temperature is back to normal, replace the wet sheet with a dry one or dry clothes.

Remember – if it's a medical problem – get medical help.
As a first aider generally all you can do is apply a plaster or dressing, put a casualty in an appropriate casualty recovery position, keep a casualty comfortable, care for someone until professional help arrives. We don't administer anything or move anyone unless they are in immediate danger – and never put ourselves at any unnecessary risk. Nothing can substitute attending a first aid course and maintaining your skills by regular training of practical scenarios which will equip you with simple, effective life-saving skills for the benefit of your friends, family members or strangers in the street.

CASUALTY POSITIONS

This position with the casualty laid down and the knees raised slightly is suggested for fractured pelvis and abdominal wounds.

This is referred to as the half-sitting position, sat up, supported against something stable, knees raised, useful for chest injuries, conscious heart attack casualty, breathing problems, massive allergic reaction (anaphylaxis). If it's in the chest – sitting is best.

Laid down with head raised, used for head injuries (unless spinal injury

FIRST AID, HEALTH & SAFETY

Laid down with head raised, used for head injuries (unless Spinal injury is suspected) or eye injuries.
If it's in the head - raise the head.

CASUALTY POSITIONS

Sat leaning forward, good for nose bleeds, fractured jaw, airway problems, some breathing problems such as asthma

ACKNOWLEGEMENT

The First Aid element of this chapter has been written for Military Pocket Books Ltd by:

Michelle Summer

Serving Sister of the Most Venerable Order of St John of Jersualem,
15 (NE) Brigade First Aid Advisor,
County Duke of Edinburgh Award officer,
North & West Yorkshire Army Cadet Force.

FIRST AID, HEALTH & SAFETY

DON'T PUT *YOUR* HEAD IN THE SAND!

The development of the contraceptive pill in the 1960's led to females taking responsibility for ensuring they did not become pregnant. Antibiotics meant that Sexually Transmitted Diseases (STDs) and Venereal Disease (VD) could be easily cured. The result was a revolution of sexual habits and social conduct across the world.

The Present is not quite so clear cut; several new sexually transmitted diseases have emerged that cannot be easily cured, such as Herpes, Chlamydia and Pelvic Inflammatory Disease, Hepatitis B and C, not forgetting the discovery of HIV and the disasterous spread of AIDS across some nations. The message is that unprotected sex can cause real discomfort, infertility or a fatal and incurable disease. Find out about these diseases, you need to know!

As a result, young people having or contemplating having sex should make sure they use a condom; "being on the pill' will not protect you. You need to learn about condoms. Learn how to use one and how to put one on the right way. Used properly they can be an enjoyable part of sex and they could even save your life.

If you cannot afford to buy them, they give them out free at the local Family Planning Clinic or Brook Advisory Centre. These places are totally confidential, you can drop in and pick some up anonymously, or stay and talk through any problems you may have in total confidence. The Brook Advisory Centre will tell you where your nearest local centre is:

Tel: 0800 0185 023

Don't be like

one of these

The above information was provided by Lifeline Publications, Manchester M4 1NA **www.lifeline.org.uk**

FIRST AID, HEALTH & SAFETY

HEALTH & SAFETY

Under this heading we are going to look at some of your actions that can affect your personal Health and Safety and contribute to wellbeing and quality of life in general.

This all sounds rather serious, yes it is. Some of you will be well aware of the information given and act accordingly, while others may not have given it a moments thought. So now is the time to consider how you can be better at taking care of your Health and Safety.

A BALANCED DIET

Means eating food from differents types of food groups. If you eat a lot of different food you will get the balance right for you to exercise to the best of your ability, to be alert, fit and feel healthy.

Types of food related 'families'

- Bread, rice, pasta, cerals, potatoes.
- Fruit & Vegetables: oranges, bananas, apples, brocoli, sweetcorn, carrots.
- Meat: Beef, lamb,pork, chicken,turkey,
- Fish: Cod, salmon, tuna, (not Fish & Chips)!
- Milk and Dairy foods,:Cheese, yoghurt.
- Food containing fat, foods and drinks that contain sugar: Chocolate, crisps, fizzy drinks.

All foods should be eaten in moderation.

CARBOHYDRATES

Provide ENERGY to your muscles, so the following should be part of your diet:-

Breakfast -cerals, shredded wheat, weeabix, bran flakes, porridge, wholemeal or brown bread, baked beans, fresh and dried fruits.

Lunch: - potatoes - mashed, boiled, jacket, bread, pasta, noodles, lasagne, rice.

Night time: breakfast cereals, toast,sandwiches, fruit juice. low fat yoghurt, fresh and dried fruit.

FIRST AID, HEALTH & SAFETY

PROTEIN

Your body needs Protein to grow and repair muscles after any active exercise.

You should include in your diet many different proteins such as lean meats, fish (fresh, frozen or canned). Poultry (chicken, duck, pheasant, pidgeon, milk. eggs, cheese, beans, lentils, nuts.

FAT

You do need some fat in your diet - not a lot. Fat is concealed in many foods especially takeaway foods. Fat can lead to serious health problems later in your life.

- The fat that is good for you is from oily fish - salmon, mackeral, herring, fresh tuna and nuts.
- The fat that NOT good for you called 'saturated fat' is from fried food, chips, burgers, pastry. CHIPS WITH EVERYTHING NO NO NO!!!

FIBRE

- Eating enough fibre helps with digestion, keeps the stomach healthy and prevents constipaton.
- So include in your diet an increased amount of wholemeal and granary breads.
- High fibre cerals, shredded wheat. whole-wheat pasta, increase vegetables. Apples wash them first then - eat the skins.
- if you must eat biscuits choose Digestive, Hob Nobs, oatcakes and bran.

VITAMINS & MINERALS
IRON

Some vitamins are added to breakfast cerals and bread.

The UK Department of Healh are doing their best to get us to eat more vitamins through their slogan 'EAT FIVE A DAY' that is fruit and vegetables.

- Iron an important mineral found in lean red meat, green leafy vegetables- runner beans, spinach brccoli. Liver and kidney.
- Pulses - peas, lentils, baked beans, red kidney beans, dried fruit.
- Oily fish - fresh tuna, salmon, mackerel, sardines, trout, herring,
- Wholemeal bread, eggs, fortified with iron breakfast cerals

CALCIUM

Calcium strengthens your bones and can help in preventing stress fractures occuring. It is important that you understand the need for

FIRST AID, HEALTH & SAFETY

calcium to be a part of your diet to prevent bones from becoming thin and brittle. In later life it can lead to a condition called osteoporosis in part through lack of calcium In the diet.

The best source for calcium is milk in all its various forms, drink it as often as you can. Generally all other ingredients already mentioned help towards building a strong bone structure in your body.

SALT

Eating too much salt can increase your blood pressure which in turn can affect the condition of your heart.

Foods to avoid as their salt content is more than is good for you are:-

- Processed ready meals, bacon, crisps, salted & roasted nuts, sweet & savoury biscuits, chips with added salt, smoked and cured meat and fish, cooking sauces, soy sauce and ketchup, olives in brine, soup, stock cubes, some breakfast cerals.
- To cut down on your salt intake;-
- Avoid the foods mentioned above.
- Don't add salt to your meal before tasting it.
- Don't add salt during cooking.

FLUID INTAKE REQUIRED

How much fluid should you drink a day? It is important that you know how much you need and the way to find out is to do the URINE TEST. Your needs will change depending upon the amount of exercise you do.

- The minimum amount of liquid a day is not less than 1.2 litres to avoid dehydratin.
- You will need more than this if you are sweating.
- You will be DEHYDRATED and become a casualty.
- DEHYDRATION causes a complete collapse of your physical ability.

SEVERE DEHYDRATION CAN BE FATAL.

URINE TEST

Check your urine colour: a good indicator of dehydration volume smell

- If you are well hydrated, your urine will be light in colour and there will be lots of it.
- If you are dehydrated, your urine will be darker in colour, and there will be less of it.

SUBSTANCE MISUSE

In First Aid, you learn that a poison is any substance that taken in sufficient quantity can cause temporary or permanent damage to your health. Believe it or not, it is quite possible to poison yourself with water. The pharmaceutical industry has invested countless billions of pounds to 'invent' drugs to assist our Doctors and Specialists in the prevention and control of medical and psychological conditions. Many of these 'drugs' have side affects; at some time you have probably taken medication that has made you feel sleepy, dizzy or worse! Taken in controlled conditions these side affects can be monitored and the dosage or drug altered. When these 'drugs' are misused, there is a real danger of 'Poisoning' your body. Who says you get what you pay for?

If you buy a CD from a shop, you know exactly what you are getting. If the CD is faulty, you return it to the shop and either have it replaced or your money refunded.

If you become a 'miss user' of substances then there is a good probability that the substances you buy are not what they seem. They may have been 'bulked up' with things like sugar, laxatives or a cheaper, more lethal cocktail of substances. What you see is not necessarily what you get; you cannot get a refund – even if you are well enough to ask for one.

Mixing Substances. Loading any drug on top of another is very risky. It requires a much lower dose of each drug to provide a 'killer cocktail' – again you do not know exactly what quantities of each substance are – or what they will do to you.

The first paragraph mentions 'any substance'; this section will cover the majority of substances that people 'misuse', what it is, how to take it and the probable side affects.

TOBACCO

Tobacco is one of the most widely used addictive substances in this country. *If you get through 20 cigarettes a day over one year, that is 365 packets costing you well over* **ONE THOUSAND POUNDS!**

What is does to you: when smoking, you take tar, nicotine and carbon monoxide into your body. Its not just smokers who inhale - of course - its those around them too. The more you smoke, the more likely you are to suffer from heart disease, blood clots, cancer, strokes bronchitis, bad circulation and ulcers.

Pregnant women who smoke a lot tend to have smaller babies and they run a greater risk of losing their child before or after birth.

FIRST AID, HEALTH & SAFETY

LSD

Also known as ACID, is a man made substance, minute quantities are impregnated into small squares of blotting paper, which are then allowed to dissolve on the tongue. The squares often have colourful designs on them. **Note:** sometimes squares sold as LSD contain none at all.

What it does to you: A trip begins about one hour after taking, and fades gradually in about twelve hours, depending on the dose. Effects depend on the user's mood, where they are, whom they are with and the strength of the dose. Trips often include distortion of vision and hearing, or a feeling of being outside the body. Bad trips can lead to depression, dizziness, even panic. Bad trips are more likely is the user is anxious or in unfamiliar surroundings. Anyone driving whilst under the influence of LSD will endanger themselves and others.

MAGIC MUSHROOMS

There are several types of wild mushroom that can produce dreams or visions. Of these the best known is the Liberty Cap, which contains hallucinogenic chemicals. It is not illegal to pick magic mushrooms and eat them raw; once you dry them or turn them into any kind of preparation you could be outside the law.

What they do to you: A magic mushroom trip is rather like an LSD trip. The difference is that it takes affect quicker and does not last as long. Magic mushrooms can also cause nausea and severe stomach cramps. In this country there are many poisonous fungi, for instance, distinguishing between the Liberty Cap and the highly poisonous Amanita is not easy.

CANNABIS

Street names: DOPE, BLOW, WACKY BACKY, SHIT, GRASS
Cannabis comes from a plant know as Cannabis Sativa. **Hash** is the commonest form in this country, is resin blocks made from the sap of the plant. Herbal cannabis or marijuana is generally mixed with tobacco, rolled into a cigarette and smoked.

What it does to you: Cannabis makes people feel more relaxed and talkative. It can also reduce the ability to carry out complicated tasks; which would make it dangerous to operate machinery or drive whilst under the effects of the substance. Inexperienced people using high doses, or taking it when depressed, may sometimes experience panic attacks. *Cannabis takes effect very quickly. It can be mixed with food or drink and it is difficult to assess how much has been taken. This can be distressing for the user, particularly if un –knowingly taken, or alcohol is taken at the same time.* Cannabis is not addictive, but users come to rely on it as a method of relaxing.

FIRST AID, HEALTH & SAFETY

SOLVENTS

Solvents are found in products like glue, lighter fuel, paint, aerosols and petrol. When the vapours from these substances are inhaled, they produce a similar affect to alcohol. Some users increase the effect by inhaling inside a plastic bag placed over the head.

What is does to you: The effects are similar to being drunk (including the hangover). Vapours are absorbed through the lungs and quickly reach the brain. Repeated inhaling can cause loss of control.

A NASTY WAY TO DIE! *A number of users have died as a result of the miss use because they have squirted aerosol gases directly into their mouths, thus freezing their air passages.* Sniffers can be accidentally injured when they are 'high' because they are in an unsafe place – on a roof or by a railway line; perceptions of danger are non – existent.

Sniffers can suffocate I they inhale the solvents by putting plastic bags over their heads. The mouth and nose areas of users are often reddened and blistered. There is a real danger of Sniffers becoming unconscious and choking on their own vomit. Heavy solvent abuse can result in lasting damage to the brain, kidneys and liver.

BARBITURATES

Street names: BARBS, BLUES, REDS, SEKKIES

Barbiturates - DOWNERS, are used medically to calm people down (as sedatives) and as sleeping pills (hypnotics). Most come in powdered form and are sold in coloured capsules. Users will swallow them, occasionally with alcohol, or inject. *Injecting Barbiturates is one of the most dangerous forms of drug misuse.*

What they do to you: Users of this drug tend to develop a tolerance to them and then a physical as well as mental dependence. Sudden withdrawal can even kill. The effects can include irritability, nervousness, faintness, sleeplessness, sickness, twitching, delirium and convulsions.

TRANQUILLISERS

Street names: TRANX, BENZOS, EGGS, JELLIES

Doctors prescribe tranquillisers to control anxiety and tension, or to help people sleep. Although they are supposed to be taken in pill form, users sometimes inject them in to the body.

What they do to you: they lessen alertness and affect skills where concentration is required. They can also release aggression by lowering inhibitions. Mixed with alcohol they can even cause death. Dependence is fairly common among long-term users. Once people stop taking the drug, they can feel confused, irritable, anxious and unable to carry on with their normal routines.

HEROIN

Street names: SMACK, JUNK, 'H', SKAG

Heroin along with other opiates is made from the opium poppy. In its purest form, it is a white powder. Heroin is sometimes sniffed like cocaine, sometimes smoked, sometimes injected.

What it does to you: Heroin depresses brain activity, widens the blood vessels (giving a feeling of warmth) and causes severe constipation. Opiates create a feeling of total relaxation and detachment from pain or anxiety. They make people warm, drowsy, content, and it appears to relieve stress and discomfort. But this is where the bad news starts. Once physical dependence has established itself simply the relief of getting hold of the drug replaces this pleasure. Users find that they need more and more of the drug to get the same feeling of well being.

As the intake increases, as it inevitably must, the user feels the effects, even between doses. These include aches, tremors, sweating, chills, and sneezing, yawning and muscular spasms.

Overdosing or using a bad fix results in unconsciousness and coma: often if the user is not discovered in time, death from breathing failure. The chances of dying are even greater if other drugs such as alcohol are used at the same time. First time users often feel sick and vomit, especially if they have injected. Damage to the body is common with users. It is usually caused by repeated injections with dirty needles and by the substances mixed with the heroin by the suppliers to make more money from the batch they are selling. By this time, the user lives for the next 'fix', spending their time trying to raise the money by whatever means they can.

General Note: Users who share needles place themselves at risk of at the least, infection, at the worst, Hepatitis or contracting HIV the virus that can lead to AIDS. Most large towns and cities have chemists who have the facility of providing users with clean hypodermics and needles.

DRUG AND OTHER ABUSE POISONING

You will be well aware of the use of drugs, which is the "broad heading" given to Painkillers, Tranquillisers, Stimulants, amphetamines and LSD, Cocaine, Narcotics, Solvents and in addition Alcohol Poisoning.

It will be necessary for you to keep strictly to the Primary Survey DRAB of First Aid when dealing with them.

We set out on the following pages a chart showing the "cause" and "effect" of drug poisoning which vary depending on the drug taken and the method by which it has been taken.

FIRST AID, HEALTH & SAFETY

DRUG	EFFECT
Painkillers Aspirin (commonly swallowed)	Upper abdominal pain, nausea, and vomiting (possibly blood stained) Ringing in the ears. "Sighing" breathing. Confusion or delirium.
Paracetamol (commonly swallowed)	Little effect at first. Later, features of liver damage, upper abdominal pain and tenderness, nausea, and vomiting.
Nervous system depressants barbiturates and tranquillisers (commonly swallowed)	Lethargy and sleepiness, leading to unconsciousness. "Shallow" breathing. A weak irregular, or abnormally slow or fast pulse.
Stimulants and hallucinogens - amphetamines and LSD. (commonly swallowed) cocaine (commonly inhaled)	Excitable, hyperactive behaviour, wildness and frenzy. Sweating. Tremor of the hands. Hallucinations, casualty may be "hearing" voices, and/or "seeing" things.

FIRST AID, HEALTH & SAFETY

DRUG	EFFECT
Narcotics - morphine, heroin (commonly injected)	Constricted pupils. Sluggishness and confusion, possibly leading to unconsciousness. Slow, shallow breathing, which may cease. Needle marks may be infected, or infection may be introduced by <u>dirty</u> needles.
Solvents (commonly inhaled) - glue, lighter fuel	Nausea, vomiting and headaches. Hallucinations. Possibly unconsciousness. Rarely, cardiac arrest

TREATMENT
YOUR AIMS ARE: To maintain AIRWAY, BREATHING & CIRCULATION.   To arrange urgent removal to hospital.
CARRY OUT THE ABC of FIRST AID.
   DO NOT ATTEMPT TO INDUCE VOMITING.

ALCOHOL POISONING

Early Stage
Smell, flushed face, deep noisy breathing, full bounding pulse.
Later
Swollen face, shallow breathing, weak, rapid pulse.
DANGER The unconscious casualty may well choke on their vomit.
Hypothermia may develop *if* casualty is not kept warm.

BE AWARE - Alcohol may conceal other serious injury.

TREATMENT Carry out DRAB the Primary Survey of First Aid. *if* casualty is unconscious - place in Recovery Position.
   URGENT REMOVAL TO HOSPITAL.

FIRST AID, HEALTH & SAFETY

SELF TEST QUESTIONS

1. Name the three types of fracture.
2. Name two signs of a possible fracture.
3. When do you carry out a Head to Toe survey?
4. What causes Shock?
5. What is the treatment for Shock?
6. What must a casualty not do if suffering from Shock?
7. How do you tell if a casualty is breathing?
8. In what position do you place an Unconscious, Breathing casualty
9. What is the treatment for a burn or scald?
10. What size burn or scald requires medical attention?
11. In Casualty Management, which casualty must have priority?
12. Name the three key points in the treatment of severe bleeding.
13. What is the treatment for Heat Exhaustion?
14. What is the cause of Heat Stroke?
15. What is your action when you are on your own, and have a casualty who is not breathing and shows NO sign of physical injury or drowning?
16. How long should you check to see if a casualty is breathing?
17. Where do you find the Carotid pulse?
18. When doing Cardio Pulmonary Resuscitation, do you stop and check that there is no heart beat?
19. What is the ratio of rescue breaths to compression for C.P.R?
20. What three things do you do to check the level of consciousness?
21. Treating a casualty for shock, what are the four things you do NOT do.
22. Treating Heat Stroke,what keeps temperature down.
23. Free circulation of air near skin, prevents what.
24. What may cause a patient to have dilated pupils.
25. Give the four effects it has on a brain when its oxygen supply is weakened.
26. Who are the principal First Aid Providers in the UK
27. Explain what the initials D.R.A.B. mean and how they are applied.
28. When do you especially SHOUT HELP,
29. What are the AIMS of First Aid.

FIRST AID, HEALTH & SAFETY

30. What factors are considered when Assessing the Emergency.
31. Diagnosis, three "key words", what are they and explain the meaning of each one.
32. You can save a life by maintaining a casualties vital needs, what are they.
33. What could cause "noisy, bubbling, gasping breathing".
34. How can you tell if the casualty is breathing.
35. In an emergency what do you dial to call the emergency services.
36. Where is the Carotid artery.
37. How do you carry out Chest Compression and when is it done.
38. When is the recovery position used.
39. If the casualty has severe bleeding their vital organs are deprived of what.
40. How do you control severe bleeding.
41. A casualty with severe burns or scalds will lose what, and as a result what condition will occur.
42. What do you understand by anything constrictive in the injured area.
43. What MUST NOT be used on a burn or scald.
44. Name three types of fracture.
45. How do you immobilise an injured arm.
46. How do you immobilise an injured leg.
47. What are the symptoms of a casualty with SHOCK
48. What must you NEVER DO with an unconscious casualty.
49. Explain what DILATED PUPILS look like.
50. What affects the "CORE" temperature in the body.
51. What is HEAT EXHAUSTION, its cause and treatment.
52. What is HEATSTROKE, its cause and treatment.
53. If you are gong to make up a set of training aids for First Aid training who could you get advice from.
54. In health terms what does the abreviation 'STD' refer too.
55. List the contents your Detachment First Aid Box. and where is it kept in the Detachment.

Chapter 11
MAP AND COMPASS

INTRODUCTION
We are fortunate to have excellent maps of this country produced by the Ordnance Survey.

The Military Survey, a specialist branch of the Royal Engineers, undertakes the provision of maps, charts, hydrographical, and other geographical products for all three of the armed services. The ATC use the maps made available by the MOD.

RELIABILITY OF MAPS
A map is literally a "Bird's eye view" of the ground drawn on paper. It is accurate only at the time it was drawn. Today, maps are produced from aerial photographs, which ensures their accuracy.

In just a few years, the shape of a landscape can change, villages may disappear under a reservoir, new roads may appear, and whole woods may disappear. For practical map reading purposes this will not affect the accuracy as far as you will be concerned, any map produced within the last few years may be relied upon unless specifically stated otherwise.

CARE OF MAPS
Maps should be treated carefully or they soon become useless. When using outdoors, it is advisable to fold the map to the area required and place it in a map case or plastic bag to protect it. When planning routes, place a transparent film over the map; writing directly on to the map ruins it for further use. Ensure you learn how to fold a new map correctly; it will prolong its useful life.

WHAT YOU WILL FIND ON MAPS

Marginal Information
On most maps you will find a part set aside for 'marginal information', find this as soon as you unfold your map, it provides

MAP & COMPASS

useful information and guidance on how to interpret the detail on the map.

Until you have been map reading for some time, you will constantly refer to this section – until you have a good understanding of what all the symbols or CONVENTIONAL SIGNS mean.

The reference number and scale of the map is to be found at the top of the map.

The index giving adjoining sheet numbers is usually shown near the bottom right hand corner of the map. You will need this info if the route you are planning "Goes off the map".

Most maps now use metres as the "Unit of Elevation", this scale is to be found in the margin at the bottom of the map as "ELEVATION IN METRES".

THE GRID SYSTEM

The British National Grid System divides the whole country into large squares which are sub – divided and finish up as the GRID LINES printed on maps that you would normally use.

Grid Lines are used to 'pin point' a specific spot on the map by using the numbers of each line as shown in the margins around the outside of the map. Maps are printed with the North at the top of the sheet, one set of GRID LINES run up and down the map (North and South), the others run across the map (East and West). It is important that you are able to find a point on the map and then be able to go out and find it on the ground. It is vital to be able to indicate on the map the exact place where you are standing on the ground.

To assist in the accurate use of the grid system it is advisable to obtain a Pathfinder Protractor/Romer, it provides two of the different scales of GRID SQUARES found on Ordnance Survey maps. The Romer is made of rigid plastic that you place on the GRID SQUARE of the map and read off the figures as described below, to the exact pinpoint position.

FOUR AND SIX FIGURE REFERENCES

When giving a reference there are a few simple rules to remember:
1. FIRST, count the figures along the BOTTOM of the map, from **left** (West), to **right** (East); these are called **"EASTINGS"**.
2. Next, count the figures up the side of the map from the bottom (South) to the top (North) these are called **"NORTHINGS"**

MAP & COMPASS

3. A reference must always contain an even number of figures.

4. GRID REFERENCES are always given with the "EASTINGS" value first, followed by the "NORTHINGS' value.

The example given in the diagram shows a black square that can be given the reference as square **8040** (*'A four figure reference'*)

This square could represent a whole square kilometre of ground, not exactly a 'pinpoint' location on a map or ground.

Should you use a four-figure reference you must add a feature such as a cross roads, a church or prominent physical feature to indicate exactly where you mean within the four-figure square.

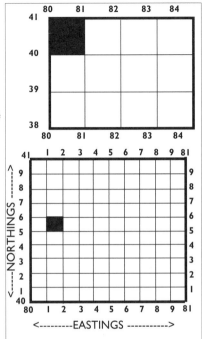

To get an exact position, the square can be further sub-divided into 10 squares in both directions. The bottom diagram illustrates this sub-division the black square is 'square 1- 5' these figures when added as explained below make up a *'six figure reference'*.

The first two figures of the EASTING value followed by the sub-divided square figure, then the two NORTHING value figures, followed again by the sub-divided figure to make up a six-figure reference of 801405

MAP & COMPASS

SETTING A MAP

The first and essential task on the ground with a map is to **'Set it'** or **'Orientating the map'**. It means aligning your map with the features on the ground. Until you have mastered this, you will not get the enjoyment out of map reading.

Setting your map using a Silva type Compass

Lay your map out flat, then find the MAGNETIC NORTH ARROW – usually in the margin of the map as shown at 'A' in the diagram.

Lay the base of the compass on the map with the DIRECTION OF TRAVEL ARROW, ('B' in the diagram), in line with the MAGNETIC NORTH. (See diagram 'line-up').

Carefully turn the map and compass round – watching the compass needle swinging until the

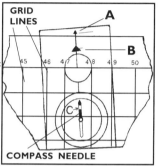

RED MAGNETIC END of the compass needle 'C' coincides with the DIRECTION OF TRAVEL ARROW 'B' and the MAGNETIC NORTH ARROW 'A' on the map. Your map is now **'Set'** or **'Orientated'** in relation to the ground.

MAP & COMPASS

FIRST THINGS - FIRST - ALWAYS SET - ORIENTATE THE MAP

SETTING A MAP WITHOUT A COMPASS
BY CAREFUL OBSERVATION

This can be easy, once you have identified exactly where you are on the map, and if you are standing on a straight road, line up the road on your map with the road you are standing on.

Make certain that the map is pointing in the right direction, i.e the right way round.

If not on a road, you will need to find other objects on the ground such as a road/track junction, church, prominent hill top or farm buildings.

You must also find the same objects on your map, using them as shown in the diagram by turning your map to set or orientate it in relation to the ground

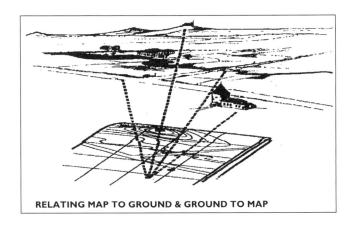

RELATING MAP TO GROUND & GROUND TO MAP

MAP & COMPASS

THE SILVA COMPASS

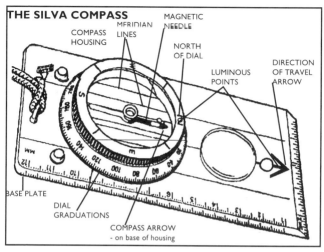

MERIDIAN LINES

MAGNETIC NEEDLE

COMPASS HOUSING

NORTH OF DIAL

DIRECTION OF TRAVEL ARROW

LUMINOUS POINTS

BASE PLATE

DIAL GRADUATIONS

COMPASS ARROW
- on base of housing

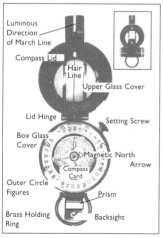

Luminous Direction of March Line

Compass Lid

Hair Line

Upper Glass Cover

Lid Hinge

Setting Screw

Box Glass Cover

Magnetic North Arrow

Compass Card

Outer Circle Figures

Prism

Brass Holding Ring

Backsight

THE PRISMATIC COMPASS

This is the compass that the Army uses. It is a very accurate instrument and therefore costly to make.
Not issued to cadets, but we include it for interest only.

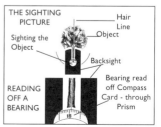

THE SIGHTING PICTURE

Hair Line

Object

Sighting the Object

Backsight

READING OFF A BEARING

Bearing read off Compass Card - through Prism

MAP & COMPASS

CARDINAL POINTS of the compass.

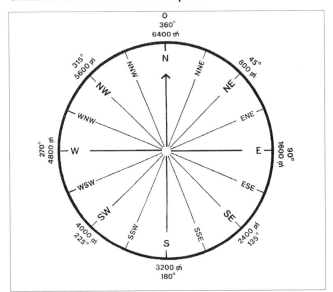

CARDINAL POINTS of the compass.

There are 32 points of the compass, but only 16 of them are normally used in map reading for the description of direction.

These 16 are the four Cardinal Points and 12 intermediate points as shown in the diagram above.

The **INTERMEDIATE POINTS** are combined with the Cardinal points, e.g. **SE** is **SOUTH EAST**, **NNW** is **NORTH NORTH WEST** etc.

These points describe direction only to within one sixteenth of the full circle. For more accurate indication of direction it is necessary to use sub-divisions of the circle using **'mils'** or **'degrees'**.

The **MILS SYSTEM** divides the circle of the compass into 6400 MILS, the zero being the North Point. The **Degrees system** divides the circle into 360^0 degrees.

MAP & COMPASS

The MILS system is used by the services to give greater accuracy than degrees. Cadet Forces work in Degrees - 360 degrees in a circle. The four quadrants or quarters of the circle are each 90°, and so the East, South and West points fall at 180°, 270°, 360° degrees respectively, as illustrated on the previous page.

The symbol normally used for Degrees is the ° as shown above.

NORTH POINTS

There are THREE NORTH POINTS

1. **TRUE NORTH** – the actual direction of the geographical North Pole
2. **GRID NORTH** - the direction of the vertical GRID LINES on a map. For all practical purposes, TRUE and GRID are the same.
3. **MAGNETIC NORTH** – the direction towards which the compass needle is attracted is the **MAGNETIC NORTH POLE** – see the diagram.

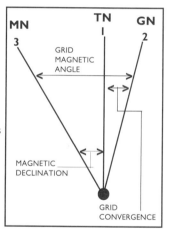

ANGLES BETWEEN NORTH POINTS (GMA)
Grid Magnetic Angles

This is sometimes called the **magnetic variation;** it is the angle between GRID NORTH and MAGNETIC NORTH; it depends on two factors:

1. **TIME:** as the position of the Magnetic North Pole moves slightly eastwards, so the GMA (Grid Magnetic Angle) changes. This is called the **ANNUAL MAGNETIC CHANGE** and must be taken into account when converting MAGNETIC BEARINGS to GRID BEARINGS and vice versa.
2. **PLACE:** The GMA **(Grid Magnetic Angle)** also varies from one part of the country to another. These two factors are included in the marginal information on a map.

MAP & COMPASS

MAGNETIC DELINATION
This is the angle between MAGNETIC and TRUE NORTH as shown on the diagram on the previous page.

GRID CONVERGENCE
This is the angle between GRID NORTH and TRUE NORTH which can in practice, be ignored since for practical map reading purposes TRUE NORTH and MAGNETIC NORTH are the same.

BEARINGS – TYPES OF BEARINGS
There are three kinds of bearings according to the North point from which they have been measured:
1. **A MAGNETIC BEARING** is one taken with a compass (an accurate compass needle always points towards MAGNETIC NORTH)
2. **A GRID BEARING** is one measured on a map with the Silva compass used as a protractor or using your Pathfinder Protractor/ Romer.
3. **A TRUE BEARING** cannot be measured direct, it must be calculated from the other two. However this can be ignored for practical map reading purposes.

NOTE: INDIVIDUAL COMPASS ERROR (ICE)
The accuracy of each compass is subject to error, it is important that you should check your own compass to establish the INDIVIDUAL COMPASS ERROR by checking it against other compasses. Having done so, make a note of the ICE on a small sticky label stuck on to the base of your compass. **Don't forget to allow for it!**

TO TAKE A MAGNETIC BEARING
1. Point the compass direction of march arrow at the object.
2. Turn the compass housing until the red arrow is under the needle.
3. Read off the MAGNETIC BEARING on the compass housing.

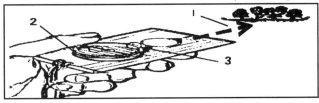

MAP & COMPASS

NOTE: IGNORE THE COMPASS NEEDLE.

One of the most common uses of taking bearings is to take one from the
map to find the bearing to march on. This is done by using a SILVA
compass or a protractor it is quite simple.

TO TAKE A GRID BEARING FROM A MAP

a. Place the long edge of the compass along the desired line of travel,
   making sure that the DIRECTION OF TRAVEL ARROW **(1)** on the
   compass POINTS IN THE DIRECTION of your LINE OF TRAVEL
   (2)

b. Turn the COMPASS NEEDLE HOUSING **(3)**, so that NORTH on
   the housing rim points to NORTH on the map.

   You will notice that the MERIDIAN LINES **(4)** on the COMPASS are
   parallel to the GRID LINES **(5)** on the map - or they should be.

c. Read the number of mils/degrees against the DIRECTION OF
   TRAVEL LINE at **(6)**, this is the GRID BEARING. Having taken a
   GRID BEARING from the map, you must take into account and make
   allowances for the GRID MAGNETIC ANGLE (GMA)

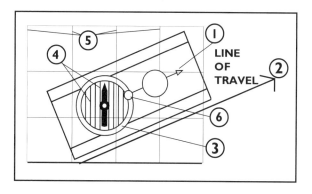

MAP & COMPASS

FORWARD AND BACK BEARINGS

When marching on a bearing - especially at night - over some distance you may often have a doubt in your mind that you may go wandering off course and finish up being lost.

The ability to use your compass and to trust it by taking a back bearing on to the point from which you started, will prevent you getting into difficulties.

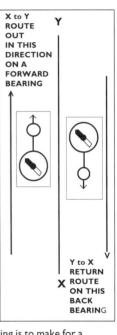

To use your Silva compass for a **BACK BEARING,** keep the compass on the bearing you have taken (as '**X**' to '**Y**' in the diagram), rotate the **COMPASS HOUSING** through 180⁰ (180 degrees) The compass is now **SET** to march on the **BACK BEARING** (in the direction of '**Y**' as shown in the diagram) of your original **FORWARD BEARING.**

To retrace your route – (from '**Y**' to '**X**') march on the bearing given as your **BACK BEARING.**

This is a very important skill, easily learned with your Silva Compass.

Using Forward and Back bearings is one of the best methods of preventing yourself from getting hopelessly lost;

remember practice makes pefect

AID TO KEEPING DIRECTION

A simple method of keeping on the right bearing is to make for a prominent object(s) on the line of march or put two or three cadets spaced, say 50 metres apart on the line of march, cover them off, when you get to the nearest one send them off to become the distant marker. It is important that they stay put and cover off each other.

MAP & COMPASS

FIND YOUR POSITION BY COMPASS - RESECTION

There may be times when you need to find your exact position both on the map and on the ground. This could be as a result of being "dropped-off" on an exercise or if you were unfortunate enough to crash land in wild country. You could find your position by using a compass and following the instructions set out below.

You will need to refer to the diagram on this page.

1. Set/orientate your map. Select TWO prominent objects or features which you can be sure of identifying on the map. These objects/ features need to be a good distance away, more than 1000 metres and also be separated by an angle of approximately 10 o'clock to 2 o'clock - see diagram opposite.

2. On the "plastic" cover of your map, mark the objects/ feature at **"A"** and **"B"**. From the position at which you are standing, (call it **"C"**) take a bearing on to each of the objects/features in turn, writing down the bearings.

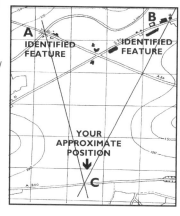

   As this has to be accurate, don't move from your position and take a further two bearings on both of the objects/features. Add together the three bearings to each object/feature and divide by three to get the average bearing to each. It is important to do this as accuracy is essential.

3. These are COMPASS Bearings, therefore they are MAGNETIC Bearings.

   As you are to use them to 'plot on a map', they have to be converted from MAGNETIC to GRID Bearings.

MAP & COMPASS

NOTE: You will always be best advised to draw a small diagram - until you become familiar with working with bearings - showing the NORTH POINTS as shown on page 5.14, this will remind you to make an allowance for the GMA (Grid Magnetic Angle).

The current GMA is approximately 100 mils (6^0) This is the figure that you would subtract from the MAGNETIC BEARING.

REMEMBER: "MAG TO GRID - GET RID"

4. Check the resulting bearing and adjust it to the nearest 25 mils. Remember the settings or divisions on the compass card of a Silva or Light Weight Compass are 25 mils.

5. Now set up the GRID BEARING on your compass for bearing **"A"**. Use a wax pencil with a fine point , put the point on **"A"** . Hold it in a vertical position, place the long edge of the compass against the pencil with the DIRECTION OF TRAVEL ARROW pointing in the direction of **"A"**, and the NORTH ARROW pointing approximately to the top of the map.

6. Using the pencil still in a vertical position, pivot the compass about the pencil point until the NORTH ARROW points exactly towards the top of the map, with the edge of the compass or any of the red setting lines on the compass base parallel to the nearest GRID LINES on the map.

7. Hold the compass firmly in this position while you draw a line along the side of the compass.
Repeat the same procedure from point **"B"**.
Where the two lines you have drawn from **"A"** and **"B"** cross each other is your calculated position on the map/ground. Now work out your exact six figure GRID reference of your location.

ONLY WITH CONSTANT USE AND PRACTICE WILL YOU LEARN TO TRUST YOUR COMPASS

MAP & COMPASS

IDENTIFYING A FEATURE

Set/orientate your map, use the edge of your protractor or a pencil, place it on the map with the edge running through your position, swing it across the map until it lines up with the feature you can identify on the ground.

The feature should be easy to pick out, provided it is not too far away and that it is on your map!.

This like so many Map Reading skills need constant practice until you carry it out as a "drill" and second nature.

After a while you will be able to locate and identify features by just looking across the map.

In setting your map, no matter what method you use, it is the constant relating and comparison of the map and ground which will build a good foundation for your navigational skills.

We remind you that this skill above all will go a long way to prevent you getting lost on your D of E expedition.

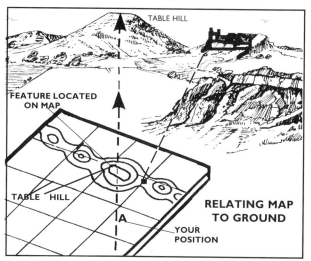

TABLE HILL

FEATURE LOCATED ON MAP

TABLE HILL

A

YOUR POSITION

RELATING MAP TO GROUND

MAP & COMPASS

GRID MAGNETIC ANGLE

(GMA) in UK is as follows:

GMA = 3° or 50 mils West in 2008*
(*approx.)

GMA changes yearly and you can get an accurate GMA reading from:
http://www.geomag.bgs.ac.uk/cgi-bin/gma_calc

> **REMEMBER**
> "Grid to Mag - ADD"
> "Mag to Grid get RID"

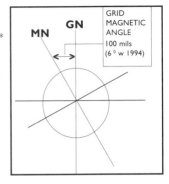

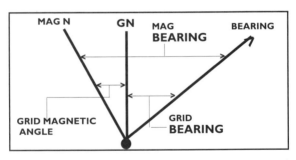

Remember all bearings are measured in a clockwise direction from the NORTH point. A MAG bearing will always be GREATER than the GRID bearing taken, by the amount of the GRID MAGNETIC ANGLE.

Therefore to convert GRID to MAG ADD the GRID MAGNETIC ANGLE.

To convert a MAG bearing to a GRID, SUBTRACT the GRID MAGNETIC ANGLE.

MAP & COMPASS

TO MARCH ON A BEARING

Having converted your GRID BEARING to a MAGNETIC BEARING, set the graduated circle on you compass to read the MAGNETIC BEARING at the DIRECTION OF TRAVEL line.

Then turn the whole COMPASS until the NORTH end of the NEEDLE coincides with the NORTH ARROW and is par allel to the MERIDIAN LINES on the COMPASS HOUSING, holding the COMPASS in front of you march in the direction indicated by the LINE OF TAVEL ARROW.

So long as the compass needle and the NORTH ARROW are kept together, the DIRECTION OF TRAVEL ARROW will remain on the required bearing.

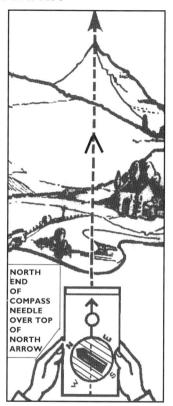

NORTH END OF COMPASS NEEDLE OVER TOP OF NORTH ARROW

HILLS AND VALLEYS

The method of showing how the ground is shaped in terms of hills and valleys (termed as **RELIEF**), appear as thin brown lines on the map and are called **CONTOUR LINES.** They are described as "An imaginary line joining all points of equal height above sea level". You must check the information at the bottom of the map near the

MAP & COMPASS

scale diagram to find the **"Contour Interval"**, that is the height between each contour.

The following information will give you a better understanding of how contour lines can give a three dimensional view of the area covered by the map.

UNDERSTANDING AND INTERPRETING CONTOURS

Firstly, you must understand that contour lines follow the same height round hills. They do not immediately provide a picture of the shape of the land, but with practice you will begin to interpret the shape of the land in your mind.

SPURS AND RE-ENTRANTS

A **SPUR** projects out from the landmass, a **RE-ENTRANT** is exactly the opposite, a shallow valley running up into the mass. It is not always possible to tell which is the top of the slope and which is the bottom without being able to find the contour figures. When the contour figures can be read with both the map and the figures the correct way up you will be able to tell if the ground is rising or falling.

A general idea of which way the slopes run can be obtained by looking at other features; particularly lakes, ponds, rivers, streams and railway lines. A stream running near a set of contours indicates at once which is the bottom of the slope.

Features such as railways, villages and large woods are more likely to be found at the bottom of a hill than at the top.

CONVEX AND CONCAVE SLOPES

A **CONVEX** slope is one that 'bulges' outwards, a **CONCAVE** slope is one that curves inwards. Standing at the top of a CONVEX slope you would not be able to see all the way down to the bottom, because the outward slope would obscure your view. It is important to recognise that this is 'dead ground', and as such can hide obstacles.

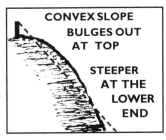

CONVEX SLOPE
BULGES OUT
AT TOP

STEEPER
AT THE
LOWER
END

MAP & COMPASS

When standing on the top of a CONCAVE slope There will be a clear view down to the bottom (unless it is heavily wooded).

CONCAVE SLOPE STEEPER AT TOP THAN LOWER DOWN

DEAD GROUND

CONTOUR VALUES

If you had several paths around a hill, each one keeping at the same level, and were walking round one of them, you would find that where the paths were near to each other the ground would be steep between the paths.

Where the paths are some distance apart, the ground will slope gently; the further they were apart, the less the slope would be.

MORE ABOUT CONTOURS

On gentle slopes the CONTOURS are far apart, on steep slopes the CONTOURS are close together. If the ground is broken and rugged there will be many **SPURS** and **RE-ENTRANTS**, a path would be constantly turning in and out. Irregular, sharply turning contours shows broken and rugged country. Where the slopes are smooth, the path will curve gently, bending out as it follows the line of a SPUR and swinging in at a RE-ENTRANT. On gentle slopes the contours appear as smooth flowing curves. Contours may appear to wander about all over, but if you follow them they naturally come back to where they started from; the only exception is when you find a cliff

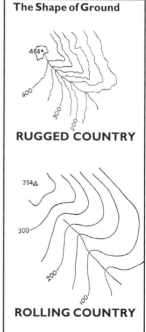

The Shape of Ground

464

400

300

200

RUGGED COUNTRY

354△

300

200

100

ROLLING COUNTRY

face with a sheer drop, then all the contour lines are so close together they appear to be one.

Every curve or bend in a contour indicates a SPUR or a valley, a rise or fall in the ground, just as it does on the side of a hill. Remember - the distance apart the contours are still indicates the steepness or flatness of the ground.

Each contour is drawn at a specific height above sea level and each one is the same vertical height above the one below. The difference in height between the contours is called the **VERTICAL INTERVAL (V.I.) See illustration on next page.**

These heights are written into the contour lines at intervals along their length. On Ordnance Survey maps figures showing the height of contours are always printed so that they read facing up the hill. It is useful to remember this so that you may quickly find out which direction the ground is sloping.

Check the information in the margins of the map to find out if the VI (Vertical Interval) is in Feet or Metres.

Whenever you are 'out and about' look at the ground in the area and draw imaginary contour lines around the hills and valleys. Make a rough sketch and then get a map of the area and see how accurately you have interpreted the ground.

Practice as much as you can, interpreting contours correctly is important when you are planning the route of an expedition, or trying to find a different route out of a difficult area.

MAP & COMPASS

UNDERSTANDING VERTICAL INTERVAL (V.I.)

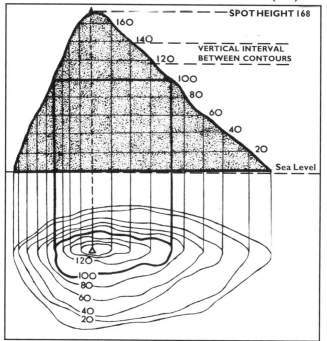

SPOT HEIGHTS

Apart from contours, height is shown by **SPOT HEIGHTS**
which is marked on a map by a dot and number ● 168. This is the
exact height in metres or feet above sea level.

You will also find **TRIG POINTS**, shown on the map as a small
blue triangle with a number next to it ▲ 576, this again is the
exact height above sea level.

MAP & COMPASS

Contours and the shape of ground

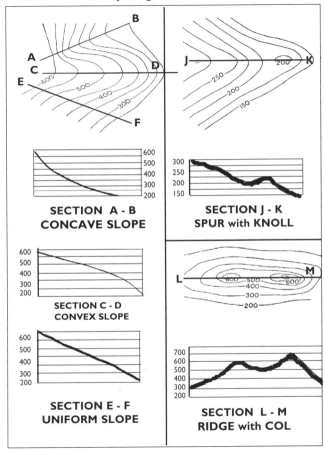

SECTION A - B
CONCAVE SLOPE

SECTION C - D
CONVEX SLOPE

SECTION E - F
UNIFORM SLOPE

SECTION J - K
SPUR with KNOLL

SECTION L - M
RIDGE with COL

MAP & COMPASS

KNOW YOUR CONTOUR PATTERNS

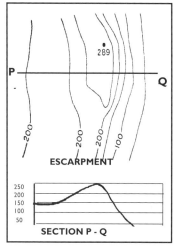

ESCARPMENT

SECTION P - Q

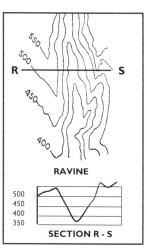

RAVINE

SECTION R - S

1. Contours close together mean steep slopes.
2. Contours far apart mean gentle slopes.
3. When contours are evenly spaced the slope is uniform, thes slopes have small undulations and pockets of dead ground.
4. When the spacing of the contours, reading from high ground to low, decreases, the slope is convex. Convex slopes mean short visibility; dead ground becomes very close.
5. When spacing of contours, reading from high to low, increases, the slope is concave.
   Concave slopes mean good visibility and little dead ground.
6. Wandering contours at various distances apart and never close, mean undulating ground. Important to note the general direction of the fall in the ground.
7. Gently curving contours indicate an area of country of rounded slopes. As the ground becomes steeper the contours come closer together; as it becomes more rugged the curves disappear and the contours take on 'jagged' shapes.

MAP & COMPASS

SCALES AND MEASURING DISTANCE

The scale of a map is the relationship between the actual distance measured from one point to another on the ground and the distance between the same two points on a map. The way that the 'scale' of a map is expressed is by the **Representative Fraction.** It used to be expressed in words, "one inch to a mile" or "four miles to one inch".

The **Representative Fraction (RF)** is the standard method used on all continental maps and wherever the metric system is used.

Most British maps are now expressed in metric. It is simple to use if you remember that the RF is 1/X, one unit of distance on the map represents X units of distance on the ground. For example, a scale of 1/50,000 means that one inch/centimetre/metre on the map represents 50,000 inches/centimetres/metre on the ground.

The essential connection is that the SAME unit of measurement applies both to the map and to the ground measurement. A distance of 2cms on a 1/50,000 map therefore represents 2 x 50,000 cm on the ground = 100,000cm = 1000 metres.

All maps are printed with graphic linear scales, usually in the centre of the bottom margin, from which any horizontal distance may be measured on the map in kilometres and metres, or in miles and yards.

A linear map scale is always shown in the form of a diagram, you will notice that the zero mark is set from the left of the scale by one major division, which is then subdivided into ten (or other suitable) sub-divisions usually not longer than about 4mm each.

SCALE   1 : 50 000
2 Centimetres to 1 Kilometres (one grid square)

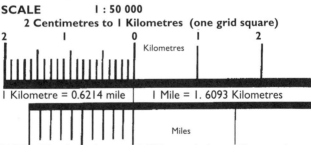

NOTE: The above diagram is NOT to scale, but to illustrate the scale found on a 1: 50 000 map. Any measurements falling between these sub-divisions must be estimated.

MAP & COMPASS

PACING

Pacing is necessary because you must always know how exactly far you have gone when counting a number of your own 'paces'. You should know your 'Pacing Scale', over different types of conditions, I.E tarmac roads, tracks, grasslands, woodlands etc. To find your PACING SCALE, put two markers out 100m apart. Walk the distance between them as you would on a patrol, counting the paces as you go.

If it has taken you 120 paces to cover the 100m, then that is your

PACING SCALE.

It follows, to use this scale if you were on a patrol and had to go a distance of 300m, you would have to count out 360 paces. Under some conditions you can use a specific length of string, tying knots at every 120 paces. Having used the length of string, un-tie the knots and repeat the process on the next 'leg' of your route. It is always advisable to have a CHECK PACER, remembering to check that your PACING SCALE is the same by day and night. You will have to make adjustments according to the terrain, weayher, wind, temperature, rain etc.

MAP & COMPASS

LINEAR MAP SCALE

How To Measure Distance

Make a mark on the straight edge of a piece of paper, put the mark on the point you wish to measure from and make successive marks along the edge of the paper as y you follow the route from your starting point to the final point.

This is easy if you just wish to measure along a straight road, but if it means going round corners you will have to pivot the paper and make several marks as you progress.

The total distance is recorded along the edge of the paper.

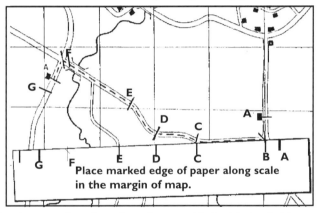

Place marked edge of paper along scale in the margin of map.

Lay the paper along the scale on the map, with the right hand, tick against one of the major divisions, so that the left hand tick lies against the sub-divisions to the left of the zero mark. The total distance is then the number of major divisions plus the distance to the left of the zero.

With practice this is quite an accurate method of measuring distances.

MAP & COMPASS

MOVING ROUND OBSTACLES

Obstacles are often found on a route and in order to keep a really
accurate direction you should go round them by plotting a series of
right angles and measuring by paces as illustrated in the diagram, **200 x
500 x 200**

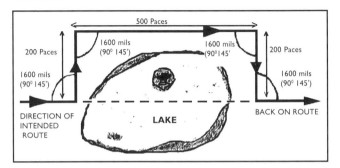

FINDING TRUE NORTH FROM THE SUN USING A WATCH

When you do not have a map or
are map reading without a
compass, it can help if you are
able to find the rough direction
of TRUE NORTH or SOUTH.
The method explained will give
you an approximate direction –
not accurate enough for reading
bearings or other measurements.

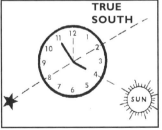

INFORMATION – as the sun rises in the EAST, and moves (in the
Northern Hemisphere) through the Southern sky, setting in the
WEST, the position of the Sun, when visible, is always a rough guide to
the direction of NORTH.

MAP & COMPASS

A watch, when set to Greenwich Mean Time (GMT) for UK (or to local time for other areas some distance EAST or WEST of Greenwich may be used.

If summertime or other artificial time is in local use, your watch should be adjusted to Greenwich Mean Time (GMT) or to the local standard time.

METHOD – lay your watch flat, with the HOUR HAND pointing to the Sun.

In the NORTHERN Hemisphere, TRUE SOUTH will then be midway between the hour hand and twelve o'clock on the watch – see the diagram.

In the SOUTHERN Hemisphere, lay your watch with twelve o'clock pointing to the Sun.

TRUE NORTH then lies midway between the hour hand and twelve o'clock.

When the Sun is high up in the sky, this method cannot be used with any success. In any case the result is unlikely to be accurate to better than five degrees.

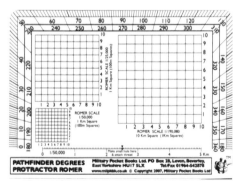

Available direct from
www.milpkbk.co.uk

MAP & COMPASS

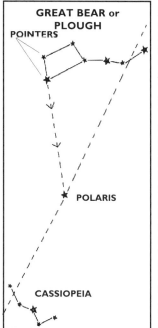

GREAT BEAR or PLOUGH

POINTERS

POLARIS

CASSIOPEIA

FINDING TRUE NORTH – by the stars (Northern Latitude)
In latitudes less than 60^0 the **POLE STAR** is never more than about 40 miles away from the **TRUE NORTH**.

The position of the **POLE STAR** is indicated by the "pointers" of **The Great Bear or Plough – see diagram.**

All stars revolve round the POLE STAR and the Plough may be either below it low down near the horizon and "right way up" or above it in the sky and "upside down" or in any position between. If the Plough is obscured or below the horizon, **Cassiopeia** which is shaped like a **'W'** and is on the opposite side of the POLE STAR from the Plough, may be visible; the POLE STAR is the nearest bright star within the arms of the 'W'. Above 60^0 the POLE STAR is too high in the sky to be a good guide to NORTH.

At the NORTH POLE it is vertically overhead.

The only way to learn night navigation is to get out in the dark, identify the constellations shown in the diagram on the left and practice moving in different directions by using stars and then checking with your compass. As with all map reading and compass work – *PRACTICE MAKES PERFECT*

MAP & COMPASS

ROUTE CARDS

The purpose of a ROUTE CARD is to ensure that you plan the route you are taking and from the start become aware of the distances you are proposing to travel, the obstacles that you will encounter, either overcoming them or taking action to find a route round them. RV's and the locations for your campsites, approximate timings. Always ensure that you give a copy of your Route Card to a responsible person to ensure that if there is an emergency the rescuers know where to start looking.

The illustration of the route card on the next page is self-explanatory; you need plenty of space in each column to write your information. Never be short on detail, it is better to have more information than you need rather than not enough. List mobile phone numbers and names

If you are in a group, ensure that each member of the group has a good copy of the route card, again we stress that it is important to ensure that you leave a copy with someone you will be in contact with during your expedition.

Remember, always include your CHECK POINTS and the **expected TIMES** that you will be there on your Route Card.

ROUTE CARD								
				Date_____				
Produced by_____ Start Point Grid Ref _____ ETD _____								
Date finish_____ Finishing Point GridRef_____ ETA _____								

Leg	From		To		Bearings		Distance	Remarks Landmarks Hazards
	Location	Grid Ref	Location	Grid Ref	Grid	Mag	Distance	
			Example of headings and layout of a Route Card - reduced in size.					

MAP & COMPASS

THE 24 HOUR CLOCK SYSTEM

The hands on the diagram of a clock face are pointing to a quarter past eight.

If it was in the morning (Ante Meridian - **AM** - before noon), you would call it 0815 hours.

If it was in the evening, (Post Meridian – **PM** - after noon), you would call it 2015 hours.

The importance of using the 24 hour clock system cannot be ignored as it avoids any confusion over timings and is explicit in its meaning. The Armed Services use what is know as the date/time group, which includes the date as two figures in front of the time.

Examples: 122200 June would be 2200hrs on the 12th of June, i.e. 10pm in the evening of the 12th of June.

This system is used when timings cover several days,
e.g. START Exercise 170600 END Exercise 201000
The Exercise will begin at 6am on the 17th and end at
10am on the 20th.

As with any new skill, make use of the 24 hour clock when giving the time - practice makes perfect!

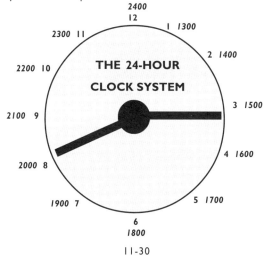

MAP & COMPASS
ORIENTEERING

Orienteering is like a car rally on foot, and as a sport has become well established in the UK. It can be over a mile or two or made to cover a vast area. It can be a morning's fun, last a day or several days. "Tough" orienteering can include crossing mountains, or be "improved" by including rafting or even canoes. It can take the form of a 'Treasure Hunt', or finding 'escaped prisoners'.
It will depend upon the imagination of your instructors to make it fun.

It is a highly competitive sport testing your map reading skills and your ability to think quickly on your feet. You need to be physically fit and have determination to safely navigate around a set course laid out by the organisers. The 'event' is judged by the shortest time it takes competitors to navigate and complete the course with the most correct points scored. Your progress is recorded on a Control Card that contains spaces for the individual checkpoint marks.

HOW IT IS ORGANISED

A **MASTER MAP** of the area in which the orienteering is to take place will be set up for all competitors to see. Normally you will be given a list of **MAP REFERENCES** that are the **CONTROL POINTS.** You will be issued with your own map in a plastic cover or case. You are given time to plot the CONTROL references on your map from the Master Map, and then when it is time for you to begin, set out for your first CONTROL.

CHECK POINTS OR CONTROLS

The CHECK POINTS or CONTROLS, which make up the route, are usually marked in some way to distinguish between them. In some Forestry Commission areas these markers are diamond shape painted red and white, fixed to posts each one being separately numbered.
In competitions moveable CONTROLS are put out before the competition. This allows the organisers to use different areas and different courses. To prove you have been to the CONTROL you have to make a note of the number or symbol carved into the top of each post or use a special punch called a Swedish marker punch on your event card. These will be checked on your return, time penalties are added for incorrect CONTROL marks.

MAP & COMPASS

The Controls are not easy to find, more often than not they can only be seen from a close distance, usually less than 30m, therefore accurate map reading is essential if you are to find them.

It is a good idea to chose an easily Identified point like a track junction near to the CONTROL (this is called an ATTACK POINT) and then pace the distance on a bearing to the CONTROL.

EQUIPMENT

To Orienteer safely you normally require: Map and Map Case (or plastic cover), Compass (Silva type), Pen/Pencil, and Whistle.

CLOTHING

The type of clothing you wear depends on the time of year, the location of the course, the type of country and how long the event is to last. Check with the organisers, some will refuse entry to competitors inadequately dressed for the area. If you really enjoy the sport and wish to make it a hobby you may wish to buy special kit. Remember, experienced Orienteers take only what they need.

The following list may be useful.

Wool or cotton shirt or vest

A lightweight waterproof cagoule

Long trousers/track suit bottoms to protect legs against thorns, nettles bracken, etc.

Cotton or wool socks

Strong walking/running shoes (spare laces)

A towel for when you return to base

A change of clothing and shoes, (you may be very wet and dirty).

KEEPING DIRECTION

To Orienteer successfully you must be able to keep going in the correct direction. This can be achieved in two ways:

1. USING A COMPASS. This will always tell you where NORTH is and by SETTING the compass you can find the direction in which you want to go. This is only useful in open country like moor land.

2. USING THE MAP. This is perhaps the best method since it is hard to get lost if you use your map correctly. The compass is only used to orientate the map, (point the map North). Once the map is orientated always use known features to get you to your destination. This involves planning your route in advance and in a number of short, easily navigated "legs". If there is a leg with no easily identified features, trust your compass.

GETTING LOST

Even the best navigators can sometimes get lost, however this is not usually the disaster it may seem, since it is not too difficult to find yourself again.

If you do get lost, **STOP AND THINK IT THROUGH.**

1. Don't panic – a cool head is needed.
2. Use the compass and orientate your map, try and trace your route.
3. Try to identify the ground around you and match it to the map. If you succeed, then you are no longer lost, plan your route onward.
4. If you cannot identify the ground, then try and re-trace your route to the previous Checkpoint.
5. If this also fails, set your compass and walk toward a road or other easily identifiable line on the ground then stay there until found.

MAP & COMPASS

THE ORIENTEERING MAP

The map is usually a large scale, (1:10000 or 1:15000 scale)
representation of the land, the information around the margin of the
map will tell you what the colours and symbols mean. Study your
map and identify everything.

Colours on the SPECIAL ORIENTEERING MAPS are used to
indicate the speed at which you can MOVE, not the TYPE OF
GROUND, for instance an area shaded dark green might indicate
ground which would be very difficult to move through, usually
known as "FIGHT" because you would have to fight your way
through it, whereas a light green area could indicate close woodland
or very rough ground through which you would walk.

White may indicate where you could run, perhaps grassland or very
mature woodland where the trees are well spaced.

Because of it's scale, the orienteering map shows great detail and will
accurately position depressions in the ground, holes and mounds,
earth walls and embankments which would normally not be shown.
Learn these new symbols as soon as you can, identifying them on the
ground could be the difference between being lost and finishing the
course. You must know exactly where you are at all times, you will
only achieve this by checking your map and always keeping it
orientated.

NAVIGATION TECHNIQUES, CHOOSING A ROUTE

When you chose your
route try and find the
best way of getting to
the first CONTROL by
selecting a good, easily
identifiable **ATTACK
POINT** like a track
junction and then plan
your route to this
ATTACK POINT

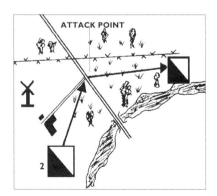

MAP & COMPASS

using easily followed features like tracks, fence lines, forest edges and streams. These features are known as **COLLECTION POINTS** because as you move around the course you can 'collect them'. Attempting to go directly to a **CONTROL** is not a good idea since they are easily missed.

Continue to plan your route round the course in the way described, chose a route that has as many **COLLECTION POINTS** on it as possible. Remember to periodically check your route with your compass.

Try to avoid bogs, dense forest and very steep hills, as these will either slow you down or prove to be impassable. It will often be better to go round an obstacle, even if the distance covered is greater, it may well be easier and faster. To help you decide, remember the following:

The Short Hard Route versus The Long Easy Route; swim across a lake or go around it: climb up and over a mountain or go round the valley. Remember to periodically check your route with your compass.

A good runner will typically take the following amounts of time to complete 400 metres over differing terrain:

a. Path – 2 mins.
b. Heath land – 4 mins
c. Open Forest – 6 mins
d. Thick Firs - 10 mins or more.

The Steep Short Route versus The Long Flat Route

When orienteering in hilly country you will often find that the course has a number of **CONTROLS** at opposite sides of a steep hill or valley. You must then make the decision whether or not it will be quicker to go over the top or to 'contour' round. To help you make your choice, a 25-metre height gain will be the equivalent to 100 metres on the flat.

AIMING OFF

Sometimes the **CONTROL** you are aiming for is on a linear feature such as a track or stream at right angles to your line of approach. This will mean that the **CONTROL** may be difficult to find since if you aim straight for it, you will not know for sure whether it is North or South, for example.

MAP & COMPASS

Simply AIMING OFF to one side of the **CONTROL** can overcome this problem, let us say the North, then when you reach the stream/track you will know that the **CONTROL** is to the South. This will cut down time spent searching for the **CONTROL.**

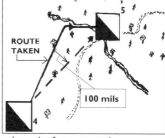

Many ATC Wings run their own competitions, some WINGS organise 'finals'. The RAF organise the cadet forces annual orienteering competition. Why not try and arrange a 'challenge' at your squadron, Cadets v. Adult Instructors. You may even win!

ON MAPS

The majority of maps in your squadron will be Ordnance Survey 1:50000 scale.

Most Military Maps used on Annual Camps, and at weekends on military land will be produced as 1:25000 scale (some are 1:50000 so do check them)

You will find that the actual sheet size of some maps are large and difficult to handle. They require careful folding to leave exposed the area you are working on. Keep them in a plastic cover or a proper Map Case to keep them clean and dry.

Points to note

1. The marginal information is usually at the bottom of the map, and the information includes extra items, such as "No Go' and 'Out of Bounds' areas.
2. "No Go" areas are subject to frequent change in some areas, so ensure that your map is the latest issue before you start planning routes.
3. Remember that contour lines that appear to be further apart are NOT, it is a larger scale map than the 1:25000; don't be caught out and find you have a steep climb instead of a gentle slope.
4. Because of the larger scale, there will be far more information given; this may be rather confusing for a while.

> *Remember as always "practice makes perfect"*

MAP & COMPASS

TERMS USED IN MAP READING

BEARING: The angle, measured clockwise, that a line makes with a fixed zero line. It may be a True Bearing, measured from True North - a Magnetic Bearing measured with a compass from Magnetic North, or a Grid Bearing measured from Grid North.

COL (SADDLE): The low land or ridge, connecting two hilltops.

CONTOUR: An imaginary line on the surface of theground at the same height above mean sea level throughout its length. Contour line are drawn a map to show the shape of the ground.

CREST: The highest part of a hill or range of hills.

DETAIL: All the topographical information on a map.

ESCARPMENT: The steep hillside formed by a drop in land level, usually at the edge of a plateau.

GRADIENT: A slope described by a percentage, mostly used on roads to indicate a steep hill.

GRID: Lines drawn on the map forming squares as a basis for a system of map references.

LEFT or RIGHT BANK: The appropriate bank of a stream or river when facing DOWN stream.

LOCAL MAGNETIC ATTRACTION: Attraction of the compass needle due to presence of metal or magnetic iron ore. NOT to be confused with Magnetic Variation.

MAGNETIC VARIATION or DECLINATION: The angle between True North and Magnetic North.

MAGNETIC NORTH: The point in far north of Canada, to which a compass needle points.

MERIDIAN: A true north and south line.

MAP & COMPASS

ORIENTATING A MAP: Placing it so that its True North line points True North (or Magnetic or Grid North line points to Magnetic or Grid North), also called "Setting the Map".

PLATEAU: A raised plain, usually quite flat, above a level of the land

PLOTTING: Transferring to a map bearings and other measurements.

RAY: A line drawn from the position of an observer to fix the direction of an object.

RE-ENTRANT: A shallow valley running into a hill, usually between two spurs, found where a stream runs off a hillside.

RE-SECTION: The process of finding a position by taking bearings on two identifiable points and plotting them on a map, also by fixing a position by observation of at least two previously fixed points.

SPOT HEIGHT: A point on a map whose height has been found by survey methods, identified on a map by a dot with figure against it.

SLOPES: (Concave and Convex): Convex "bulges out", Concave "caves in".

SPUR: A hill feature or low ridge, running out from a hill or high ground, often found between two re-entrants.

TRIG POINT: A concrete pillar with a brass mounting used by Ordnance Survey for their survey work. The correct name is a Triangulation Point. Marked on a map by a small triangle with the height above sea level shown next to it.

TRUE NORTH: The direction of the North pole from that point.

VERTICAL INTERVAL (V.I.): The difference in height between two adjacent contours.

WATERSHED: The line, usually mountain range where waters divide to flow in different directions.

Deception using a large scale maps
A tip to remember when using large scale maps, contour lines close together indicate steep sloping ground, but due to the scale you may be misled as to the severity of the slope on the ground

MAP & COMPASS

GLOBAL POSITIONING SYSTEM

GPS is a simple concept involving a complex system of ground stations, satellites and receivers. The first GPS satellite was launched by the Americans for military use by the in 1989.

For the civilian user, GPS accuracy has improved greatly over the years. Refinements in technology and removal of selective availability by the US government mean that the average user can now pinpoint their position to within 20 yards. However, GPS is still only a navigational aid; it does not work indoors because a clear view of the sky is needed.

Now, 24 satellites (soon to be 30), orbit the earth every 12 hours from a distance of 11,000 miles, sending signals to a GPS receiver to compute velocity, time and position. The receiver must lock on to four of the satellite signals to compute a 3-D position fix for accurate reading.

A typical GPS device consists of a 12 channel parallel receiver, an antenna, internal memory, and a LCD screen. Many sizes and configurations are available. GPS planning programs contain so much information that is has become virtually impossible to get lost, with over a million waypoints (latitude/longitude coordinates) that translate into markers on a GPS unit. There are web – enabled packages that provide up to date weather and construction warnings along your route, hiking trails, hospitals and much more. Some of the more sophisticated programs include spoken and voice – activated commands for use with multimedia laptops and PDAs.

GPS technology is similar to the internet in that both were created by the United States Government for government use. In the near future, GPS will be part of our everyday life; un – manned vehicle navigation may be closer than we think!

If you are planning to buy a GPS, do some research before you buy; consumer GPS units are produced by several manufacturers, PC software manufacturers are integrating GPS support into many of their trip – planning and mapping programs.

If you loose your GPS, it breaks down or run over by a car - you'll still need to read a map.

MAP & COMPASS
PATHFINDER PROTRACTOR/ROMER
IMPROVE YOUR MAP READING TRAINING & SKILLS

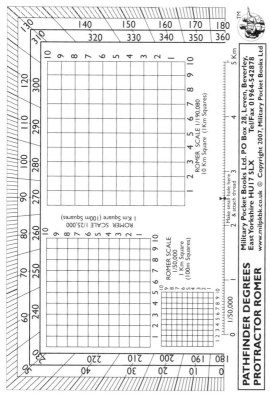

Available from
Military Pocket Books Ltd
www.milpkbk.co.uk

MAP & COMPASS
SELF TEST QUESTIONS.

1. Who produces maps for the Army.
2. Where will you find the Map Sheet number.
3. What is the Grid System used for.
4. Do you normally use a four or six figure reference to pin point a item.
5. On a map sheet where is North.
6. What is a Romer used for.
7. What is to Orientate a map for.
8. Where do you find Meridian lines on a Silva compass.
9. How can you set a map without a compass.
10. Name eight Cardinal Points.
11. How many North's are there.
12. What do you understand by the GMA.
13. What is Grid Convergence.
14. How many types of Bearings are there, and what are they called.
15. What is I.C.E, and what do you do about it.
16. Taking a bearing, which two arrows on a compass do you "line-up".
17. Taking a Grid bearing, what do you do with the compass needle.
18. Complete the sentence: "Grid to Mag Add, _ _ _ _ _".
19. What is the reverse of a forward bearing.
20. What use has a contour line, give a definition.
21. Concave and Convex slopes, which "bulges" out, which has good visibility.
22. Where are you most likely to find a re-entrant.
23. What type of ground will you find if contours are close together.
24. What is the name given to the height between contours.
25. It says; "one unit of measure on the map, equals X on the ground". Explain what is this about.
26. When finding North with a watch (that has hands) which hand is pointed to the sun.
27. Without a compass, how would you find North on a clear night.
28. You are to make out a Route Card, give the headings required to do so.
29. When do you use a Master Map.
30. When Orienteering, why do you "Aim Off
31. What is the scale of most MILITARY maps you will be given to use on military training areas.

Chapter 12

AIRCRAFT OPERATION
PREPARATION FOR FLIGHT Part I

Introduction

The successful completion of any flight depends largely on the thoroughness of the preparation made before take-off.

The basic essentials are:

a. The provision of a serviceable aircraft, correctly fuelled and loaded for the flight, properly positioned on the Aircraft Servicing Platform (ASP) or dispersal so that the pilot may start the engines and be marshalled out to the airfield taxiway.

b. Thorough briefing of the crew and passengers with full flight planning by the crew.

c. Correct authorization for the flight (Form 3562 and completion of Form 700 (Aircraft Servicing Record).

Servicing

In the RAF "servicing" covers the technical activities of inspection, repair, reconditioning, modification, salvage, arming and refuelling. Because of the complexity of modern aircraft the development of a system of servicing that reduces to a minimum the time an aircraft is grounded for servicing has been essential.

This system depends for its success on the co-operation of both the ground staff and the aircrew.

The development of this team spirit is the keystone of the RAF servicing system which comprises:

a. **First Line Servicing.** Daily inspection; replenishing and re-arming; repair and ground handling.

b. **Second Line Servicing.** The Station Engineering Wing undertakes work requiring more complicated and extensive technical operations e.g. major and minor periodic servicing, replacement of engines, wings and other major components.

c. **Third Line Servicing.** The Station's capacity is augmented by the temporary attachment of airmen and specialist equipment for non-periodic servicing such as minor rebuilds of damaged aircraft.

d. **Fourth Line Servicing.** When an aircraft reaches the state of being ready for complete re-conditioning and re-building, it is relocated to a centralised servicing unit which specialises in these tasks. The aircraft then begins a new life and the servicing cycles begin anew.

Ground Handling

Aircraft are never taxied into or out of hangars; they must be towed or man-handled. The normal method is to tow it with a suitable vehicle.

When man-handling is required, great care must be taken to push only against the strong parts of the airframe; damage could be caused by pushing on vulnerable parts such as ailerons, elevators or lightly made fairings.

Parking

The aircraft must be parked facing into the wind with the wheels chocked (fore & aft), the brakes off, the ignition switches and fuel cocks off, control locks applied and covers fitted to the pilot and static vent.

Refuelling

Aircraft are refuelled after every flight. This prevents condensation in empty tanks and thus reduces the tendency for water contamination of the fuel.

Refuelling may be by hand, by bowsers, from high pressure ground installations, or, while still in flight, from a "tanker" aircraft.

The risk of fire is high during refuelling and a standard precaution is to prevent a spark from static electricity. This is done as shown in the diagram with the aid of an earthing cable and an Earth Spike into the ground:

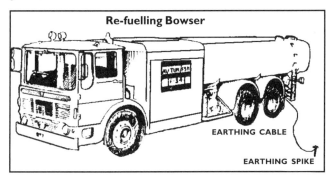

Re-fuelling Bowser

EARTHING CABLE

EARTHING SPIKE

AIRCRAFT OPERATION

Other precautions include:

a. Only the correct grades of fuel and oil are used.

b. Aircraft are never refuelled in a hangar or with the engine running.

c. Fuel must pass through a filter before entering the aircraft tanks.

d. No naked light or flames (smoking included which is a silly habit anyway!) within 30 metres.

e. Extinguishers are placed ready for use.

Loading In Strike Command

It is the responsibility of the Air Loadmaster to supervise the loading and security of loads. He ensures that the load is evenly distributed, securely stowed and that the centre of gravity (CofG) is within limits.

Marshalling

Directions to the pilot for taxying and parking may be given by hand signals; this practice is known as marshalling. The marshaller is there to assist the pilot. It must be clearly understood that the pilot is in command of the aircraft and is at all times responsible for its safety. The type of marshalling varies with circumstances.

To park an aircraft where the approaches are clear, the only information required by the pilot is an indication of where the aircraft should be finally stopped.

If obstructions exist, two additional marshallers may be required to walk on either side of the aircraft ahead of the wing tips and signal to the pilot what clearance exists.

If the taxi path is long or tortuous, it may be necessary to have a number of marshallers stationed at intervals to act as signposts.

Marshallers must position themselves so they can be seen by the pilot at all times.

Marshallers usually place themselves ahead of the aircraft and faces the centre of the left wing.

On the following pages you will see the standard hand signals used for marshalling aircraft, followed by a description of the hand signals given by the pilot to the marshaller.

SHUTTLEWORTH
OLD WARDEN PARK

Its so easy to see the attraction!

Ideal For Group Outings

Shuttleworth Old Warden Park
Nr Biggleswade
Bedfordshire SG18 9EP
01767 627927

Shuttleworth Collection Of Historic Aeroplanes
Play Centre - Swiss Garden - Bird Of Prey Centre
Gift Shop - Restaurant - Ample Parking - Open Daily

12-4

AIRCRAFT OPERATION

MARSHALLING SIGNALS
FROM MARSHALLER TO PILOT
FIXED WING AIRCRAFT

Description of Signal	Meaning of Signal
Right or left arm down, the other arm moved across body and extended to indicate position of the other marshaller.	Proceed under guidance of another marshaller 
Arms repeatedly moved upwards and backward, beckoning onward.	Move ahead 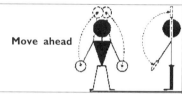
Right arm down, left arm repeatedly moved upward and backward. The speed of arm movement indicates the rate of turn.	Open up starboard engine or turn to port
Left arm down, the right arm repeatedly moved upward and backward. The speed of arm movement indicates the rate of turn.	Open up port engine or turn to starboard

AIRCRAFT OPERATION

Arms repeatedly crossed above the head. The speed of arm movement indicates the urgency of the stop.	**Stop**	
A circular motion of the right hand at head level, with the left arm pointing to the appropriate engine.	**Start Engines**	
Arms extended, the palms facing inwards, then swung from the extended position inwards.	**Chocks inserted**	
Arms down, the palms facing outwards, then swung outwards.	**Chocks away**	
Either arm and hand placed level with the chest, then moved laterally with the palm downward.	**Cut engines**	

AIRCRAFT OPERATION

Arms placed down, with the palms toward the ground, then moved up and down several times.	**Slow down**	
Arms placed down, with the palms towards the ground, then either the right or left arm moved up and down indicating that the motors on the left or right side, as the case may be, should be slowed down.	**Slow down engines on indicated side.**	
Arms placed above the head in a vertical position.	**This bay.**	
The right arm raised at the elbow with the arm facing forward.	**All clear. Marshalling finished**	
ROTARY WING Arms placed horizontally	**Hover. sideways.**	

AIRCRAFT OPERATION

Arms placed down and crossed in front of the body.	**Land.**	
Arms placed horizontally sideways with the palms. up beckoning upwards. The speed of the arm movement indicates the rate of ascent	**Move Upwards**	
Arms placed horizontally sideways with palms down beckoning downwards. The speed of the movement indicates the rate of descent.	**Move Downwards**	
Either arm placed horizontally sideways, then the other arm moved in front of the body to that side, in the direction of the movement, indicating that the helicopter should move horizontally to the left or right side, as the case may be, repeated several times.	**Move horizontally**	
Arms placed down, the palms facing forward, then repeatedly swept up and down to shoulder level.	**Move back**	

AIRCRAFT OPERATION

Left arm extended horizontally forward then right arm making a horizontal slicing movement below left arm.	**Release load.**	
Raise arm and fist, clenched, horizontally in front of the body, then extend fingers.	**Release brakes.**	
Raise arm and hand, with fingers extended, horizontally in front of body, then clench fist.	**Engage brakes.**	
Left hand overhead with the number of fingers extended, to indicate the number of the engine to be started, and circular motion of right hand at head level.	**Start engine(s).**	
Point left arm down, move right arm down from overhead vertical position to horizontal forward position, repeating right arm movement.	**Back aircraft tail to starboard**	

AIRCRAFT OPERATION

Point right arm down, move left arm down from overhead vertical position to horizontal forward position, repeating left arm movement.	**Back aircraft tail to port.**	

MARSHALLING SIGNALS
FROM PILOT TO MARSHALLER
FIXED WING

Description of signal	Meaning of Signal
Raise arm and hand with fingers extended horizontally in front of face, then clench fist.	**Brakes engaged.**
Raise arm with fist clenched horizontally in front of face, then extend fingers.	**Brakes released.**
Arms extended palms facing outwards, move hands inwards to cross in front of face.	**Insert chocks.**
Hands crossed in front of face, palms facing outwards, move arms outwards.	**Remove chocks.**

AIRCRAFT OPERATION

Description of Signal	Meaning of Signal
Raise the number of fingers on one hand indicating the number of the engine to be started. For this purpose the aircraft engines shall be numbered in relation to the marshaller facing the aircraft, from his right to his left. For example No 1 engine shall be the port outer engine, No 2 shall be the port inner, No 3 shall be the starboard inner, and No 4 shall be the starboard outer.	**Ready** **to** **start** **engines.**

2. PREPARATION FOR FLIGHT - Part 2

Aircraft Captain

Normally this is the pilot but may be any member of the crew. At all times there must be only one person in charge.

Personal Preparation

The captain of the aircraft must ensure adequate preparation for the flight and his crew. He will make certain that:

a. He and the crew fully understand the objective of the flight.

b. He is fit and safe to carry out the flight.

c. The relevant order books have been read and understood.

d. The flying clothing and safety equipment of all the crew is complete and serviceable. Serviceability checks should be carried out by each user before each flight.

AIRCRAFT OPERATION

Flight Planning

Before a flight the following must be determined:

a. The current weather conditions and a forecast of how it the weather will change during the flight - taking into account both time and position.

b. Clearance by Air Traffic Control - including details of diversion airfields and restricted airspaces.

c. Preparation of maps and charts.

The captain will fully brief his passengers and crew and will also be responsible for obtaining formal authorization for the flight.

This is done by completing and entry in the Flight Authorization Book (Form 3562) and obtaining the signature of a nominated officer (normally the flight commander or squadron commander).

This book is the official record of flying times and exercises carried out and will be completed by the captain on completion of the flight.

MOD Form 700

These important documents are the official records of the servicing of the aircraft and comprise the F700A which is the Engineering Record and F700B which contains the information required for the operation of the aircraft.

F770B tells the pilot:

a. Whether or not the aircraft is serviceable for flight.

b. The quantities of fuel and oil in the tanks.

c. The armament and oxygen states.

d. The hours run by the engine.

e. The flying hours remaining to the next periodic servicing.

The captain signs the F700 before each flight to signify that he has carried out his own inspection of the aircraft.

He also signs the F700 on completion of the flight to certify the state of the aircraft for the next flight.

Pre-Flight Checks

These are an important safety measure and the pilot checks all aspects of the position and condition of the aircraft prior to entry.

He will look for loose articles that may be picked up by the engine and will ensure that there is sufficient room to manoeuvre the aircraft for take off.

AIRCRAFT OPERATION

Detailed checks for the type of aircraft are found in Pilot's Notes for the type and will normally include:-
    a. External checks
    b. Cockpit checks before starting engines
    c. Warming/running up (piston engines)
    d. Pre-take off checks.

These checks are often in a "card" form and are "called off" by the pilot to another crew member who responds to ensure nothing is overlooked.

Checks are the final step necessary to ensure that all is ready for take-off.

RULES OF THE AIR

Just as cars obey the rules of the road, then aircraft must also follow a set of rules in order to avoid mid-air collisions.

Because airspace in the UK is particularly crowded, pilots of all types of aircraft must obey them.

Right of Way Rules for Different Type of Aircraft

There are four main types:-

1. Balloons which cannot be steered and therefore all other type of aircraft must give way to them.

2. Gliders can take evasive action but are slow and have no engine to help them get out of trouble. Airships and powered aircraft therefore always give way to them.

3. Airships, although fairly rare are quite manoeuvrable so give way to balloons and gliders.

4. Powered Aircraft, either piston or jet engined are the most manoeuvrable type of craft and therefore must take avoiding action when encountering any of the other three types.

Right of Way Rules

When Aircraft of the Same Type Meet The rules of the air are based on the rules of the sea.

a. If aircraft meet head-on, then they both must turn to the right.

b. When a faster aircraft overtakes a slower one, then he passes on its starboard (right) side - exactly as do cars on the British roads.

c. When two aircraft are at the same height on a converging course, the aircraft which has the other on its left has right of way.

The following apply when flying in airfield circuits:-

AIRCRAFT OPERATION

a. An aircraft which is landing has priority over one in flight or waiting to take-off.

b. When two aircraft are trying to land at the same time, the lower one usually has the right of way.

Rules at Night

The above rules apply equally in daylight or darkness. At night aircraft display navigation lights which may be steady or flashing but in either case are intended to draw attention to both their position and direction.

In general, a red light indicates port (left), a green light shows starboard (right) and a white light is shown at the rear of the aircraft.

Instrument Flight Rules

In good weather pilots use their eyes and are said to be flying in Visual Meteorological Conditions (VMC).

This is defined as being more than one nautical mile from cloud, 1,000 feet vertically from cloud and a visibility of more than five nautical miles. If any one of these conditions is not met, then the aircraft is in Instrument Meteorological Conditions (IMC) and the pilot must spend much of there time flying on instruments.

In these conditions the pilot ha too obey Instrument Flight Rules which lay down the procedures to be followed. This applies particularly in controlled air space in which case he is closely controlled by ground stations to avoid collisions.

Low Flying

This can be both noisy and dangerous and is not at all popular with certain sections of our community. Because of this pilots are normally forbidden to fly lower than 2,000 feet above the ground - with some important exceptions e.g. take-off and landing!

Low flying is however an important part of any Service pilot's training and thus special areas of our country are designated "low flying areas" to allow them to practise the necessary skills to enable them to fly and fight safely at low level.

These areas are selected to avoid population density and obstructions such as high masts or chimneys.

AIRCRAFT OPERATION

Self Test Questions

1. What are forms 3562 and 700 used for.
2. Name the basic essentials required when preparing for a Flight.
3. Describe First Line Servicing.
4. If you have to "man-handle" an aircraft, what must you remember.
5. Give details of actions to be taken when Parking an aircraft.
6. When is an aircraft refuelled.
7. Describe Second Line Servicing.
8. When refuelling, what does static electricity have to do with it.
9. Name the five special precautions to take when refuelling.
10. The Loadmaster supervises loading an aircraft, what do they have to ensure about the load.
11. What do you understand by "Marshalling".
12. Where does a Marshaller usually place themselves.
13. Give the Marshalling signals for "Stop", "Cut Engines", "Hover", "Release Load".
14. Who is the "Aircraft Captain".
15. Explain the Personal Preparation for Flight checks carried out by the aircraft Captain.
16. Describe Third Line Servicing.
17. What purpose are the MOD Form "F700A" and MOD Form F700B used.
18. What does the Captain sign before and after a flight and for what reason.
19. Who carries out the "Pre-Flight Checks" and how is it done.
20. The "Rules of the Air" name FOUR TYPES of aircraft: and give their descriptions.
21. If two aircraft meet head-on, which way do the pilots turn.
22. Define Visual Meteorological Conditions (VMC).
23. Describe Fourth Line Servicing.
24. Apart from take-off and landing, pilots are normally forbidden to fly lower than ....ft above the ground.
25. In Flight Planning, what must be established before and who obtains permission for the flight.

Chapter 13

Aircraft Recognition

HISTORY OF AIRCRAFT RECOGNITION

Aircraft recognition has its origins in World War I. Soldiers were taught to identify aircraft, whether they were friend or foe, so as to avoid shooting down their own aircraft. This continued through into World War II when there was a much more diverse range of aircraft which required identification. Observers were required to report incoming aircraft types to their superiors and, where possible their strength in numbers and any reportable ordnance (bombs) they were carrying.

In modern times a battlefield identification system, Identification Friend or Foe (IFF), reduces the need for Visual Aircraft recognition – but it is not completely obsolete. Photographic Interpreters and intelligence specialists still use aircraft recognition when examining satellite images. It enables them to gauge the strength of an enemy force, and assess their air assets and capabilities. It is important that they do this accurately to ensure that pilots know what aircraft the enemy have should their IFF system fail.

Within the Air Cadets aircraft recognition is still taught, and a number of competitions are held each year, testing cadets' skills at correctly identifying aircraft under pressure.

Aircraft Names

There is no set overall system for naming aircraft. Depending on the manufacturers, the type will either have a name and/or designation following the company title.

Examples are the Boeing 747 and the Fokker F28 Fellowship. The former type is in service, but was never given a name whilst the latter has a designation, F28, and a name, Fellowship.

In the RAF designations are given to the aircraft which reflect their roles. Designations are made up of letters and numbers – the letter describes the role, the number the mark. For example Tornado F3 is a Fighter ('F') version 3. A similar system is employed in the USA.

For reporting purposes, the name only is used as the whole designation takes too long to say and would be difficult to memorise. Names are easier to remember than designations.

AIRCRAFT RECOGNITION

IDENTIFICATION OF AIRCRAFT

Camouflage

An aircraft's camouflage or paint scheme may also give clues as to its identity. Commonly ground attack aircraft fly low to the ground, so need to be camouflaged from above. As such they are painted a green colour for temperate or tropical climates, sand/pink for desert, and grey/white for arctic conditions. Air defence and air superiority fighters are high altitude aircraft and are painted a blue/grey colour. Rescue aircraft are commonly painted yellow as they need to be highly visible. To help in remembering aircraft you can break the aircraft down into its component parts, known by the acronym *WEFT*: **Wings, Engines, Fuselage and Tail**.

Wings

Wing shapes of an aircraft vary dramatically – they may be swept, delta wing, a delta wing with tailplane, or a delta wing with canards. They may have a double delta shape, or be variable geometry. Are the wings tapered, straight, or swept forward?
The position of the wings may be high, midset or low. They may simply be a flying wing – for example, the B2 Spirit.
Wing form terms, see illustratins on next page.
In some cases they may have a "gull wing" shape. The wings may point up (dihedral) or down (anhedral) – or they may have no attitude change at all.

Wing positions – see diagram on next page.

There may also be more than one wing – the aircraft could be a Bi, or even a Triplane!
The aircraft may not have wings at all – it may be a helicopter or autogiro. In which case, how many rotor blades does it have – and how many sets? Are they coaxial, or intermeshed, see diagram on page 13-3.
Are there any armaments, stores or pods present on the wings which could be altering the aircraft's shape?

Engines

The location and type of engines can vary considerably between aircraft, The position of the engine and the number of engines can give you a quick idea of the type of aircraft.

AIRCRAFT RECOGNITION

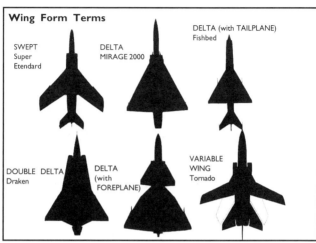

Wing Form Terms

SWEPT
Super Etendard

DELTA
MIRAGE 2000

DELTA (with TAILPLANE)
Fishbed

DOUBLE DELTA
Draken

DELTA
(with FOREPLANE)

VARIABLE WING
Tornado

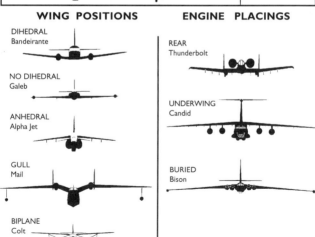

WING POSITIONS

DIHEDRAL
Bandeirante

NO DIHEDRAL
Galeb

ANHEDRAL
Alpha Jet

GULL
Mail

BIPLANE
Colt

ENGINE PLACINGS

REAR
Thunderbolt

UNDERWING
Candid

BURIED
Bison

AIRCRAFT RECOGNITION

ROTOR TYPES

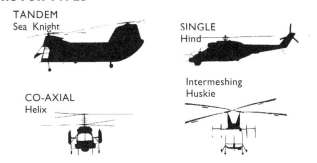

TANDEM
Sea Knight

SINGLE
Hind

Intermeshing
Huskie

CO-AXIAL
Helix

ENGINE PLACINGS

Are the engines on the fuselage, wing, nose, or mounted in the tail fin? In some cases the only visible differences between different marks of aircraft could be the number of propeller blades on their turboprop engines!

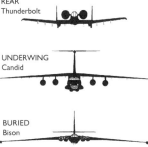

REAR
Thunderbolt

UNDERWING
Candid

BURIED
Bison

Fuselage

The fuselage of the aircraft can indicate to you the aircraft's role. If it is wide and big it could be a cargo or passenger aircraft like the A400M or Boeing 777. Are there any distinguishing features – for example the Radar dome on the E-3 Sentry, or the tail boom on the Nimrod? It could be a twin boom aircraft, like the Virgin Global Flyer or Cessna Skymaster.

AIRCRAFT RECOGNITION TERMS

Tail

The tail section can come in a number of arrangements – a high set 'T' tailplane, or a midset H tail. The aircraft could have a number of tail fins. The tail fins might be particularly big in relation to the rest of the aircraft, for example the Tornado, or might have a distinguishing feature, such as a Radar receiver.

Aircraft recognition terms

See diagrams on next page.– aircraft recognition terms

Problems identifying aircraft

There are a number of factors affecting how quickly you can identify an aircraft. These are:

Size: Some aircraft, such as heavy transports, are four times as large as light ground-attack aircraft and therefore more likely to be identified at a greater distance.

Viewing Angle: An aircraft banking and presenting a distinctive wing shape can be identified much more readily than one where you can only see a slim side profile, or approaching you head on.

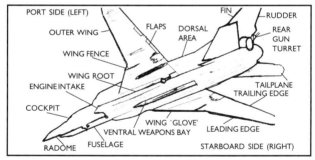

Visibility conditions: Rain, mist, position of the sun, all have a bearing on identifying aircraft. Bright sun on a high-tailed aircraft may cause the fin to "disappear" by shadow etc.

Aircraft finish: Where an aircraft has a natural metal or highly polished finish, its reflective surfaces may cause some areas to seem to disappear. Camouflage, while very effective in observation from above, may render an airborne aircraft more conspicuous when viewed from the ground.

AIRCRAFT RECOGNITION

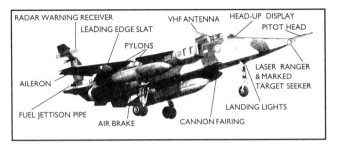

RADAR WARNING RECEIVER
LEADING EDGE SLAT
PYLONS
VHF ANTENNA
HEAD-UP DISPLAY
PITOT HEAD
AILERON
LASER RANGER & MARKED TARGET SEEKER
FUEL JETTISON PIPE
AIR BRAKE
CANNON FAIRING
LANDING LIGHTS

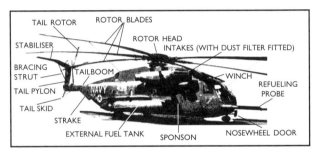

TAIL ROTOR
ROTOR BLADES
ROTOR HEAD
INTAKES (WITH DUST FILTER FITTED)
STABILISER
BRACING STRUT
TAILBOOM
WINCH
REFUELING PROBE
TAIL PYLON
TAIL SKID
STRAKE
EXTERNAL FUEL TANK
SPONSON
NOSEWHEEL DOOR

Roundels

Aircraft can be identified using a number of techniques. **Roundels,** for example, are distinctive mostly round markings painted on military aircraft to indicate which air force, army or navy they belong to.

AIRCRAFT RECOGNITION

Observing aircraft

There are plenty of opportunities to observe aircraft in general, the more this is practised, the quicker it will become evident that different types of aircraft have different visual characteristics that can be recognised in the air, and at considerable distances.

There are a number of ways to learn about aircraft; the internet contains a number of very good resources. Your squadron may have aircraft recognition slides which you can use. You could also visit airport viewing areas to watch and identify aircraft.

When learning new aircraft recognition it's best to learn about a small number first, for example aircraft of the Royal Air Force, and then introduce new aircraft gradually.

SELF TEST QUESTIONS

1. When did Aircraft Recognition have it's origins.
2. Why did it become necessary.
3. What is the modern aircraft recognition system known as.
4. What system is now used to identify aircraft.
5. What does the acronym WEFT tell you.
6. The position of wings bay be ......
7. Name four Wing Form Terms.
8. Name six wing positions.
9. Name two 'engine placings'
10. How could the fuselage shape indicate the type of aircraft
11. Where would you most likely find a Radar Warning Receiver.
12. Name four factors that can affect how quickly you can identify an aircraft.
13. Name four different configurations of aircraft wing types.
14. What is the name given to gull wings that point up.

FLYING

Chapter 14

FLYING

The likelihood is being an Air Cadet you already have some interest in flying. The opportunities open to you within the ATC are dependent on your efforts on squadron, and your attempts to reach the required standards of training. You must qualify as a First Class Cadet to be considered for any flight training (or as a minimum, pass your Airmanship, Navigation and Communications modules).

Flying with the ATC is free, so take advantage of it. There is no other organisation that gives you an opportunity like this! It is also a chance to put into practice some of the skills and knowledge you have learnt at your squadron.

Before you can get airborne, there is one very important document that you have to have signed and completed; that is the Parent or Guardian's Consent to Fly form. This forms part of your 3822A, held at your squadron.

In the following paragraphs we will set out some of the opportunities to fly within the Corps, from your first AEF through to a Flying Scholarship.

AIR EXPERIENCE FLYING

Opportunities for cadets to fly were provided from 1958 to encourage an interest in aviation. These flights are available at many different locations within the RAF. Air Experience Flights (AEF) are commanded by RAF pilots, assisted by staff pilots who are members of the RAF and RAF Volunteer Reserve, with previous experience as full time pilots.

They fly the Grob 115e, known in the RAF as the Tutor T1. It is a two-seat, single-engine aircraft with dual controls. Usually, the pilot sits in the left seat and you will sit in the right seat. The aircraft is fully aerobatic, so as well as learning standard manoeuvres, you may be invited to experience some aerobatic flight.

FLYING

The Tutor has side-by-side seating with dual controls, which enables you to take control of the aircraft when asked, so as to put into practice what you have learnt.

You can expect to fly at least once a year with the local AEF, as well as on annual camps to other RAF stations.

Before you fly, try to think about what you would like to learn from each flight, as the pilot will probably ask if you have any specific requests.

FLIGHT SAFETY

Before you are allowed to fly in the Tutor, you will be given a full safety brief. This includes what to do in an emergency. You will get the brief every time you attend the AEF, and you must pay attention. The brief may have changed from your last visit, and you won't remember everything anyway. The brief will tell you the following information:

a. Donning of your parachute and LSJ (Life Saving Jacket) if needed
b. How to enter the aircraft, and where it is safe to tread
c. Where to sit in the aircraft, with assistance from ground crew
d. How to fasten your harness
e. Use of the radio communication equipment

EQUIPMENT

You will be provided with a flying suit, parachute, LSJ if flying near water, helmet, gloves, boots and a sick bag. A safety equipment fitter, or "Squipper" for short, will assist the fitting of your parachute, and adjust your helmet accordingly. Your sick bag is important - if you are sick you must tell your pilot immediately, who will fly straight and level and provide ventilation to help. If you think you will be sick, get your sick bag out immediately. If you make a mess of the aircraft, it may be rendered unserviceable for a day or two. Many people feel airsick when they fly, even very experienced pilots, so don't feel embarrassed if you do feel unwell.

ENTERING THE AIRCRAFT

You will be escorted to the aircraft, and approach from the rear of the aircraft, to enter the right hand side of it. The wings of a Tutor are glass-reinforced plastic (GRP), and therefore are very fragile. Marked in black are the areas where it is safe to tread on.

Your escort will also help you get strapped into the aircraft.

FLYING

The seat harness is fitted securely to the aircraft, and ensures you won't fall out of the seat if inverted. It consists of two waist straps, which should be connected first, two shoulder straps and one "g" strap which go between your legs. The harness straps all connect to one Quick Release Box, or QRB. Your headset lead will be plugged into the aircraft's communication system.

YOUR FLIGHT

When the pilot is ready he will taxi the aircraft away from the dispersal, and get permission from Air Traffic Control to take off. On average, you should get 30 minutes flying, with some hands-on experience. When the pilot is not busy talking to Air Traffic Control or other aircraft, make sure you talk to them and try to observe as much as possible in flight. On returning to the airfield, you should ensure your 3822 is updated with your flight details.

TUTOR T1: GROB 115e

The TUTOR entered RAF service in 1999 and serves the RAF's Elementary Flying Training Schools (EFTS), University Air Squadrons (UAS), and Air Experience Flights (AEF). It replaced the Scottish Aviation Bulldog T1, itself successor to the long-serving de Havilland Chipmunk. It is a side-by-side, single-engine aircraft with dual controls. It offers superb visibility and is fully aerobatic.

Technical Details:

Wingspan	10m
Length	7.4m
Crew	2
Normal Operating Speed	100kts ASL
Engine	1 Avro Lycoming
	4-cylinder piston engine

FLYING

The Parachute

This is a seat type parachute with a soft rubber seat cushion on which you sit.
The two shoulder straps **(A)** are brought over the shoulders and
allowed to hang vertically.

The leg straps **(B)** are brought over the thighs and passed through
the leg loop **(C)** which protrudes from the parachute pack itself.

The leg straps must pass up through the loop and the metal lugs **(D)** are
pushed into the bottom slots of the quick-release box **(E)** which is fitted to
the large webbing strap **(F)** which comes round the left of the body.

The operating knob **(E)** of the quick-release box has three positions -
fastening, locked and unlocked. When pushing in the lugs, this knob
must be turned anti-clockwise and held in the fastening position where
it is spring loaded and will
automatically return to the locked
position when released.

When the lugs of both leg straps
are correctly in place in the quick-
release box, the lugs of the
shoulder straps are inserted into
the top slots of the quick-release
box - again holding the knob in
the fastening position.

The harness is now adjusted by
first tightening the leg straps by
pulling up on the loose ends then
tightening the shoulder straps by
pulling down on the loose ends.
The harness should be a good,
tight fit such that you should be
able to stand only in a stooped
position.

To release the parachute harness
after your flight, rotate the
operating knob **(E)** of the quick
release box to the unlocked
position and PRESS.

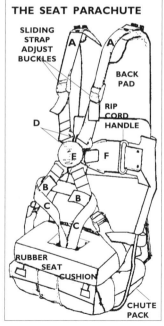

THE SEAT PARACHUTE

SLIDING
STRAP
ADJUST
BUCKLES

A   A

BACK
PAD

RIP
CORD
HANDLE

D

E   F

B

B

C

C

RUBBER
SEAT
CUSHION

CHUTE
PACK

FLYING

Life Preserver (or Mae West)

If you are liable to fly over water, you will be supplied with a life preserver waistcoat. If you need to use it, will be inflated by a carbon monoxide cylinder when the beaded handle is pulled downwards. It will enable you to float in a safe and comfortable position in the water.

Headset and Microphone

You will be provided with a headset and a safety helmet. The headset plugs into the aircraft communications system by means of a jack plug. There is an on-off switch on the microphone which should be kept in the 'off' position except when you are speaking in order to minimise the level of engine noise for the pilot.

Loose Articles

Ensure that you remove everything from your pockets before a flight since loose articles can lead to jammed controls which could be disastrous.

Air Sickness

You will be provided with a sick bag in case you feel unwell at any stage during the flight. Should this occur, tell the pilot you feel unwell, he will then fly the aircraft straight and level and open the cockpit slightly to give you some fresh air. If you are sick, remember to catch it all in the sick bag otherwise if you make a mess of the aircraft no one else will be able to fly today.

In order to avoid the possibility of air sickness, you should tell the pilot if it is your first flight and he will fly accordingly. Remember, you do not have to do aerobatics unless you wish to and if these should cause you to become unwell, tell the pilot immediately.

Action In an Emergency

Emergencies in the Tudor T1 are extremely rare. However accidents can happen. If an emergency arises:-

> a. Do not panic.
> b. Do as you are told.

If an emergency arises the pilot will tell you about it and give the order "Check parachutes" - do so by ensuring that the parachute straps are tightened.

The pilot will then, at the appropriate time, open the cockpit by sliding the canopy back as far as he can.

You must slide it back to its full extent by grabbing the handle marked with black and yellow stripes and sliding the canopy right back.

When the pilot decides that the aircraft must be abandoned, he will give the order "Jump, Jump" upon which you will:

a. release the aircraft safety harness (this is the blue one - do not release the parachute harness)

b. unplug your headset and microphone

c. stand up in the cockpit

d. jump head first over the side of the aircraft aiming to clear the trailing edge of the wing. It is vital that you do this immediately the pilot has ordered "Jump, Jump".

e. when clear of the aircraft, look at and pull the metal rip chord handle as far as you can - it comes out a l-o-n-g way. (the rip cord handle is known as the "D" Ring)

This releases the parachute which will allow you to float safely to the ground with an impact rather like jumping off a wall 3 - 4 metres high.

OPPORTUNITY FLIGHTS
When on summer camp or a station visit, it is very common for cadets to receive flights in multi-engine or rotary-wing aircraft with an operational or training squadron.

THE AIR CADET PILOT SCHEME
This award has three "streams", AEF, civil powered and civil microlight.

AEF
On an AEF, flying the Tutor, you will undertake a residential course, usually a couple of weeks long. You will complete a course of around 12 hours, covering a syllabus similar to the RAF's EFT course up to solo standard (but due to safety regulations, Air Cadets cannot fly the Tutor solo).

CIVIL
At a selected flying school, you will learn to fly a single-engine light aircraft, and if you are competent, fly solo. These courses are usually residential.

Both of these courses when successfully completed, will gain your Flying Scholarship wings, with a "P" in the centre.

FLYING

MICROLIGHT

This course offers 12 hours instruction on a microlight aircraft at a civilian school, with the chance to fly solo. On completion, you will receive microlight wings with an "M" in the centre.

THE AIR CADET PILOT NAVIGATION SCHEME (ACPNS)

This course provides you with flying and ground instruction in navigation techniques for pilots. It is only available at certain AEFs. On completion you are awarded an Air Cadet Navigator's Brevet.

CIVILIAN FLYING SCHOLARSHIPS
ROYAL AIR FORCES ASSOCIATION

The RAFA offers four scholarships a year, one for a full NPPL and three smaller awards of 12-15 hours. The scheme is open to all cadets of the ACO aged 17 and over, subject to academic and medical requirements. The scholarships are provided as a thank you for support given in past Wings Appeal campaigns, and will go to the cadets who they feel deserve it most. Selection is usually through a short aptitude test and interview. Application forms and up to date details can be found at: **www.rafa.org.uk**

THE AIR LEAGUE EDUCATIONAL TRUST

The ALET offers about 50 scholarships a year of about 12 hours each, with one winner deemed to have made the most progress awarded funding for a full NPPL the following year. These scholarships are advertised late in the year, to be flown the following summer. All are gifts from members of the Air League or sponsored by outside bodies. The scheme is open to Air League members over 17 and under 26. Selection includes an interview and a short aptitude test.
The ALET also offers a bursary scheme for young PPL holders, as well as one full balloon PPL scholarship.
Details can be found on their website: **www.airleague.co.uk**

GUILD OF AIR PILOTS AND AIR NAVIGATORS

GAPAN offer about six scholarships a year for a full PPL. Selection includes an interview and a short aptitude test. Applicants must be between 17 and 26 years old. Details can be found on their website: **www.gapan.org**

FLYING

SELF TEST QUESTIONS

1. What are the requirements expected for an Air Cadet to be considered for flying?
2. What are the minimum standards required for flight consideration?
3. What is the important document you must have before being considered for flying?
4. What is a '3822A'?
5. What does the acronym AEF refer to?
6. In what year did the first opportunities for Air cadets to fly come into being?
7. When cadets reach the stage of being accepted to fly, who commands such flights?
8. Which aircraft is used by Cadets on training flights?
9. Are the seating positions side by side or front to back?
10. How many sets of controls does the training aircraft have?
11. Name five areas of flight safety you can expect to be told in a pre-flight briefing?
12. What equipment would you be provided with before a flight?
13. What / Who is a 'Squipper'?
14. What would you do if sick on a flight?
15. From which direction do you approach an aircraft?
16. What are the aircraft wings made from?
17. What colour are the aircraft wing 'Safe Areas' where you may tread?
18. Name the component parts of the seat harness and how it is fitted?
19. What is a QRB?
20. The Parachute is important for your safety, learn how it works, then name the parts and what they do!
21. What is a 'Mae West'?
22. Why must you remove all loose articles from your pockets?
23. In the unlikely event of an in flight emergency, what are the main things to remember? (List)
24. After a flight what needs to be updated?
25. What does the acronym ACPNS mean?
26. What is the RAFA?
27. What is ALET? How can it help you.?
28. What is GAPAN? How can it help you?
28. What is the difference between a Grob 115E and a Tutor T

Chapter 15

FLYING AND GLIDING

You would obviously not be an Air Cadet if you were not interested in flying. The opportunities open to you are dependent upon your efforts to achieve the required standards of training.

You must qualify as a First Class Cadet or better to be considered for the first steps to get yourself "off the ground".

Before you get airborne there is one very important document that you have to conform with, that is, the Parents or Guardian's Consent to Fly form.

All service forms/documents have a number, and in this case it is RAF Form 3822A, is held in your Squadron and contains - amongst other data - your parent or guardians consent to join the Corps and to fly. In the following paragraphs we set out some of the opportunities for flying that are available to you through the Corps.

POWERED FLYING

This was started in 1958 to encourage interest in flying and today provides powered flying for you as an Air Cadet as a part of your training syllabus.

These flight are available at many different RAF locations. They are commanded by serving RAF Pilots, assisted by Staff Pilots who are unpaid part-time members of the Volunteer Reserve, all of whom have served previously as Pilots in one of the three armed services.

The Chipmunk aircraft is equipped with tandem seats which have dual controls which enable you to take control of the aircraft and put all that you have learned into practice in a controlled situation.

You are not allowed to take part in powered flying until you are a First Class Cadet or above and be over 13 years 3 months old.

THE AIR CADET PILOT NAVIGATION TRAINING SCHEME (ACPNTS)

This course provides you with flying and ground instruction in navigation techniques for pilots. It is only available at certain Air Experience Flight stations.

FLYING AND GLIDING

THE ROYAL AIR FORCES ASSOCIATION
FLYING SCHOLARSHIP SCHEME

INTRODUCTION

The RAF ASSOCIATION Flying Scholarship scheme provides the winning candidate a course of up to 35 hours flying training, and up to 12 hours for the four runners up, in light aircraft primarily to encourage young people of high calibre to obtain a National Private Pilots Licence. The scheme is open to male and female members of the Air Training Corps.

These scholarships are provided as a thank you to members of the Air Training Corps for all the support they give to the RAF Association each year in helping to raise funds for the Wings Appeal.

Training is given at selected clubs throughout the UK and covers all/ part of the tuition needed for the award-holder to obtain or go towards the completion of a National Private Pilots Licence (NPPL) up to a maximum of 35 hours flying.

This is not open to those who already hold an NPPL or PPL with a single Engine Piston-engined (SEP) aircraft rating.

ELIGIBILITY

1. A candidate must have been a member of the Air Training Corps for at least 12 months immediately prior to applying.

Nationality Requirements

2. A candidate must have been a Commonwealth citizen or a citizen of the Republic of Ireland since birth or have been born in a country or territory, which is (or then was) within the Commonwealth or Republic of Ireland.

3. Each parent of a candidate must have born in a country or territory which is (or then was) within the Commonwealth or Republic of Ireland and each parent must be (or was at death) a Commonwealth citizen or a citizen of the Republic of Ireland and is, or has been, one or the other at all times since birth.

4. The term 'Commonwealth citizen' includes:

> a British citizen a British Dependent Territory citizen
> a British overseas citizen
> a British subject under British Nationality Act 1981
> a citizen of an independent Commonwealth country

5. A waiver of the nationality requirements above may be granted under exceptional circumstances by application to the Royal Air Forces Association.

FLYING AND GLIDING

RESIDENCE REQUIREMENTS

6. Candidates, whether or not they are of UK origin, should normally have resided in the UK for a minimum of 5 years immediately preceding their application. In certain circumstances, particularly where an applicant is of UK origin, a shorter period of residence may be accepted and a waiver of part of the residence requirement may be granted provided that evidence of assimilation into the UK can be demonstrated.

EDUCATIONAL QUALIFICATIONS

7. A candidate must, at the time of application, hold GCSE awards at Grade C or higher in English Language, Mathematics and 3 other subjects, only one of which may be non-academic (eg art, music), or the equivalent of such passes.

AGE LIMITS

8. A candidate must be at least 17 years of age and under 22 years of age at the First of January of the year of application.

9. Flying training will not commence before the age of 17 and will not be undertaken without the written consent of a parent or guardian where the candidate is under the age of 18.

GENERAL REQUIREMENTS

10. A candidate must be medically fit and able to obtain a UK NPPL medical declaration of health from his/hers doctor.

11. A candidate must be prepared to undergo a Flying Scholarship aptitude test.

12. Winning candidates must be able to attend a course of flying training for a continuous period of up to 45 days.

Due to winter weather conditions it is assumed that the training will normally take place between the first of June and the end of October.

13. Winning candidates will be expected to attend the RAF Association Annual Conference at either Blackpool or Bournemouth, to be presented with their scholarships personally by the RAF Chief of Staff or his representative.

SELECTION PROCEDURE

Method of Application

14. Applicants are to be nominated by a RAF Association Branch or Squadron Commander and applications must be submitted by 31st

FLYING AND GLIDING

January for consideration in that year. However, applications from unsuccessful candidates will not be considered until at least 12 months have elapsed from the date of the previous application. Application forms can be obtained from the RAF Association Area HQ or the RAF Association CHQ, or from the web site **www.rafa.org.uk.**

Application forms should be submitted by a RAF Association Branch or Air Training Corps Squadron to the RAF Association Central HQ, 117½ Loughborough Road, Leicester, LE4 5ND, and short-listed candidates will be informed by mid March of the year of application.

SELECTION

15. Short listed candidates will be invited to the RAF Officers and Aircrew Selection Centre (OASC), RAF Cranwell, Lincs for a board interview that includes flying scholarship aptitude tests and an interview. Candidates will then be debriefed and advised in writing whether or not they have been successful.

The decision of the selection board is final.

Expenses

16. Second class rail fare will be paid from a candidate's place of residence to RAF OASC. Meals and accommodation will be provided for the duration of the tests.

The maximum allowances will be notified separately. Similar arrangements apply to award winning candidates attending the RAF Association Annual Conference venues.

TRAINING

17. Practical arrangements for the implementation of flying scholarship awards are made by the RAF Association in conjunction with the Air League Educational Trust.

18. Flying courses must be completed by the end of March the following year. However, training normally takes place during the spring or summer of that year with a view to completion of training by the end of the year.

19. If the flying school is beyond daily travelling from the candidate's home, the RAF Association may contribute towards board and lodging. However, candidates will be expected to pay for their own transport costs to the flying school.

20. Flying scholarships are valid only until the end of March the following year from the award. An award not completed or taken up within this period cannot be carried over to the following year, unless

it is due to circumstances beyond the candidate's control (eg sudden illness or exceptional weather conditions).

21. A candidate who fails to meet the required standard and cannot complete the course will not be given a second chance.

Note:

The Royal Air Forces Association reserves the right to vary the terms and conditions of the scheme outlined above.

A serving Air Cadet who attains the age of 18 is offered a one year free subscription to become a member of the Royal Airforce Association.

The address of The Royal Air Forces Association,
117 Loughborough Road, Leicester, LE4 5ND
The Association is a Charity Registration No. 226686

NON SERVICE OPPORTUNITY FLIGHT SCHEME.

Cadets who are over the age of 15 may be given flights by civil aircraft within the UK and Europe.

These flights - when available - are allocated by Wing HQ's to Squadrons.

OVERSEAS FLIGHTS

The object of this scheme is to enable selected cadets to see the operation of RAF transport aircraft at first hand and visit one of our overseas bases usually in Germany or Cyprus.

PRIVATE FLYING

You are not normally permitted to fly in private aircraft **under Corps sponsorship and insurance**, but of course this does not stop you from making your own arrangements and flying as a private individual.

FLYING AND GLIDING

ATC GLIDING COMMITMENT

The combined strength of the Air Cadet Central Gliding School (ACCGS) and a nationwide network of Volunteer Gliding Squadrons (VGS) provides the Air Cadet Organisation with the largest glider training organisation in the world. ACCGS is located at RAF Syerston, Nottinghamshire. The school carries out continuous Gliding Scholarship and Advanced Glider Training courses during the week, as well as instruction courses for staff. There are currently 28 VGSs, staffed mainly by officers of the RAF VR(T) and Civilian Gliding Instructors (CGI).

Many cadets learn to glide to solo standard each year, and are awarded their silver gliding wings soon after their 16th birthday. Glider training began in 1939 when some cadets were given training at Dunstable Downs. By 1945, some 84 schools were in existence. Initial training was given through theory lessons, and flights in single-seater aircraft. The methods of teaching have come on a long way with the introduction of two-seater gliders and the development of a structured training syllabus.

The following chapter describes what courses are available to cadets, to be flown in Viking and Vigilant gliders.

GLIDING COURSES

1. GLIDING INDUCTION COURSE (GIC)

The GIC serves as an introductory course with three levels. Each level (1, 2 and 3) will introduce you to basic manoeuvres and procedures in a glider. The course will include up to 5 launches in a Viking, or 30 minutes in a Vigilant. You must be 13 years and 3 months old to attend a GIC, and First Class qualified. Your squadron will be allocated a visit to the local VGS at least once a year.

2. GLIDING SCHOLARSHIP

To attend this course you must be 16, Leading Cadet, and pass a simple medical. This training may enable you to glide solo, subject to satisfactory completion of the course. If you solo, you are awarded silver wings with an "S" in the centre. If you complete the course but cannot solo, you areawarded blue wings with 'GS' in the centre.

3. ADVANCED GLIDER TRAINING

This course is subject to gliding solo and being recommended by the VGS (or ACCGS) you have trained at. The course aims to extend your skills, including instruction on soaring flight. Completion of the course will gain you your gold wings, with an "A" in the centre.

FLYING AND GLIDING

GROB B109B VIGILANT

The VIGILANT entered service with the Air Cadets in March 1990 replacing the previous motor glider, the FalkeT61F: Venture T2.
It is a side-by-side, single engine aircraft with dual controls, but do not be fooled by the similarities to the Tudor - it is a very different aircraft! The aircraft is self-launching, and the engine can be set to idle to fly as a glider.

Technical Details

Wingspan	17.6m
Length	7.9m
Crew	2
Operating Speed	60 Kts
Engine	1 Grob G2500 piston engine.

GROB103a VIKING

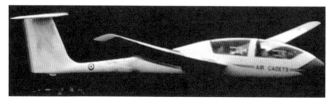

The Viking's tough construction should give years of safe flying and easy maintenance.
The VIKING is a conventional glider (with no engine) and has been in service since 1984. It is a tandem glider, with the instructor usually sitting in the rear, giving the student the best visibility in the front.

FLYING AND GLIDING

The usual method of launching is by winch, but it can also be launched by aerotow. Its forgiving nature and excellent soaring capabilities make it an ideal trainer for Air Cadets. Its GRP construction provides easy maintenance.

Technical Details:

Wingspan	7.5m
Length	8.18m
Crew	2
Operating Speed	50-55kts
Engine	None

GLIDING AS A SPORT

Having the opportunity to take part in Gliding Training can provide you with a life long interest. Training available to Cadets is a good starting point to take up Gliding as a sport, though a local civilian club. of which there area great many across the country.

Becoming a member of a Gliding Club is considered one of the best ways of developing your skills. You must be aware that in Gliding you pay for the training yourself and benefit from individual attention, so your training can go on for as long as you like - provided you can afford it.

To fly once a week you will find that some sessions are lost because of bad weather. As a result of this you will spend most flights getting back to your previous level, failing to make progress.

Being an Air Cadet gives you this opportunity to get some experience, if you enjoy it then there is no reason why you should not become a Qualified Glider Pilot.

There are many books on Gliding which can be of great help and you would be well advise to spend some time at your local Library or write to the British Gliding Association, Kimberley House, Vaughan Way, Leicester LE1 4SE.

APTITUDE

To start with, the aptitudes required for flying are very complicated and vary according to each stage of your training. It is very much like learning to drive a car you need the aptitude and co-ordination to keep it at the correct speed, and look where you are going.

Next you have to learn how to judge the angles and rates of decent,

FLYING AND GLIDING

in order to fly around the circuit and then get down in the right place. Later on you would be expected to develop these skills taking in other factors such as the wind-gradient to land safely. You have to show the ability to sort out problems in the air and make wise decisions before you will be allowed to fly solo.

PREPARATION

It is important to note that gliding demands self reliance: to become a solo pilot you will need to manage everthing yourself, and back on the ground you will be expected to run the airfield. While waiting for your flight, you will spend a lot of time at the launch point assisting with log book keeping and the launching of gliders.

You will probably fly with more than one instructor in a variety of aircraft, but do not be put off by this.

Different approaches to teaching combined with different gliders to learn in will help broaden your skills, make your enthusaism clear.

If your instructors see you are keen to learn, they will be more willing to help you progress.

You will be provided with a log book, and most probably a training progress card. You will always be expected to have these documents with you.

You do not fly for too long at a time as it is not possible to concentrate for a long period, 45 minutes is a sensible limit for normal training.

COMMITMENT TO TRAINING

It is most important to make your training a regular commitment, as progress can be very slow if your training is too intermittent. If you aim to fly once a week, you will find some sessions are lost because of bad weather. As a result of this, you may spend most of your flights getting back to your previous level. However, being an Air Cadet can give you some experience as an advantage, and with determination, focus and commitment, you can expect to glide solo and beyond with a civilian club.

PROGRESS

Although you cannot get a glider pilot licence in the UK, in time you may progress through the various recognised stages, marked as certificates. These are A for solo, B for soaring flight, and from then onwards you can gain a Cross Country qualification. The later, more prestigious certificates are accomplished through height, distance and duration goals, rated as Bronze, Silver, Gold, and Diamond.

FLYING AND GLIDING

SUPPORT

There are many books on gliding available; a good one to start with is Derek Piggott's "Gliding". You may also like to write to the British Gliding Association for support, at Kimberley House, Vaughan Way, Leicester LEI 4SE. Or visit their website: **www.gliding.co.uk.**

CIVILIAN GLIDING SCHOLARSHIPS

You may be interested to know that the ALET offers a gliding scholarship catering for all gliding abilities, available to members of the Air League under 26. **www.airleague.co.uk**

SELF TEST QUESTIONS

Name these Gliders below?

FLYING AND GLIDING

SELF TEST QUESTIONS

1. Explain what is meant by 'LIFT'. Demonstrate with a simple example.
2. Draw a diagram of a wing showing THRUST, LIFT & DRAG.
3. The amount of LIFT a wing giges depends upon five factors. What are they.
4. Explain what is meant by DRAG.
5. What are the three main causes of DRAG.
6. When are both LIFT and DRAG equal.
7. What are the four factors that influence the STALLING SPEED.
9. CONTROL COLUMN movements, what affect does it have on the aircraft when the 'STICK' is (a). pulled back, (b). pushed forward, (c). pushed to left, or (d.) pushed to right.
10. The two pedals on the floor control what.
11. An Aircraft in flight has the freedom to move in three different ways. What are they and explain their affect on the aircraft.
12. What is the main purpose of FLAPS on an aircraft.
13. What causes an aircraft to STALL.
14. What are the four factors that can affect the STALLING SPEED of an aircraft.
15. What are the four specific advantages of having FLAPS on an aircraft.
16. TRIMMING TABS, FLAPS and SLATS and AILERON TRIMMING TABS play an important part in maintaining the aircraft in
   ....
17. What is the speed of sound at sea leve.l
18. How is the MACH number calculated.
19. What do you understand by the following terms commonly used a. SUBSONIC. b. SONIC. c. SUPERSONIC.
20. How far will a Glider glide. With minimum DRAG at an angle of usually 1in19, what does this mean to the pilot.
21. Name and explain four different ways a Glider can be launched.
22. What controls and instruments will you find in a Glider.
23. What do you understand by SOARING and how is this done.

Chapter 16

METEOROLOGY

METEOROLOGICAL TERMS

ANEMOMETER. Instrument for measuring wind speed.

ANTICYCLONE. A type of pressure distribution in the atmosphere in which a central area of high pressure is surrounded by areas of lower pressure, all pressure measurements being related to the same height above mean sea level.

BACK. Change of wind direction in anti-clockwise sense.

BEAUFORT SCALE. Numerical scale for estimation of wind force varying fro m 0 (Calm) to Force 12 (Hurricane.

CLOUD Main types:-

High Cloud - Cirrus, Cirrostratus, Cirrocumulus.

Medium Cloud - Altocumulus, Altostratus.

Low Cloud - Stratocumulus, Nimbostratus, Cumulus, Cumulonimbus, Stratus.

DEPRESSION. A type of pressure distribution in the atmosphere in which a central area of low pressure is surrounded by areas of high pressure, all pressure measurements being related to the same height above mean sea level.

FOG. Visibility of less than 1,100 yards.

FRONT. Boundary between adjacent air masses characterised by some physical difference, eg. temperature, humidity, etc.

A warm front generally heralds lowering cloud with steady rain and followed by mixed cloudy weather.

A Cold front usually brings turbulent conditions but is followed by clear skies.

INVERSION. Region of atmosphere in which temperature increases with height instead of, as is usual, decreasing with height.

METEOROLOGY

ISOBAR A line on a weather map drawn through places where the barometric pressure reduced to mean sea level is the same.

LAPSE RATE. The rate at which air temperature decreases with height; the normal value is about 1.7°C per 1000 ft.

OCCLUSION. The meeting of a warm and cold front.

PRESSURE. Atmospheric pressure is usually quoted in inches of mercury or millibars (29.92 ins = 1013.2mb).

These figures are the standard Atmospheric Pressure Settings.

Near sea level pressure drops by approx, 1mb per 30 ft rise in altitude.

VEER. Change of wind direction in clockwise sense.

WEATHER REPORT. Statement of weather conditions existing at a specified place and time.

VISUAL METEOROLOGICAL CONDITIONS. (V.M.C.) Weather conditions are such that flight may be conducted in accordance with Visual Flight Rules.

INSTRUMENT METEOROLOGICAL CONDITIONS (I.M.C.) Weather conditions are such that compliance with Visual Flight Rules is precluded.

CHART MARKING SYMBOLS

CHARACTER OF FRONT	ON PRINTED CHART	ON WORKING CHART	DIRECTION OF MOVEMENT
Warm		Continuous Red Line	↑
Cold		Continuous Blue Line	↓
Occlusion		Continuous Blue Line	↑

METEOROLOGY

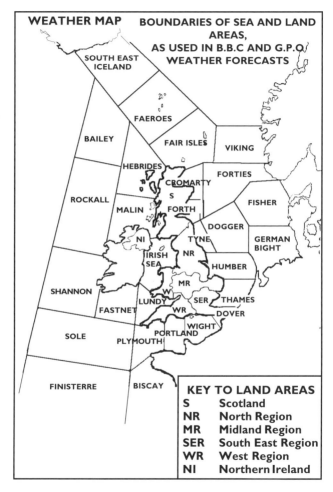

WEATHER MAP

BOUNDARIES OF SEA AND LAND AREAS, AS USED IN B.B.C AND G.P.O WEATHER FORECASTS

SOUTH EAST ICELAND
FAEROES
BAILEY
FAIR ISLES
VIKING
HEBRIDES
FORTIES
CROMARTY
ROCKALL
S
FISHER
MALIN
FORTH
DOGGER
NI
TYNE
GERMAN BIGHT
IRISH SEA
NR
HUMBER
MR
SHANNON
W
LUNDY
SER
THAMES
FASTNET
WR
DOVER
WIGHT
SOLE
PORTLAND
PLYMOUTH
FINISTERRE
BISCAY

KEY TO LAND AREAS	
S	Scotland
NR	North Region
MR	Midland Region
SER	South East Region
WR	West Region
NI	Northern Ireland

METEOROLOGY

Weather systems

On a weather chart, lines joining places with equal sea-level pressures are called isobars. Charts showing isobars are useful because they identify features such as anticyclones (areas of high pressure), depressions (areas of low pressure), troughs and ridges which are associated with particular kinds of weather.

High pressure or anticyclone

In an anticyclone (also referred to as a 'high') the winds tend to be light and blow in a clockwise direction. Also the air is descending, which inhibits the formation of cloud. The light winds and clear skies can lead to overnight fog or frost. If an anticyclone persists over northern Europe in winter, then much of the British Isles can be affected by very cold east winds from Siberia. However, in summer an anticyclone in the vicinity of the British Isles often brings fine, warm weather.

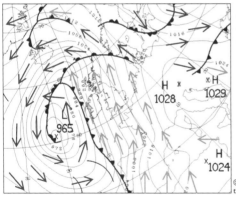

Figure 1.
The chart left shows the flow of wind around a depression situated to the west of Ireland and an anticyclone over Europe.

Low pressure or depression

In a depression (also referred to as a 'low'), air is rising. As it rises and cools, water vapour condenses to form clouds and perhaps precipitation. Consequently, the weather in a depression is often cloudy, wet and windy (with winds blowing in an anticlockwise direction around the depression). There are usually frontal systems associated with depressions.

METEOROLOGY

A rule in synoptic meteorology, enunciated in 1857 by Buys Ballot, of Utrecht, which states that if, in the northern hemisphere, one stands with one's back to the wind, pressure is lower on one's left hand than on one's right, whilst in the southern hemisphere the converse is true. This law implies that, in the northern hemisphere, the winds blow anticlockwise round a depression, and clockwise round an anticyclone; the converse is true in the southern hemisphere.

Isobars (lines of equal atmospheric pressure)
The lines shown on a weather map are isobars - they join points of equal atmospheric pressure.

The pressure is measured by a barometer, with a correction then being made to give the equivalent pressure at sea level. Meteorologists measure pressure in units of millibars (mb), though instruments sometimes give pressures in terms of inches of mercury. The term hectopascal (hPa) is often used instead of millibar, where 1 millibar equals 1 hectopascal. In the British Isles the average sea-level pressure is about 1013 mb (about 30 inches of mercury), and it is rare for pressure to rise above 1050 mb or fall below 950 mb.

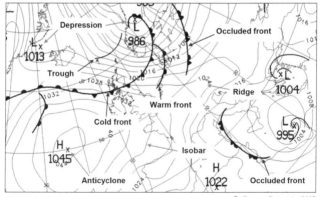

Figure 2. The chart above shows the association between depressions, anticyclones, isobars and weather fronts.

© Crown Copyright 2007, the Met Office

METEOROLOGY

Charts showing isobars are useful because they identify features such as anticyclones and ridges (areas of high pressure) and depressions and troughs (areas of low pressure), which are associated with particular kinds of weather. These features move in an essentially predictable way.

Also, wind speeds and directions are related to the spacing and orientation of the isobars.

Relationship between isobars and wind

There are two important relationships between isobars and winds.

> 1. *The closer the isobars, the stronger the wind.*
> 2. *The wind blows almost parallel to the isobars.*

These make it possible to deduce the wind flow from the isobars.

Wind speed and direction

The direction given for the wind refers to the direction from which it comes. For example, a westerly wind is blowing **from the west** towards the east.

Measurements of wind strength are made at 10 metres (33 feet) above the ground. A specified height has to be used because the wind speed decreases towards the ground. In this country winds are measured in knots (nautical miles per hour). However, forecast winds are often given in miles per hour (where 1 knot is equivalent to 1.15 mph) or in terms of the Beaufort Scale. There are rapid variations in the wind - these are referred to as gusts. Gusts are higher inland than over the sea or windward coasts, although the mean wind speeds tend to be lower inland. Typically, gusts can be 60% higher than the mean speed, although in the middle of cities this can reach 100%. Northerly winds tend to be gustier than southerly ones.

Relationship between wind direction and weather

In general, the weather is strongly influenced by the wind direction, so information about the wind provides an indication of the type of weather likely to be experienced. However, this approach is effective only if the wind is blowing from the same direction for some time. A marked change in wind direction usually indicates a change in the weather.

METEOROLOGY

Northerly winds tend to bring relatively cold air from polar regions to the British Isles. Similarly, southerly winds tend to bring relatively warm air from the tropics. The characteristics of the air are also affected by its approach to the British Isles. Air picks up moisture if it travels across the sea, but remains relatively dry if it comes across the land.

As cold polar air moves southwards over an increasingly warm sea, the heating of the air by the sea causes cumulus clouds to form. These clouds may grow sufficiently for showers to develop and, consequently, winds from the north-west, north or north-east usually bring cold, showery weather to the British Isles.

Warm air from the tropics moving northwards over the sea is cooled from below. Sometimes the cooling is sufficient for sea fog or a thin layer of stratus to form. The cloud can become thick enough for drizzle, especially on windward coasts and over high ground. In general, winds from the west or south-west are associated with overcast, wet weather.

Winds from the south and south-east mainly occur in summer and these bring warm, dry weather. However, southerly winds can sometimes bring hot, thundery weather.

Easterly winds in winter bring very cold air to the British Isles. The characteristics and path of the air determine whether it is cloudy (with perhaps rain, sleet or snow) or fine and sunny. In summer, an easterly wind will mean it is cool on the east coast but warm elsewhere, usually with clear skies.

Fronts
The boundary between two different types of air mass is called a front. In our latitudes a front usually separates warm, moist air from the tropics and cold, relatively dry air from Polar Regions. On a weather chart, the round (warm front) or pointed (cold front) symbols on the front point in the direction of the front's movement. Fronts move with the wind, so they usually travel from the west to the east. At a front, the heavier cold air undercuts the less dense warm air, causing the warm air to rise over the wedge of cold air.

METEOROLOGY

As the air rises there is cooling and condensation, thus leading to the formation of clouds. If the cloud becomes sufficiently thick, rain will form. Consequently, fronts tend to be associated with cloud and rain. In winter, there can be sleet or snow if the temperature near the ground is close to freezing. It is convenient to distinguish between warm fronts, cold fronts and occluded fronts.

A front which is moving in such a way that the warm air is advancing to replace the cold air is called a **warm front**. As the warm front approaches, there is thickening cloud and eventually it starts to rain. The belt of rain extends 100-200 miles ahead of the front. Behind the front the rain usually becomes lighter, or ceases, but it remains cloudy. As a warm front passes, the air changes from being fairly cold and cloudy to being warm and overcast (typical of warm air

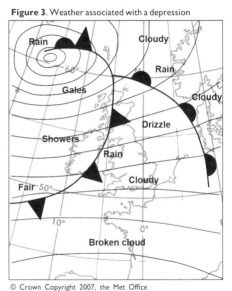

Figure 3. Weather associated with a depression

© Crown Copyright 2007, the Met Office

from the tropics travelling over the sea). Also there is a clockwise change in wind direction, and the wind is said to 'veer'.

A **cold front** moves so that the cold air is advancing to replace the warm air. This means that as a cold front passes, the weather changes from being mild and overcast to being cold and bright, possibly with showers (typical of cold polar air travelling over the sea). The passage of the front is often marked by a narrow band of rain and a veer in the wind direction.

16-8

METEOROLOGY

An **occluded front** can be thought of as being a result of the warm and cold fronts meeting. Consequently, ahead of an occlusion the weather is similar to that ahead of a warm front, whereas behind the occlusion it is similar to that behind a cold front.

The characteristics given for the fronts apply to active fronts. If the front is weak, the rain associated with it is light or non-existent, and the changes across the front are less marked.

The preceding text is adapted from Crown copyright data supplied by the Met Office.

If you would like to learn more about Meteorology in greater detail, go online at **www.metoffice.gov.uk.**

In the Education section you will see *Fact Sheets. Select No 11 and others.*

Chapter 17
PROPULSION

Introduction

Piston engines have been employed for aircraft propulsion from the earliest days of flying. Today in the Royal Air Force they have been almost totally replaced by gas turbine (jet) engines. After a description of the piston engine, the following will concentrate on the principles of the gas turbine and give examples of their use in the aircraft of today.

The Piston Engine

This is based upon the four-stroke internal combustion engine. The diagram below shows the four strokes of the sliding piston which harness the power of the expansion of air and fuel vapour when burned in the cylinder.

The crankshaft converts the linear force into a rotary power or torque. The crankshaft is connected directly or via a gearbox to the propeller which then converts the torque into linear thrust.

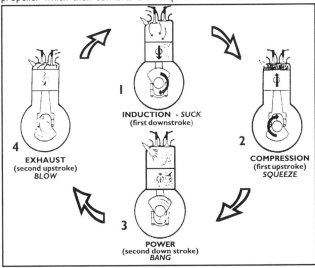

1 INDUCTION - *SUCK*
(first downstroke)

2 COMPRESSION
(first upstroke)
SQUEEZE

3 POWER
(second down stroke)
BANG

4 EXHAUST
(second upstroke)
BLOW

PROPULSION

In practice a single cylinder engine as shown would not work as the single power impulse in every two revolutions of the shaft would not produce an even flow of power.

To overcome this, multi-cylinder engine have been developed with cylinders in various layouts. The main configurations are shown in the illustrations on the next page.

THE FOUR STROKE CYCLE

1. INDUCTION - *(SUCK)* first downstroke. Inlet valve is open. Piston moves down the cylinder, from Top Dead Centre (TDC) to bottom dead centre (BDC).
Fuel air mixture is drawn into cylinder (the charge).

2. COMPRESSION - *(SQUEEZE)* first upstroke. Both valves are closed. Piston moves back up the cylinder (from BDC to TDC).
Fuel air mixture is compressed into the top of the cylinder (the combustion chamber).

3. POWER - *(BANG)* second downstroke. Both valves remain closed. Spark occurs igniting the compressed fuel air mixture. Rapid expansion of the burning mixture forces the piston back downthe cylinder from TDC to BDC.

4. EXHAUST - **(BLOW)** second upstroke. Exhaust valve is open.Piston moves back up the cylinder from BDC to TDC.
The burnt (exhaust) gases having now performed their useful work on the power stroke, escape into the atmosphere via the exhaust pipe.

PROPULSION

As mentioned on the previous page, the propeller is employed to convert the torque into thrust to propel the aircraft through the air. The two illustrations on the next page show the mechanics of how this is achieved.

Examples of piston engined aircraft in service today are the TUTOR T1 CHIPMUNK used by Air cadets for Air Experience Flying it is powered by one Lycoming 360 engine.
VIGILANT T1 used by some Volunteer Gliding Squadrons. It is powered by the GrobG2500 engine.

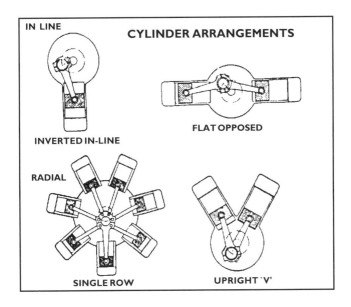

PROPULSION

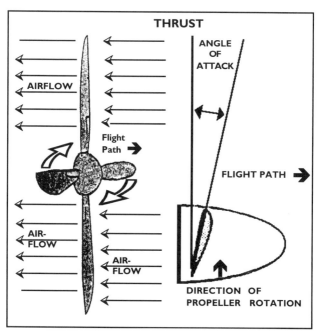

THRUST

ANGLE OF ATTACK

AIRFLOW

Flight Path

AIR-FLOW

AIR-FLOW

FLIGHT PATH

DIRECTION OF PROPELLER ROTATION

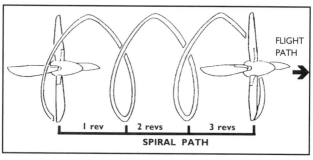

FLIGHT PATH

1 rev   2 revs   3 revs

SPIRAL PATH

17-4

PROPULSION

Gas Turbine Engines

In the piston engine petrol vapour and air are burned in the cylinder and the expanding gases move the pistons and the crankshaft to turn the propeller. Towards the end of the Second World war piston engines had come to the end of their development and began to be supplanted by gas turbines (or jets as they have now become known). The first jet aircraft entering RAF service were the De Haviland Vampire and the Gloster Meteor. These aircraft had no propellers, thrust was obtained from the reaction to the discharge of the stream of exhaust gases from their rearward facing jet pipes.

In comparison to the piston engine the gas turbine power unit is simple.

A **compressor** fan blows air into a tubular housing where it is directed to a number of combustion chambers arranged around the central shaft which couples the compressor to a turbine. In the combustion chambers fuel is atomised through high pressure nozzles and mixed with the airflow before being ignited by high voltage electric sparks. Once ignition has been achieved, combustion is continuous provided the fuel supply is maintained.

The ignition of the atomised fuel, mixed with the pressurised air, causes a rapid temperature rise and considerable expansion which escapes into the atmosphere via the rearward facing jet pipe.

As the hot gasses escape they pass through the TURBINE which consists of rotating aerofoil section blades fixed radially on a hub at one end of the central rive **SHAFT.** The drive shaft runs right through the engine to the front where it s connected to the compressor fans. The function of the rearward turbine is to rotate the central drive shaft, the rotation being provided by the exhaust gasses passing over the aerofoil.

This motion translates along the drive shaft to the compressor blades

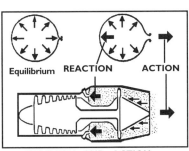

Equilibrium **REACTION**   **ACTION**

REACTION AND ACTION

which in turn draws in more air, compressing it and feeding this air into the combustion chamber - and so the cycle starts again.

These three components (Compressor, Shaft and Turbine) are referred to as a SPOOL. Multi-spool engines have concentric shafts each connecting a compressor to its respective turbine - see the diagram on left.

Main Types

There are four main types of gas turbine engines.

The first two, **TURBOJET** and **TURBOFAN** are reaction engines

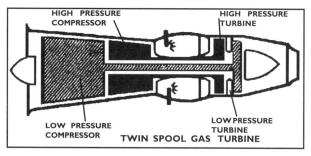

TWIN SPOOL GAS TURBINE

that is they derive their power from the reaction of the jet efflux. The second two, the **TURBOPROP** and **TURBOSHAFT**, operate on an entirely different principle where the energy of the expanding gas stream powers an additional turbine which is connected to a propeller or output drive shaft.

Applications of Gas Turbine Engine Types
1. TURBOJET

This is the simplest and earliest form of gas turbine power unit. It is employed mainly in high speed, high
altitude aircraft where small frontal area and high jet velocity are an advantage.

Examples are the 'Olympus 593' in the Concorde and the 'Viper' in various military aircraft.

PROPULSION

2. TURBOFAN

This is a "by-pass" engine in which only part of the intake air is fully compressed and passed to the combustion chambers. The remainder is compressed to a lesser degree and ducted round the hot section of the engine to rejoin the exhaust gases in the jet pipe. This gives reduced overall jet velocity, better propulsive efficiency at lower aircraft speeds, lower noise levels and improved fuel consumption. Examples are the 'RB 211' in the Boeing 747 and 757, the 'Ardour' in the Jaguar and Hawk and the 'RB 199' in the Tornado.

3. TURBOPROP

This is a turbojet with an extra turbine designed to absorb all the energy remaining in the gas stream after sufficient has been removed to drive the compressor. This power turbine drives the propeller through a reduction gearbox. The turboprop is a very efficient engine for relatively low speed, low altitude aircraft - 400 mph, 40,000 feet. Examples are the 'Dart' in the HS 748 and F27 and the 'Tyne' in the Transall C160 and Atlantic.

4. TURBOSHAFT

This can be considered as a turboprop without a propeller. The power turbine is coupled to a reduction gearbox or directly to an output shaft. As with the turboprop, the power turbine absorbs as much of the remaining gas energy as possible and the residual thrust is very low.

The turboshaft is used extensively in helicopters where the engine drives both main and tail rotors.

Examples are the 'Gem' in the Lynx and the 'Gnome' in the Sea King and Chinook helicopters.

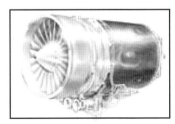

**Rolls Royce
Turbofan Engine**

PROPULSION

VECTOR THRUST

This is a variation of the turbofan where the ability to vary the direction of the jet pipe - and hence the line of action of the resultant thrust. Vector thrusting is employed in a number of aircraft, but is generally associated with VSTOL (Vertical or Short Take Off and Landing) aircraft.

The "Pegasus" turbofan which powers the Harrier has four linked swivelling nozzles which direct the jet downwards for VTOL or through an arc to the rearward position for forward flight - see the diagram below. In the "Pegasus" the fan or by-pass (cool) air is discharged through the two front nozzles and the exhaust (hot) gas through the two at the rear.

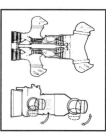

Vector thrusting has been developed extensively over recent years to make aircraft more manoeuvrable in flight, enabling them to change direction faster, and at much higher speeds.

Unlike the Harrier, aircraft such as the Su-30 Flanker and the F22 Raptor have 2 and 3-demensional jet pipes in place of conventional jet pipes.

The V-22 Osprey is also a thrust vectored aircraft, but in this case, it's entire turboprop engine rotates around it's wing section to allow it to operate as either a helicopter, or as a conventional aircraft.

VECTORED THRUST

V22 OSPREY

Ramjet

The final engine type to be considered is the Ramjet. This is a high velocity, high altitude engine. It is unlike the other engines considered since it has very few moving parts. The ramjet relies on the speed of

PROPULSION

the aircraft to cause the compression of the air into the engine,
doing this by passing it over a cone and into a small opening. Here it is
mixed with atomised fuel and passed into an ignition phase in a
combustion chamber. The thrust is then provided by exhaust gases
through a jet pipe.

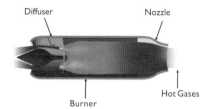

The Ramjet requires an aircraft to be at high speeds for it to work
efficiently.
Ramjet engines are generally found in missiles where they use solid fuel
rocket to propel them to speeds where the ramjet engine can work
efficiently. An example of this is the Sea Dart surface-to-air missile.

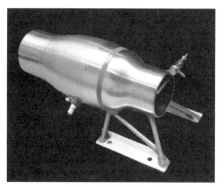

A Ramjet Engine

PROPULSION

Self Test Questions

1. What is the drawback with a single cylinder piston engine when used for aircraft power
2. What is the correct name for a 'jet' engine
3. Why does a gas turbine engine have a compressor
4. Why does a gas turbine engine have a turbine
5. What is a 'spool'
6. Name the four types of gas turbine engine, name their applications.
7. What does VSTOL stand for.
8. What does a CRANK SHAFT do
9. How is a CRANKSHAFT connected to the engine.
10. What opens and closes the inlet and outlet valves.
11. What converts TORQUE into THRUST.
12. Name the four types of cylinder aircraft engines.
13. Draw a diagram of of the AIR FLOW across a Propeller.
14. Explain how a gas turbine jet engine compressor works
15. Name a VSTOL aircraft.
16. What aircraft are you most likely to find a Ram Jet engine in service.
17. What do the following have to do with a Piston Engine:
    Suck - Sqeeze -Bang - Exhaust.
18. There are four configurations of piston engine cylinder designs. What are each of these cylinder arrangements named.

Chapter 18

AIRFRAMES

AIRCRAFT MAJOR COMPONENTS

The 4 main components of a fixed wing aircraft are: Fuselarge, Main Plane, Tail Unit and Alighting Gear illustrated and explained below:

1. FUSELAGE

This is the body of an aircraft to which the other components are attached. It also contains the cockpit or cabin, weapons, fuel tanks avionic and electrical systems and sometimes engines.
The Fuselage accommodates the crew and passengers and may be provided with space for cargo.

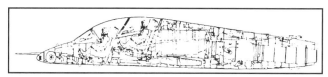

2. MAIN PLANE

The aircraft is fitted with left and right main planes known as wings. The primary function of the wings is to support the aircraft in flight but they may contain or support the fuel tanks, bomb racks, missile rails or in commercial aircraft the engines.

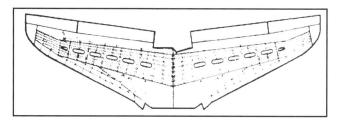

AIRFRAMES

3. TAIL UNIT
This unit is generally made up of the following components:

a. TAILPLANE
This is the horizontal stabiliser and prevents the aircraft from pitching in flight. It may consist of a single plane, orseperate left and right planes. It may be fixed, or may be equipped with suitable mechanisms to alter the angle to the airflow in flight.

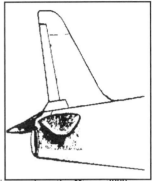

The tailplane may be mounted at the base of the fuselage, midway throughthe fin, or on top of the fin - giving a 'T' tail configuration.

In some aircraft - particularly delta wings such as the Mirage 2000 - the tail plane is removed completely. in others, for example the Typhoon, the tail plane is replaced by CANNARDS which do the same job as the tailplane, but are mounted forward of the main wings.

b. FIN.
The tailfin prevents the aircraft from yawing from left to right during flight. some aircraft, for example the Tornado are equipped with only one fin. Others, such as the FA18 Hornet, F14 Tomcat or Mig-29 Fulcrum are equipped with two tailfins.

c. ELEVATORS
These are hinged surfaces attached to the tail plane which, when operated, cause the aircraft to rise or fall.

d. RUDDER
This is a hinged surface attached to the fin which, when operated, causes the aircraft to turn left or right.

4. ALIGHTING GEAR
This consists of a main undercarriage and a nose or tail wheel undercarriage which absorb the shock of landing and supports the weight of the aircraft when it is on the ground.

AIRFRAMES

AIRCRAFT CONSTRUCTION

Stressed Skin Construction

Almost all aircraft are manufactured to a type of construction known as "stressed skin" which provides a structure with good strength-to-weight ratio. For ease of construction, transportation and repair the airframe is built in sections. The fuselage may consist of nose, front, centre and rear sections which are bolted or riveted together to form the whole. The main advantages of this type of construction are:-

    a. The skin takes the stress in flight.

    b. Relatively lightweight covering providing rigidity.

    c. Provides a good streamlined shape.

In this type of construction the FUSELAGE (see diagram below) consists of *transverse frames or formers* with lengthwise members called *stringers*. The whole is covered with light alloy sheeting.

The frames resist the compression loads and give the fuselage its shape. The stringers resist the bending loads and provide a means of riveting the skin onto the fuselage.

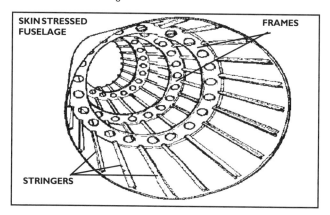

SKIN STRESSED FUSELAGE   FRAMES

STRINGERS

AIRFRAMES

The **MAIN PLANES** have greater thickness at the root (fuselage) end and here the stresses are greater. The wing (see diagram below) is made up of spars which are the main strength members that extend from the root end to the wing tip and resist the torsional loads on the main plane. The ribs provide the wing with the correct aerofoil shape and resist compression loads. The skin covering is riveted to the ribs and stringers.

THE SANDWICH METHOD OF CONSTRUCTION

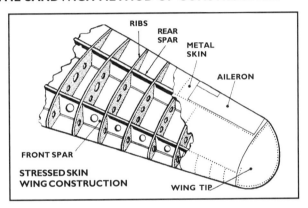

This is used to cover the main surfaces and consists of inner and outer light alloy sheets attached to a core of corrugated sheet. It provides a rigid structure where heavy spars are not necessary. The number of rivets can be reduced and the surface finish is very smooth.

THE INTEGRAL METHOD OF CONSTRUCTION

This is achieved by machining or chemically etching a solid block of material to provide a skin with integral stringers. This provides a much stronger and more rigid structure without compromising the wing's overall weight.

AIRFRAMES

AIRCRAFT SHAPE AND MATERIALS

The shape of the aircraft since their first flight in December 1903 has changed dramatically from the light wooden framed, linen covered, bi-plane of the Wright Brothers to the gleaming Mach 2+ swept. delta and variable geometry aircraft of the 21st Century.

The biplane was light and slow with a short wing span but a large wing area and therefore great manoeuvrability. The strut and bracing wires between the wings provided a light but strong structure having a low wing loading and hence a safe, low landing speed without resorting to complex flaps and slats arrangement to help generate low speed lift. Unfortunately the early biplane airframes were inefficient at speeds in excess of 150mph, and ultimately replaced by the monoplane.

The monoplane can have a braced or a cantilever (i.e. supported at one end only) type of wing which can be placed high, middle or low on the fuselage.

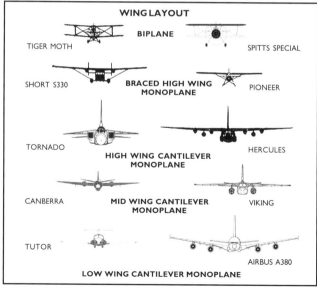

WING LAYOUT

BIPLANE

TIGER MOTH   SPITTS SPECIAL

SHORT S330   **BRACED HIGH WING MONOPLANE**   PIONEER

TORNADO   HERCULES

HIGH WING CANTILEVER MONOPLANE

CANBERRA   **MID WING CANTILEVER MONOPLANE**   VIKING

TUTOR

AIRBUS A380

LOW WING CANTILEVER MONOPLANE

AIRFRAMES

Because of the need for greater speed, the monoplane became more complicated and therefore more expensive to build. It required retractable undercarriages, the piston engine was replaced by a turbojet engine and a swept wing became a necessity, all of which increased the weight of the aircraft.

To overcome these problems, the efficiency of the aerofoil needed to be increased, and extra lift inducing devices were needed to be fitted.

Materials have changed significantly over the history of aviation - from the wood and linen construction of the early aircraft, to the light alloys of World War II, and then the steels, fibreglass, carbon fibre, titanium and composites of modern day aircraft.

Because of the stresses and strains that are applied to an aircraft in flight, every safeguard is applied and all major components are "lifted" causing them to be replaced after a certain number of flying hours to ensure safety and to extend the life of the aircraft concerned.

ENGINE INSTALLATION

When considering where to put the engines on a new aircraft, the designer has to consider a number of factors:-

a. What is the specific role of the aircraft?
b. What are the performance requirements?d
c. How many engines are needed to meet the performance requirements?
d. What engines are appropriate to meet these needs, and what are their size and weight?
e. How and where will the engines be mounted?
f. Will this be easy to remove for maintenance and engineering?
g. How efficient is the engine - how much fuel will the aircraft need and where can it be stored?
h. Will the engine(s) positioning affect the centre of gravity
i. Will the engine(s) positioning affect the directional stability of the aircraft?

These, as well as many other questions, will allow the designer to use the most appropriate engine, and in the right place on the aircraft. Engines can be fitted in the fuselage, outside the fuselage, inside the wings, on the wings or suspended under the wings in pods. In fact they can go in almost any place on an aircraft and have done so over the past 90 years. See illustrations on next page

AIRFRAMES

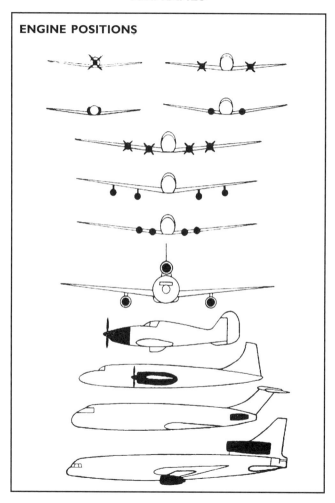

ENGINE POSITIONS

UNDERCARRIAGE

From the skids of early biplanes and gliders, the floats upon seaplanes and through the complex multiwheeled, jockey units of modern cargo aircraft such as the AN225, undercarriages are an essential component of all aircraft. They are required to:-

a. support the aircraft when it is on the ground
b. Keep the engines and sensitive components clear of any obstructions.
c   Absorb the shock of landing and provide reasonably smooth taxying.
d. withstand side loads of crosswinds at takeoff and landing.

Modern aircraft tend to have main and nose wheel units and the number of wheels and type of undercarriage leg is dependent on the aircraft's size and role.

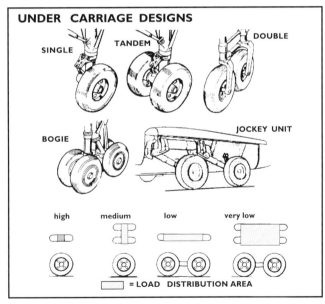

AIRCRAFT CONTROLS

All aircraft have to be fitted with a system that will enable the pilot to control and manoeuvre the aircraft in flight. There are 3 main control surfaces:-

ELEVATORS on the Tailplane control the **PITCH** axis movement.
AILERONS on the Wing controls the **ROLL** axis movement.
RUDDER on the Fin controls the **YAW** axis movement.

Depending on an aircrafts shape and configuration some of these control surface can be merged - for example Tailerons, Elevons and variable incidence of tailplanes. Canards are another example of where the control surfaces has been moved and no longer fits the traditional aircraft shape - but they still do the job of a tailplane.

The aircraft's control surfaces are operated from the Control Column and Rudder Bar via a number of alternative systems.

- **mechanical linkages** - the control column is linked directly to the control surfaces by wires', the Viking glider is an example of such systems, but it is also used in aircraft such as the Boeing 707.
- **power assisted hydraulics** - The pilot's movement of a control causes the mechanical circuit to open the matching servo valves in the hydraulic circuit. The hydraulic circuit powers the actuators which then move the control surfaces. This arrangement is found in most jet transports and high performance aircraft. These include the Antonov An-225, the Lockheed SR-71 and most aircraft in-between.
- **Fly-by-wire:** (FBW) electronic signals from the control column operate signal transducers which generate the appropriate commands and transmit them to controllers at the control surfaces. This reduces the need for heavy, complex and high maintenance hydraulic systems. An early form of this system was used in the Avro Vulcan. Modern aircraft which use it include Airbus 320 and the Boeing 777.
- **Fly-by-light:** Fly-by-light or Fly-by-optics (FBL) is sometimes used instead of fly-by-wire because it can transfer data at higher speeds, and it is immune to electromagnetic interference. In most cases, the cables are just changed from electrical to fiber optic cables. The data generated by the software and interpreted by the controller remain the same.

AIRFRAMES

As aircraft move towards FBW and FBL systems so the need for heavy mechanical circuits is removed The next step is to eliminate the bulky and heavy hydraulic circuits which move the control surfaces.

The absence of hydraulics greatly reduces maintenance costs, and also decreases the aircrafts overall weight. This system is used in the Lockheed Martin F-35 and in Airbus A380 backup flight controls.

Autopilot

Because of the distances that aircraft travel and the length of time they are in the air, aircrews need to be relieved of the mental and physical strain that occurs in controlling the aircraft. This is the primary function of the autopilot. It is a mechanism that, when switched on, can sense a disturbance of the control surfaces, the aircraft's attitude or heading, and apply immediate counter movements to maintain the course and height set by the pilot.

Aircraft Systems

Unlike a house, an aircraft is not connected to common services such as electricity, gas or mains water. Therefore each aircraft has to be independent and provide its own services. These cover all aspects of the aircraft's working parts and the following are the major systems involved:

Hydraulics are used for retractable undercarriages, flaps, bomb bays, wheel brakes etc

Pneumatics (or compressed air) has similar uses to the hydraulic systems above, and for the use of control airflow to the wing surfaces to help in improving lift.

Electricals Most aircraft flying today require electrical power and this is usually provided by a generator driven by the aircraft's engine. AC and DC voltages of various frequencies are provided by *Transformers, Rectifiers, Invertors* or *Frequency Changers*. Typical systems requiring electrical power include radios, radar, instruments, actuators and a host of other systems.

Ice Protection When flying in all weather conditions and at high altitudes ice can form on parts of the aircraft. This is particularly dangerous if it forms on the control surfaces or wing as it can change the shape of the aerofoil, so reducing lift, or stop the control surfaces

AIRFRAMES

Airspeed Indicator: This, as the name implies, gives the pilot his Indicated Air Speed (IAS). This is the speed of the aircraft relative to the air.+n which it is flowing over. It is not the aircrafts ground speed - i.e. how fast it is travelling over the ground. IAS is obtained by measuring the air pressure caused by the aircraft's movement.

Altimeter: This instrument gives the height of the aircraft above a certain reference point determined by a known barometric pressure. It measures the difference between the pressures of the free air surrounding the aircraft with-that of the reference point.

Artificial Horizon: By using a gyroscope rotating at very high speed, this instrument will indicate the natural horizon whatever the aircraft's attitude in flight.

Compass: This is one of man's oldest means of navigation. It will give the direction of magnetic north, regardless of the aircraffis attitude.

Other navigation instruments will very between aircrafts. Some will rely on ground based equipment, whilst others are satellite based - for example an Instrument Landing System (ILS), Automatic Direction Finding (ADF), Distance Measure Equipment (DME) or a Global Positioning System (GPS).

Rate of climb and descent indicator: This instrument gives the pilot an indication of how fast they are descending

Turn and slip indicator: This instrument shows the rate of turn. The rate of turn is indicated gyroscopically and the coordination of the turn is shown by an inclinometer, which works in a way similar to a simple pendulum. No pitch information is provided. The rate of turn is the actual rate at which the airplan is rotating.

Other Instruments: A number of other instruments may also be present. These will indicate engine information, include temperatures, engine revolutions, oil levels, pressures. These may also be fuel or battery information present. Other instruments may involve navigation aid, radio and communications.
You should not touch these unless you have been specifically told to do so by the pilot.

AIRFRAMES

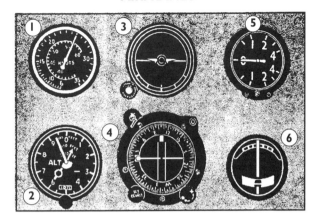

AIRCRAFT INSTRUMENTS

A description of the numbered instruments shown in the illustration on the previous page are explained in the following numbered paragraphs:

1. AIRSPEED INDICATOR
This, as its name implies, gives the pilot his Indicated Air Speed (IAS) which is the speed of the aircraft in relation to the air which is flowing over it and is not its speed over the ground. IAS is obtained by measuring the air pressure caused by the aircraft's movement.

2. ALTIMETER This instrument gives the height of the aircraft above a certain reference point determined by a known barometric pressure. It measures the difference between the pressure of the free air surrounding the aircraft and that of the reference point.

3. ARTIFICIAL HORIZON By use of a gyroscope rotating at very high speed, this instrument will indicate the natural horizon what ever the attitude of the aircraft in flight.

4. COMPASS This is one of man's oldest means of navigating across the earth's surface. It is therefore not surprising that an aircraft should have one.

Other instruments used are aimed at navigation, communication and landing e.g. Instrument Landing System (ILS), Automatic Direction Finding

AIRFRAMES

(ADF), Distance measuring Equipment (DME) and in these days of computers and satellites, more and more of this type of electronic equipment is being used.

5. RATE OF CLIMB AND DESCENT the rate of climb **RoC** is the speed at which an aircraft increases it's altitude.

6. TURN and SLIP INDICATOR The TURN and SLIP INDICATOR shows the rate and direction of a turn. It tells the pilot if he is performing a coordinated turn using all his controls most efficiently.

Self Test Questions

1. Name the four main components of a fixed wing aircraft.
2. What are the main advantages of stressed skin construction
3. What is meant by the "life" of an aircraft component
4. What are the three main control surfaces on an aircraft
5. Why do modern aircraft need ice protection systems
6. What are the four main instruments used by a pilot
7. Tailplane, Fin, Elevators and Rudder, explain the different controls they have over the aircraft.
8. Name the five Wing Layout designs.
9. Name the different types of Undercarriage designs.
10. What is the primary function of the Auto Pilot
11. How much does a gallon of fuel weight and why is it important
12. What for and when is Auxiliary Power used
13. What is essential to have if you fly over 10,000 feet
14. To what is Indicated Air Speed related
15. When designing an aircraft, what factors have to be considered
16. What is an Undercarriage required to do
17. Where will you find Spars on an aircraft

Chapter 19

PRINCIPLES OF FLIGHT-GLIDING

"To every action there is an equal and opposite reaction" is one of Newton's famous laws. This is easily understood by thinking of a person swimming. The water is pushed backwards (that is the action) and your body is propelled forwards (equal and opposite reaction). Consider one further example: the wheels of a motor car revolve, the tyres push backwards on the road and the car moves forward.

So how can this simple idea explain whet happens to an aircraft in the air? To answer this question it should first be realised that air, too, is a substance like water and if you like - the road or ground. Consider what happens whenever there is a strong gale, for example, it may be difficult to walk or it may be possible to lean against the air currents. This proves that air is a real substance, even though it is invisible.

SIMPLE EXPERIMENT

On fixed wing aircraft, it is the wings that produce the LIFT (which balances the weight of an aircraft, if the lift of an aircraft is greater than the weight, then the aircraft rises - and vice versa). To demonstrate how 'lift' is produced by a wing, a simple experiment is shown.

A Hold a piece of card so that it is slightly raised at the front (similar to a real wing) Push the card forward fairly rapidly, and you will see the card rise and try to fold backwards.

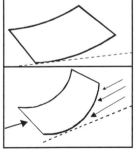

This is very similar to what happens when an aircraft speeds along the runway - the wings produce enough LIFT to carry the aircraft off the runway. It is now possible to look at all the forces that act on a real wing.

PRINCIPLES OF FLIGHT

CROSS-SECTION OF A WING
NOTE: THRUST is the result of the power from the engine(s)
DRAG is the resistance produced from the whole aircraft.
So far we have seen that LIFT is the key factor.
But how is this LIFT produced?

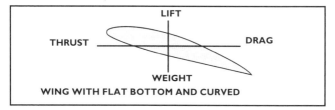

To explain this, consider another experiment.
Blow along a sheet of paper, lift is produced.
By blowing along the piece of paper, notice it rises. Now consider a typical aircraft wing:-

CENTRE OF PRESSURE

A simpler way to imagine all these forces acting on the wing, is to sum these up and show them as a single arrow. This is obviously an easier way to show the LIFT FORCE than drawing lots of arrows. It is also normal practice to show this single arrow acting at one particular point on the wing - known as the Centre of Pressure. See the diagram on the next page. This is similar to balancing a ruler on your finger by finding the centre of gravity - i.e. the middle of the ruler.

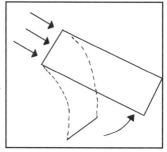

PRINCIPLES OF FLIGHT

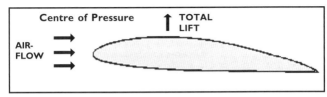

HOW LIFT VARIES

The amount of lift a wing produces depends on a number of factors:
1. The airspeeds of an aircraft.
2. The angle of attack.
3. The air density.
4. The shape of the wing cross section.
5. The total wing area.

Naturally, if the speed of an aircraft is increased (as it speeds along the runway) the more and more LIFT is produced. The angle of attack of an aircraft (that is the angle at which wing meets on-coming air) can also be varied to produce lift.

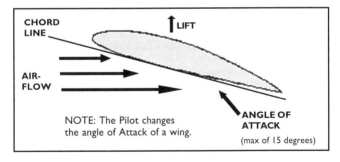

Clearly, if one was to measure the distance travelled along AIRFLOW 'A', and compare it with that travelled along 'B' then one would realise that distance for the first airflow is much greater than the second. But notice they start and finish together.

This must mean 'A' travels faster than 'B' in order to finish together because it has to travel a larger distance.

PRINCIPLES OF FLIGHT

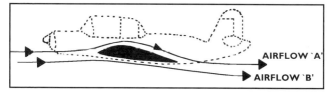

The only way 'A' can travel faster is that the pressure above the wing(path 'A') is reduced and the pressure below the wing iswing is still the same as it was at the start or the finish. This *PRESSURE DIFFERENCE* is known as **LIFT**, and since the pressure at the bottom of the wing is greater than the top, then a rise or lift is achieved.

LIFT AND WEIGHT

Consider the cross-section of a typical wing as illustrated below, it can be seen how much LIFT is produced at every point on the wing.

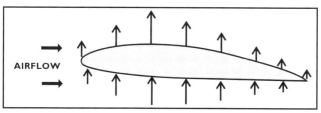

The lift forces are shown in the diagram by the length of the arrows. Greatest lift is, of course, produced in the middle of the area of the wing there.

THRUST AND DRAG

Thrust is in fact identical to what is commonly known, in the motor vehicle, as power. Just as a motor vehicle needs to produce continuous power to remain in motion, so too does an aircraft.

DRAG

Any object that moves through the air has to overcome the DRAG or the resistance before it can move in a desired direction. A car experiences two types of resistance. Firstly, there is the friction between the road and the wheels, and secondly,

PRINCIPLES OF FLIGHT

there is resistance from the air. However, in an aircraft only the air resistance need be considered. The more aerodynamic and smooth the surface of an aircraft or a car the less DRAG it produces.

There are three main parts which make-up total DRAG of an aircraft:

1. **FORM DRAG** - total DRAG caused by the parts of an aircraft.

2. **SKIN FRICTION** - smooth surfaces produce less friction.

FORWARD

MOTION

AIR

PUSHED

BACK

3. **INDUCED DRAG** - double the air speed, four times the DRAG; similarly, treble the airspeed, nine times the DRAG, and so on.

LIFT AND WEIGHT IN STRAIGHT AND LEVEL FLIGHT

If the LIFT is greater than the WEIGHT, an aircraft will CLIMB; and if the WEIGHT is more than the LIFT an aircraft will DESCEND. However, in straight and level flight, both the LIFT and Weight are equal.

STALLING

The Stall

Normally, air flows smoothly and continuously over and under the wings in flight, with some amount of Angle of Attack. However, if this angle of attack is increased beyond 15° then the airflow round the wing suddenly becomes

turbulent, which causes the LIFT to DECREASE rapidly. This sudden and rapid loss of LIFT is known as the STALL. The result is that the aircraft descends rather quickly causing height loss which in some circumstances could be dangerous.

STALLING SPEED

The stalling angle of a particular aircraft wing does not vary. But, the speed at which a STALL can occur varies from aircraft to aircraft. The stall can occur at high or low speeds.

Factors which influence the stalling speed are:-

1. **WEIGHT** - Higher the weight, higher the stalling speed.

2. **POWER** - Greater the power, lower the stalling speed.

3. **FLAPS** - Lowering flaps reduces stalling speed, especially when landing.

PRINCIPLES OF FLIGHT

4. **MANOEUVRES** - ALL manoeuvres increase the stalling speed, in particular, steep turns.

NOTE:

Control Column back,	nose up.
Control Column forward,	nose down.
Control Column to the left,	roll to the left.
Control Column to the right,	roll top the right.
Left Rudder,	yaw to the left.
Right Rudder,	yaw to the right.

STABILITY AND CONTROL

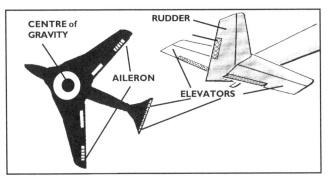

Three Plane Movements

An aircraft in flight has the freedom to move in three planes or three different ways:

PITCHING plane (lateral axis). ROLLING plane (longitudinal axis) and YAWING plane (vertical axis). Each axis passes through the centre of gravity of the aircraft, and the aircraft can rotate freely in any of these three planes. This is illustrated in the diagram next page.

To achieve movement in any one of these planes described an aircraft has three important 'SURFACES' or 'AREAS' which are used to achieve a required manoeuvre.

PRINCIPLES OF FLIGHT

The Control Column (commonly known as the 'stick') is linked to two of these surfaces - the ELEVATORS (which produce a PITCHING movement) and the AILERONS (which produce a ROLLING movement.)
The Third surface is the RUDDER (which produces a YAWING movement), and is connected to the RUDDER Pedals.

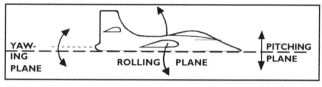

FLAPS

The main purpose of FLAPS is to enable aircraft to make landing approach at as safe and slow a speed as possible. FLAPS are lowered, used, mainly during landing, but can also be used for take-off and are raised when not in use to 'fit-in' with the rest of the wing - giving the best of two worlds.

It will be realised that at say 30°, with increased lift, the stalling speed is reduced and consequently a slower, safer approaching and landing speed is possible.
But at full FLAP, say 70° although there is a further reduction in the stalling speed, there is a most definite increase in the DRAG which results in a steeper approach angle and a better view for the Pilot as shown in the diagram, below.

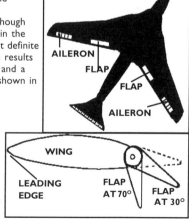

Advantages of Flap

1. Steeper slower approach, better view.
2. Lower touch-down speed, reduced landing run.
3. Braking effective more since low speed.
4. About 15° of Flap makes take-off more efficient.

PRINCIPLES OF FLIGHT

TRIMMING TABS, FLAPS AND SLATS

In the previous pages we explained how varying the position of a surface (the ELEVATORS, AILERONS or the RUDDER), causes the aircraft to move about a particular axis.

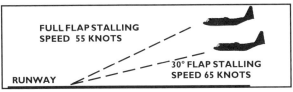

FULL FLAP STALLING
SPEED 55 KNOTS

30° FLAP STALLING
SPEED 65 KNOTS

RUNWAY

These three surfaces also have additional 'Mini-Surfaces' called TRIMMING TABS, known as the ELEVATOR, RUDDER and AILERON TRIMMING TABS, respectively. These extra parts often play an important role.

TRIMMING TABS

If a Pilot tries to maintain a particular direction by flying 'straight and level' they have to ensure that a 'BALANCED' flight is achieved. This is only achieved if the Pilot is at all time conscious of what is happening to the aircraft, and if it 'DRIFTS' the Pilot has to correct it in order to maintain his FLIGHT PATH.

To relieve the Pilot of constantly having to adjust the aircraft, the Pilot can 'TRIM-OUT' using the TRIMMING TABS to achieve a well balanced aircraft -and now of course the Pilot is free to concentrate on other important activities - such as navigation.

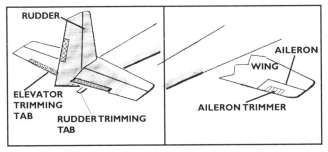

RUDDER

ELEVATOR
TRIMMING
TAB

RUDDER TRIMMING
TAB

AILERON

WING

AILERON TRIMMER

PRINCIPLES OF FLIGHT

HIGH SPEED FLIGHT - SPEED OF SOUND

You may have noticed that when a batsman strikes a cricket ball there is a delay of a fraction of a second between seeing the ball hit and actually hearing the noise of the strike. Similarly, lightening flashes can be observed several miles away yet the thunder is heard a few seconds later.

When noise is generated, at the source, air is rapidly compressed and pressure waves are formed which travel through the air until they reach the ear - these are known as sound waves. These sound waves all travel at the 'speed of sound'.

Sound Waves travel at different speeds in different air temperature. This can be realised by the fact that temperature of air falls off with height and so does the Speed of Sound. Consider the figures in the table below;

HEIGHT	SPEED OF SOUND
Sea Level	760mph
10,000	735mph
20,000	705mph
40,000	660mph

MACH NUMBER

The Mach Number is the ratio of the true airspeed of an aircraft to the 'LOCAL' speed of sound. If the local speed of sound is 600 mph and the aircraft speed is 1200 then the MACH number is 2 - displayed on a Machmeter.

$$\frac{\text{TRUE AIRSPEED}}{\text{LOCAL SPEED OF SOUND}} = \text{MACH NUMBER}$$

SOUND BARRIER AND THE SHOCK WAVE

When an aircraft is travelling below the speed of sound, air ahead is 'warned' of a approaching aircraft and makes way by separating so that the aircraft flies through smoothly. If however, the aircraft is travelling at the speed of sound then the air of course has no time to make-way and the effect is that the air strikes the aircraft and noise

PRINCIPLES OF FLIGHT

and vibration can be heard - this is known as the SHOCK WAVE.
Furthermore, the higher the speed of the aircraft above the speed of
sound the
further back the shock is relative to the aircraft.
Some terms commonly used are listed below:

>**SUBSONIC** - under the speed of sound.
>**SONIC** - at the speed of sound.
>**SUPERSONIC** - above the speed of sound.

GLIDING

On all aircraft four forces act:

>**LIFT   WEIGHT   THRUST   DRAG**

If any of these forces are disturbed (from a straight and level position)
then the aircraft will either climb or descend, accelerate or decelerate.
The forces acting on a Glider are the same as those on an aircraft with
the engine power reduced to zero.

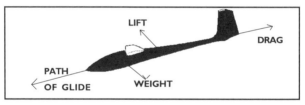

This means the aircraft or glider will descend, that is GLIDE towards
the earth due to it's own weight.

HOW FAR WILL A GLIDER GLIDE

Naturally, the Pilot wants the glider to travel as much distance as is
possible. To achieve this, the DRAG factor must be kept to a minimum
because this ensures that the ratio LIFT/DRAG is maximum and hence,
the further the glider will travel.
This minimum DRAG is attained at a angle of, usually 1 in 19 - that is,
at a height of one mile, a glider will travel 19 miles before touch down.

PRINCIPLES OF FLIGHT

GLIDER LAUNCH

There are several ways of 'launching' a glider;

AERO-TOW A powered aircraft tows the glider behind it using the tow rope and is released at whatever speed the Pilot choses.

AUTO-TOW A tow rope is attached to a car which is driven at high speed in order to launch the glider.

BUNGEE This uses the Catapult principle.
The glider is normally launched at the edge of a slope by a 'V' shaped strong elastic rope - and when released the tension on the rope is enough to raise the glider to a small height.

WINCH LAUNCH This is the most common method used. A powerful winch and engine draws a 1000 yard steel cable to which a glider is attached and quickly launched.

Typically 1000 feet is achieved with a 1000 yard cable.

CONTROLS AND INSTRUMENTS

A glider has similar type of control surfaces as any conventional aircraft, and similar controls to operate them.
The instruments usually include: Airspeed Indicator (AI), and of course a Variometer (an instrument which indicates whether an aircraft is rising or descending)
In the cockpit there is also a control which operates the spoilers - these are effectively air brakes.

SOARING

The THERMALS, or rising hot air, is used by glider pilots to remain airborne as long as possible. In fact in a relatively large area there are many thermals, on a sunny day, which a Pilot 'CONSUMES' until a certain height and then moves onto another thermal thus continuously gaining height and in the process remaining airborne for a longer period.

PRINCIPLES OF FLIGHT

IMPORTANCE OF THERMALS

A THERMAL is a mass (or a quantity) of air which moves upwards when it is warmed for, by example the sun, green fields or lakes (they take much longer to heat than tarmac or built-up areas and these result in thermals being formed as shown in the diagram below.

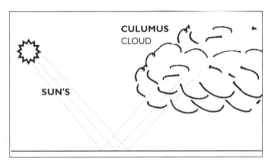

SELF TEST QUESTIONS

1. Explain what is meant by 'LIFT'. Demonstrate with a simple example.
2. Draw a diagram of a wing showing THRUST, LIFT & DRAG.
3. The amount of LIFT a wing giges depends upon five factors. What are they.
4. Explain what is meant by DRAG.
5. What are the three main causes of DRAG.
6. When are both LIFT and DRAG equal.
7. What are the four factors that influence the STALLING SPEED.
8. CONTROL COLUMN movements, what affect does it have on the aircraft when the 'STICK' is (a). pulled back, (b). pushed forward, (c). pushed to left, or (d.) pushed to right.
9. The two pedals on the floor control what.
10. An Aircraft in flight has the freedom to move in three different ways.

11. What are they and explain their affect on the aircraft.
12. What is the main purpose of FLAPS on an aircraft.
13. What causes an aircraft to STALL.
14. What are the four factors that can affect the STALLING SPEED of an aircraft.
15. What are the four specific advantages of having FLAPS on an aircraft.
16. TRIMMING TABS, FLAPS and SLATS and AILERON TRIMMING TABS play an important part in maintaining the aircraft in ....
17. What is the speed of sound at sea leve.l
18. How is the MACH number calculated.
19. What do you understand by the following terms commonly used a. SUBSONIC. b. SONIC. c. SUPERSONIC.
20. How far will a Glider glide. With minimum DRAG at an angle of usually 1in19, what does this mean to the pilot.
21. Name and explain four different ways a Glider can be launched.
22. What controls and instruments will you find in a Glider.
23. What do you understand by SOARING and how is this done.

Chapter 20

COMMUNICATIONS RADAR

Introduction

The name "radar" comes from RAdio Detection And Ranging. It is a method of using radio waves the existence of an object and its position. Most RADARS utilise short bursts of radio transmissions separated by (relatively) long time intervals.

These pulses travel out towards the target and are reflected back to be received by the radar installation. The range is calculated by measuring the time taken for the pulses to travel to and from the target.

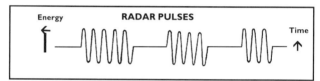

Types of Radar

There are two different types of radar, these are:-

1. **Pulsed** (pulse modulated)
2. Continuous wave (there are two types of continuous wave radars and these are:-

    a. **Doppler Radars** which utilise the change of frequency of the wave reflected from the target

    b. **Frequency Modulated Continuous Wave (FMCW)** which transmit continuous waves which vary in frequency at a controlled rate.

Radars may also be categorised by function:-

1. **Primary Radars** - these receive no co-operation from the target and rely on reflection only.
2. **Secondary Radars** - these work with the active co-operation of the target which re-transmits the signals which it receives from the radar.

COMMUNICATIONS - RADAR

Calculation of Target Range

"Time" in radar terms is usually measured in microseconds and is calculated using the velocity of radio waves in free space. They travel at 186,000 miles per second.

The table sets out the time taken by radio waves to travel the distances shown:-

Range of Target	Number of feet	Time for return of echo in microseconds
1 kilometre		6.70
1 nautical mile	6080	12.36
1 statute mile	5280	10.75

The time taken for an echo to return from a target 1 mile away is known as the *"Time for a radar Mile"* and a delay of 1 microsecond between transmission and reception corresponds to a range of 150 metres (approx. 500 feet). **Cathode Ray Tubes (CRT)** are used to measure target range and one method is illustrated in the diagram below:-

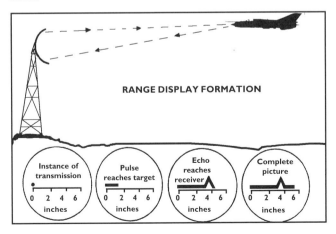

RANGE DISPLAY FORMATION

COMMUNICATIONS - RADAR

Range Indication

This is a diagram of a Type A
display range indicator:-
X - Y represents the time base
with the scale selected starting
when the transmitter fires.
X - Z represents the distance from
the transmitter of the object
providing the reflection and is
directly proportional to the target
range.

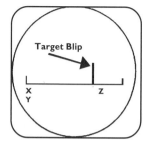

Transmission pulses are usually in
the order of 1 microsecond to
keep a steady display on the CRT
screen and, to ensure no targets
are missed, many pulses (usually
over 1,000) are   transmitted
producing a screen presentation
like the illustration on the right.
Scale markers can be either
superimposed onto the screen or
integrated with it.
A change in range scale is
obtained by increasing the velocity
of the time base sweep.

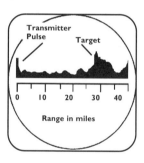

Indication and Measurement of Bearing

The bearing is the horizontal direction of the target from a reference
and is measured in degrees from North.
To obtain such a finite measurement a narrow beam of energy is
transmitted from the aerial when it is facing the target's direction.
In such instances the target is said to be "illuminated".
This technique is quite complex and is best explained by your
instructors and reference the cadet manual ACP 38.
To search for targets the beam must be rotated through 360 degrees
(called **scanning**) and when this is done continuously it is called
Continuous Rotation.

COMMUNICATIONS - RADAR

Each scanned sector joins onto the preceding one thus giving a circle of presentation. This type of display is known as a **Plan Position Indicator (PPI).**
Sections of the display can still be selected for illumination by a process known as **Sector Scanning.**
The diagram above shows a typical PPI display:-

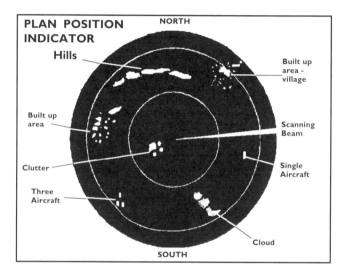

Again by changing the time base velocity and superimposing markers, range can be shown by a series of rings on the **Plan Position Indicator (PPI).**

Indication of Height

Target height is determined by measuring its angle of elevation from the transmitter. The narrow beam of energy previously explained can do this by using it to measure the **Slant Range** from ground to target. The height is then found from:-

Height = Slant Range x sin(angle of elevation)

COMMUNICATIONS - RADAR

To enable this information to be displayed, a beam of energy is transmitted in the vertical plane moving up and down (nodding). This is sometimes called a "beaver tail" beam.

Radar Installation and Performance

The main components as shown below are:-

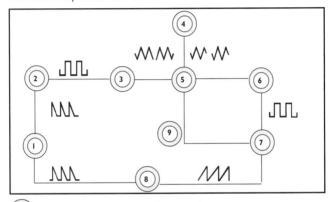

① The Master Timing Unit (MTU)
This produces regular pulses which determine the Pulse Recurrence (or Repetition) Frequency (PRF) and this is defined as the number of pulses per second. It is measured in pulses per second (PPS). The MTU controls the firing of the transmitter and the start of the time base.

② The Modulator
This determines the Pulse Duration by switching the oscillator (see below) on and off at the PRF.

③ The Oscillator
This produces pulses at the required frequency and power level to give to the aerial to convert into electromagnetic radiation for transmission.

④ The Aerial
This produces a narrow beam of radiation which it sends out to be reflected by the targets. On reflection, the same aerial is usually used to receive the energy back from the target.

(5) **The Transmit - Receive Switch (T/R Switch)**
This is an electronic switching device to connect the aerial alternately to the transmitter and receiver.

(6) **The Receiver**
This picks up and amplifies the weak target echoes and produces wide bandwidth (video) pulses which are applied to the CRT for display

(7) **The CRT Indicator**
This displays the target echoes and other relevant information.

(8) **Time Base Generator**
This produces the waveform (sawtooth) necessary for the CRT trace.

(9) **The Link**
This supplies information about the position of the aerial beam to the displays.

Secondary Radar

As previously mentioned this system relies on the target actively responding to a received radar signal.

Such systems have an interrogator and a transponder and can be either air based or ground based (e.g. TACtical Air Navigation - TACAN). The interrogator transmits pulses to a target where the transponder activates and re-transmits coded pulses back to the interrogator.

The power requirement for such systems is low as both the interrogator and transponder generate the necessary energy for transmission

Factors Affecting Radar

Radars can be affected by external factors (e.g. unwanted reflections from objects like building and clouds, jamming by enemy radars, external noise from other electronic devices) and internal factors although these can be controlled by the design of the radar itself.

COMMUNICATIONS - RADAR

Self Test Questions

1. What does RADAR stand for.
2. State the essential difference between primary and secondary radars.
3. How in RADAR terms is "TIME" measured.
4. At what speed do radio waves travel in free space.
5. What do you understand by "Time for a radar mile".
6. What in radar terms is "scanning" and "Continuous Rotation".
7. What do the initials CRT stand for.
8. What is the principle function of a beaver tail beam.
9. What is the function of the Master Timing Unit (MTU) in a primary radar.

Chapter 21

AIR NAVIGATION

INTRODUCTION

A simple definition of *"to navigate"* is *"to direct the course of a ship or aircraft"*. An even simpler one is *"being able to find your way about"* and in that sense we are all navigators. The essentials of any form of navigation are knowing where you are, where you want to go - and not getting lost in between!

Air navigation may be defined as the ability to know the aircraft's position at any given time, to calculate a heading to reach a given point, and to determine the time of arrival at that point.

The Earth and Direction

To steer an aircraft, one must first understand the earth, its form and how direction is determined. The Earth is a globe that spins around an axis running through the North Pole to the South Pole.

These are known as **Geographic Poles.** However, there are also magnetic North and South Poles. Most people are familiar with the idea of a compass pointing towards north (i.e. Magnetic North).

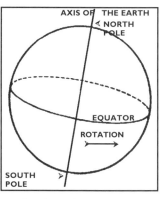

It is these two pairs of poles that are used to determine
True North and Magnetic North.

To assist in the application of this theory, a grid (termed Latitude and Longitude) is superimposed onto the globe.

AIR NAVIGATION

This helps to determine position as well as direction. This is illustrated on the previous page and in the diagram on the left.

NORTH POLE

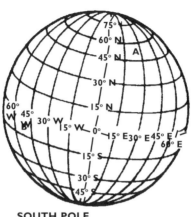

SOUTH POLE

Flight Planning

Having determined direction, the navigator must now calculate how long it will take to travel a known distance. This is done using the simple equation:-

Speed = **Distance x Time**

where the units used are:-

Speed = **Nautical miles per hour** = **Knots (kts)**
Distance = **Nautical miles**
Time = **Hours**

The next stage in planning is to calculate a heading for the aircraft in order to compensate for the affects of wind. This is achieved by using the vector triangle, see diagram and and explanation on next page.

AIR NAVIGATION

Finding the Track and Ground Speeds

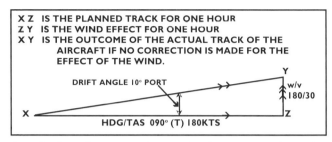

X Z   IS THE PLANNED TRACK FOR ONE HOUR
Z Y   IS THE WIND EFFECT FOR ONE HOUR
X Y   IS THE OUTCOME OF THE ACTUAL TRACK OF THE
        AIRCRAFT IF NO CORRECTION IS MADE FOR THE
        EFFECT OF THE WIND.

DRIFT ANGLE 10° PORT

w/v
180/30

X

HDG/TAS 090° (T) 180KTS

From the above diagram it can be seen that if no correction for wind is made, the aircraft would rapidly deviate from its required track over the earth's surface.

In this case the aircraft would steer a heading of 1000 (M)
in order to maintain a track of 0900 (M).

The method of solving vector triangles is described in ACP36A - Air Navigation, your instructors will soon have you conversant with them.

Navigation in the Air

Once airborne it is easy for an aircraft to become unsure of its position (e.g. think of the wind problem above).

To alleviate this problem various methods of "fixing" have been developed, for example:-

> Visual pin-point
> Beacon bearing and distance fixing
> Onboard radar fixing
> Position line fixing
> Long range navigation aids.

If an aircraft is discovered to be off track, a new heading must be determined to either:

> a) regain the required track or
> b) to fly direct to your destination from your known
>   position.

AIR NAVIGATION

Drift Lines allow a new heading to be calculated quickly with reasonable accuracy. The diagram shown below illustrates drift lines:-

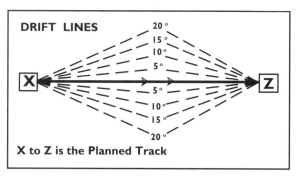

The practical use of drift lines is further illustrated in the diagram below:-

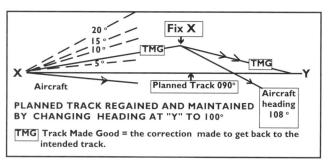

In order to calculate the **Track Error (TE)** and required heading changes, the "1 in 60 Rule" is applied.
Your instructors will explain this fully to you.
The subject is dealt with in the cadet training manual ACP36A - Air Navigation.

AIR NAVIGATION

Using these basic principles, it is now possible to navigate an aircraft from X to Z quite successfully.

It is important to note that these principles also apply to high level navigation. Obviously, at high level it is not possible to navigate by interpreting ground features on a map.

This problem is overcome by using various electrical and electronic navigation systems such as:-

TACAN
LORAN
GLOBAL POSITION INDICATORS (GPI) - these determine position using satellites.
DOPPLER.

Conclusion

The basic principles of air navigation are not in themselves difficult. Their application to real life situations is however more complicated and further ideas and principles are detailed in the course which you will be given in preparation for passing your cadet examination.

Most of the material can be found in ACP36A - Air Navigation.

Self Test Questions

1. What are the (2) simple definitions of 'To Navigate'
2. How would you define air navigation?
3. The Earth is a globe that spins around an axis running through the North Pole to the South Pole. What are these Poles known as?
4. What other name describes the North and South Poles?
5. What are the terms used to describe a grid superimposed on a globe to assist with navigation?
6. What does this grid help to determine?
7. What equation does a navigator use to determine how long it will take to travel a known distance?
8. In regard to navigation what do the following terms mean?
   (a) Speed = ? (b) Distance = ? (c) Time = ?
9. What is a vector triangle used for?
10. Give five examples of 'fixing' in relation to air navigation?
11. If an aircraft is discovered to be 'off track' a new heading must be determined for what reasons – (a) OR (b)
12. What do 'Drift Lines' allow?

Chapter 22

COMMUNICATIONS

Wireless Telegraphy (W/T) MORSE is a procedure adopted to produce a concise language for communication.
Morse has to be learned by all Air Cadet operators.
There is a great deal of practice needed to become a   proficient operator, both transmitting and receiving information accurately.

PROCEDURE

In your R/T lessons you will learned about "PROWORDS" used to abbreviate words or information used frequently, thus shortening the message.
With W/T procedure "PROSIGNS" are used for the same purpose.
A list of PROSIGNS used by the ATC are set out below.
NOTE: Any letters enclosed in brackets thus; [AA] indicates that they are transmitted as a single letter, without a pause between each letter.

LIST OF PROCEDURE PROSIGNS

Prosign	Meaning
[AA]	Unknown Station
AA	All After
AB	All Before
[AR]	End of transmission.

Prosign	Meaning
[AS]	Wait
B	More to follow
[BT]	Long Break (written = =)
C	Correct
DE	From
EEEEEE	Error
FM	Originator's sign

COMMUNICATIONS

GR (numeral)	Group Count
II	Separative sign
[IMI]	Repeat
INFO	Information addressee sign
[INT]	Interrogatory
K	Invitation to transmit
NR	Number
R	Received
T	Transmit
TO	Action Addressee
WA	Word After
WB	Word Before

PRECEDENT PROSIGNS

Z	Flash
Y	Emergency
O	Operational Immediate

NOTE: The above three Precedent Prosigns are **NOT** applicable for ATC use.

P	Priority	Normal
R	Routine	ATC
M	Deferred	use

MESSAGE COMPOSITION PROCEDURE

W/T Message Composition and the use of the correct procedure will ensure the accuracy and speed required in the handling of W/T messages.

Like R/T messages , W/T messages follow a basic standard format, they are divided into FOUR segments which are transmitted in the following sequence:-

I. The **CALL**..	2. The **PREFACE**.
3. The **TEXT**.	4. The **ENDING**.

COMMUNICATIONS

The CALL
This segment is made up of :

1. The callsign(s) of the stations to whom the message is being transmitted.

2. Who the transmission is from by using the standard PROSIGN **"DE"**.

3. The callsign of the sender.

Example: MRX99 DE MRX77

The PREFACE contains:-

1. A letter to indicate the degree of precedence, normally **"R"** for our ATC use, indicating a "Routine" message.

2. The date-time group of six figures, followed by a letter indicating the time zone ("Z" for GMT, "A" for local time).

3. The Group Count, shown by the standard PROSIGN **"GR"** followed by a numeral(s).

Example: MRX99   DE   MRX77   ZEU R 131040Z **GR5**

The TEXT contains the subject matter comprising the message and it follows the long break PROSIGN **"BT"**

(LONG BREAK SHOWN AS = = IN THIS TEXT).

The text can be in plain language or in code.

The end of the text is indicated by a second long break standard PROSIGN **"BT"**. See example over page.

Example text transmission:

MRX99 DE MRC77 R 131040Z GR5

= = details of message abc def ghi jkl mno pqr stu = =

COMMUNICATIONS

The ENDING

This segment of your message could include final instructions.
The use of standard PROSIGNS to condense frequently used
instructions saves valuable time and aids accuracy.

Examples of this are:

"B" indicating that more is to follow.

"C ...." to indicate a correction.

The last PROSIGN to be sent is **"K"**, which indicates the very end of the
message. It also invites the receiving station to transmit, to either
confirm correct receipt of the message, or to ask for a repetition of the
whole or part of the message as necessary.

Example of a complete message:

    MRX99 DE MRX77 R 131040Z GR5
= = DETAILS OF MESSAGE ABC DEF GHI JKL = = K

THE PRELIMINARY CALL
Acknowledging receipt and confirming readability.

Before traffic - transmissions - can be passed safely between
stations it is necessary to establish contact and check on the
"readability" of transmissions, this is carried out by a preliminary
call.
The PROSIGN **"R"** is used to acknowledge "Call Received" and the
readability is indicated by using one of the **"Q"** codes as set out

below: **Q R K 1 Scarcely Readable**

                        Q R K 2 Weak
                        Q R K 3 Fairly Good
                        Q R K 4 Good
                        Q R K 5 Very Good

Example of Preliminary Call and Response:
                 MRX99 DE MRX77 K
            MRX77 DE MRX99 R **QRK 3** K
      MRX99 DE MRX77 R **QRK 4** [AR](end of TX)

COMMUNICATIONS

PARTICIPATION IN A CONTROLLED NETWORK
Preliminary Call and Responses

With a Controlled Network it is normal for the Control Station to make a Preliminary Call, addressing all stations of the network.
Each station is required to reply in the callsign sequence used by the Control Stations.
In the example below the Control Station is MRX01.

MRA99 MRB38 MRC99 DE MRX01 K

MRX01 DE MRA99 R QRK 3 K

MRX01 DE MRB38 R QRK 4 K

MRX01 DE MRC99 R QRK 5 K

The Control Station would then in turn confirm the readability of responses from each of the network stations, using the letters **"C C"** meaning all stations on the network, see example below:

C C DE MRX01 R, MRA99 QRK4, MRB 38

QSA5,   MRC99 QSA3 [AR]

PASSING TRAFFIC

Once preliminary calls have been made and satisfactory communications established, the NETWORK is ready for passing traffic between stations.
For example if station MRB38 has a message to send they would call the control station: MRX01 DE MRB38 K
In response the Control Station would reply in one of two ways as in the examples that follow:
1. If **ready** to accept transmission:

MRB38 DE MRX01 R K

2. If **not** ready to accept transmission:
MRB38 DE MRX01 R [AS] [AS] (**AS** PROSIGN Wait)
followed by (when ready)

MR38 DE MRX01 R K

When the message is then passed from MRB38 to MRX01 the Control Station can reply as follows acknowledging that:
1. The message has been fully received, example:

MRBN38 DE MRX01 R [AR]

(using PROSIGN **AR** to indicate completed traffic).
2. If the whole or part of the message **has not been received,** example:

MRB3D DE MRX01 [IMI] GR2 K

COMMUNICATIONS

Where the PROSIGN **IMI** (repeat) followed by **GR2** indicates a request for Group No 2 to be repeated.

As alternatives after the PROSIGN [IMI] other PROSIGNS can be used to state the exact part of a message which the receiving station wishes the sending station to repeat.

Examples of this are as follows:

       1. [IMI] WB ......means `repeat word before'.

       2. [IMI] WA ...... means `repeat word after'.

       3. [IMI] AA .... means `repeat all after'.

       4. [IMI] AB .... means `repeat all before'.

In the following example transmission:

    [VE] MRB38 DE MRX01 [IMI] AA

                        SERIAL NUMBER .... K

`[IMI] AA SERIAL NUMBER .... ' therefore means ,

          "repeat all after Serial Number ....".

PRACTICE AND EXERCISE MESSAGES

When preparing plain language practice messages great care must be taken to ensure that any stations listening out during your transmission (

      MRX01 DE MRB38 R 134 5Z = = DRILL
      CONFIRM TX AND RX TYPES IN USE DRILL = = K

COMMUNICATIONS

MORSE CODE

A	·▬	N	▬·	1	·▬▬▬▬	
B	▬···	O	▬▬▬	2	··▬▬▬	
C	▬·▬·	P	·▬▬·	3	···▬▬	
D	▬··	Q	▬▬·▬	4	····▬	
E	·	R	·▬·	5	·····	
F	··▬·	S	···	6	▬····	
G	▬▬·	T	▬	7	▬▬···	
H	····	U	··▬	8	▬▬▬··	
I	··	V	···▬	9	▬▬▬▬·	
J	·▬▬▬	W	·▬▬	0	▬▬▬▬▬	
K	▬·▬	X	▬··▬			
L	·▬··	Y	▬·▬▬			
M	▬▬	Z	▬▬··			

COMMUNICATIONS

SELF TEST QUESTIONS

1. What is W/T.
2. What are 'PROSIGNS'.
3. Letters enclosed in 'brackets' indicate what
4. Which are the 'precedent prosigns NOT applicable for ATC use.
5. List procedure prosigns and their meanings.
6. List the basic standard format of four segments of W/T messages in their correct order.
7. List the separate parts of the four segments.
8. What is the prosign used at the very end of a message.
9. What prosign is used to acknowledge a "Call Received".
10. What is meant by 'readability' of transmissions.
11. Write out the alphabet and count 1-0 in morse code.
12. What should the segment of your ending message include.
13. What is the purpose of the Preliminary call.
14. When operating in a Controlled Network why, when and how is a Preliminary Call made.

Chapter 23

THE Royal Air Force Regiment

IN THE BEGINNING

The RAF Regiment is to the RAF, what the Royal Marines are to the Royal Navy; it is the ground fighting force that enables its parent Service to operate effectively from a safe environment. The RAF Regiment has its roots in the RAF Armoured Car Squadrons that protected the RAF in its Air Control role of preserving the peace of the Middle East Mandate after the Great War of 1914-18. Nos 1 and 2 Armoured Car Squadrons are direct ancestors of today's Nos 1 and II Squadrons RAF Regiment.

2 Armoured Car Company
RAF – HMAC Cerberus RR AC

In the post-war years, the fledgling RAF operated in relatively benign environments; however, the German shock tactics developed in the Spanish Civil War and in the approach to World War II, coupled with the British Army's focus on rebuilding itself after the debacle of the British Expeditionary Force's evacuation from Dunkirk in 1940, forced a different and radical review of RAF ground defence. A specialist RAF 'Ground Gunner' organization was established but its *ad hoc* and ill-defined tactics were no match for the enemy's capabilities.

THE RAF REGIMENT

Prime Minister Winston S Churchill observed, in 1941 – following the Battle of Crete debacle - that, *'Every Airfield should be a stronghold of fighting airgroundmen, and not the abode of uniformed civilians in the prime of life protected by detachments of soldiers'*. Recognizing that the RAF needed its own specialist ground defence force, the RAF Regiment was formed by the Royal Warrant of HM King George VI in February 1942, as a unique Corps within the RAF. While the strategic function of the Corps was to be inherently defensive, it was deemed essential that it should be trained to act tactically on the offensive and that its title should be one which will foster a fighting spirit and high morale and not lay emphasis on the defensive role. Its initial tasks were essentially the ground and low-level air defence of the UK-based airfields facing imminent Nazi invasion. However, the role expanded rapidly to include more offensive action as the direct invasion threat to the UK mainland diminished and the focus moved to mainland Europe, the Middle East and - with the entry of Japan int the war in December 1941 - the Far East.

RAF Regt Armoured Cars in NWE during WWII

THE POST-WAR YEARS

The Regiment served in every theatre of the war and quickly gained a reputation as a highly effective fighting force. It fought in the Battle of El Alamein with the British 8th Army and was present at the final victory over the Axis forces in North Africa. The Regiment then went on to serve with distinction in Italy, Greece and Yugoslavia. It was involved fully in the D-Day landings in June 1944, where the Regiment fought alongside - and frequently in advance of - its sister Army units,

THE RAF REGIMENT

providing route defence and securing German airfields and equipment before they could be destroyed. It also comprised the first Allied forces to enter Denmark. The Regiment also fought a highly successful campaign in Burma and was responsible for maintaining the security of the forward jungle airstrips that were crucial to the air-logistics support of the land forces in the fight against Japanese forces. At its height, the Regiment comprised some 85,000 personnel, but at the end of World War II, its strength was drastically reduced by the wholesale demobilisation of the Wartime armed forces.

RAF Regt – Malaya

In the post war years, despite frequent UK Government and budget threats to its very existence, the Regiment continued to provide effective defence of RAF assets worldwide. It played a significant part in the RAF Levies (Iraq), RAF Regiment (Malaya) and the Aden Protectorate Levies, which it commanded for a 10-year period. It provided field forces in support of the Army continuously during OPERATION BANNER in Northern Ireland (1969-2007) and deployed its *Tigercat* surface-to-air missile systems to British Honduras (now Belize), Central America, when Guatemala threatened to invade the British Dependency in 1972 and again in 1978. In 1982, No63 Squadron RAF Regiment, armed with the *Rapier* short-range air defence system, deployed with 5 Infantry Brigade to defend the RAF's *Harrier* Force - at Port San Carlos and then Port Stanley - against Argentinean air attack during the Falklands Conflict. Units of the RAF Regiment remained in the Falklands providing continuous, 24-hour air defence of the RAF airfields there for the following 24 years.

The RAF Regiment relinquished its air defence role in 2008, leaving it with its mainstay field squadrons in the infantry role. One unit – No II Squadron RAF Regiment – has a fully-fledged parachute capability to enable it to secure hostile airfields in advance of the land forces. That Squadron is, currently, the only British unit to have parachuted into an active operational theatre - in Sierra Leone - since the Suez Crisis in 1956. Another unit, The Queen's Colour Squadron (No 63 Squadron RAF Regiment) is responsible for the custody and escort of The Queen's Colour for the RAF in the UK. Although technically a RAF

THE RAF REGIMENT

unit, it is commanded and manned by the RAF Regiment; it is dual-roled as a field squadron and has been deployed on operations in Cyprus, Iraq, the former Republic of Yugoslavia and Afghanistan. The RAF Regiment also deployed *en masse* to protect RAF assets during Gulf War I, the Allied recapture of Kuwait, in 1991 and returned there in 1997 when Iraq once again threatened its neighbours. It was also fully involved in Gulf War II, the invasion of Iraq, and the United Nation's counter-terrorist operation in Afghanistan from 2002. Elsewhere, the RAF Regiment has also provided a significant number of officers in support of United Nations' peace-support and peacekeeping operations; these have included Cyprus, Bosnia-Herzegovina, Kosovo, Cambodia, Sierra Leone, former Soviet Union Republics and many others over several decades. The Regiment is also provides a combat element of the UK Special Forces Support Group and individual personnel in the Special Air Service; it has also participated in a highly effective Officer Exchange Programme with the USAF Combat Security Police and Security Force since 1965.

On its formation, the home of the RAF Regiment was at Belton Park, Leicestershire, but it moved in 1946 to RAF Catterick, North Yorkshire, where it stayed until it transferred to its current location at RAF Honington, Suffolk, in 1994. The Corps was presented with its first Queen's Colour by HM Queen Elizabeth II in 1953; since then, four other Queen's Colours for the RAF Regiment have been presented, the last one - together with The Queen's Colour for the RAF in the UK - at RAF Fairford in July 2008, celebrating the 90th Anniversary of the formation of the RAF. The Corps sets great store in the community of the Regimental Family. Military ethos, traditions and *esprit de corps* are viewed as

Queen's Colour Presentation at RAF Fairford in 2008

THE RAF REGIMENT

powerful motivators and are emphasised throughout an individual's time with the Corps and afterwards as a veteran. A competitive spirit is patently visible in all aspects of the RAF Regiment.

CORPS ORGANIZATION

The Corps is commanded from Headquarters RAF Air Command at RAF High Wycombe in Buckinghamshire. At its head is the Commandant General, an Air Commodore. It is a diverse Regiment, since although the majority of its manpower is vested in the RAF's Force Protection Force, many others occupy positions within the wider NATO, Ministry of Defence, Joint Service and RAF operations and training organizations. For example, the RAF Regiment is responsible for the organization and implementation of all RAF station and operational Force Protection

training for the RAF. Additionally, it provides the command and core element to the Joint Service (JS) Chemical, Biological, Radiological and Nuclear (CBRN) Defence Centre at Winterbourne Gunner in Wiltshire, and a significant element of the JS CBRN Regiment at RAF

General Purpose Machine Gun in the Sustained Fire

Honington. It also provides other Corps assets in support of UK Special Forces. The RAF Regiment was responsible for developing NATO's *Survive to Operate (STO)* concept for its international air forces; the STO concept was later developed into NATO's and the British Armed Forces' *Force Protection (FP)* concept which provides a comprehensive and coordinated approach to the defence of military assets. The RAF Regiment is widely recognized as the world leader in specialist FP and CBRN operations.

With the loss of the air defence role in 2008, the Regiment is now focussed mainly on providing its infantry capabilities. There are currently seven field squadrons (with an eighth in prospect), all under the operational command of a RAF Force Protection Wing Headquarters and supported by a commensurate number of Royal Auxiliary Air Force (RAuxAF) and RAuxAF Regiment units.

THE RAF REGIMENT

Further manpower, equipment and unit enhancements to the Force are planned to cater for the Corps' ongoing operational commitments in Iraq and Afghanistan.

The RAF Regiment, on operations, is primarily responsible for the ground defence of RAF facilities 'outside of the wire' and this role involves the active patrolling and *'domination of ground'* out to a certain distance to deter and prevent hostile forces from launching direct or indirect attacks upon the airbase. Internal base defence is generally undertaken by the wider RAF contingent and the RAF Police, supported by the RAF Regiment. Regiment field squadrons are generally better equipped than their British Army counterparts, notably in the provision of integral indirect fire support (ie mortars) and CBRN areas. Of note, the RAF Regiment is, reputedly, the only force in the British Armed Forces to have been on uninterrupted operations since its inception in 1942.

Queen's Colour Squadron (No. 63 Squadron RAF Regiment) on Parade at Buckingham Palace - 2008

CEREMONIAL DUTIES

Another, more public, role of the RAF Regiment is providing the professional ceremonial support for the RAF. This role is undertaken primarily by The Queen's Colour Squadron (No 63 Squadron RAF Regiment). With its origins in the RAF Regiment's Demonstration Flight and then the RAF Drill Unit, The Queen's Colour Squadron was formed on 1st November 1960 and has since gained a worldwide reputation for drill and ceremonial excellence. It represents the RAF at all major ceremonial occasions and, as mentioned earlier, is the Escort Squadron to

THE RAF REGIMENT

The Queen's Colour for the RAF in the UK, whenever it is paraded. The Squadron also provides Guards of Honour for visiting Heads of State and military dignitaries. It also has the honour, since 1943, of carrying out Public Duties on behalf of the RAF at Buckingham Palace, St James' Palace, Windsor Castle and Edinburgh Castle on a regular basis. However, the Squadron is probably best known for its continuity drill displays, which have been performed before audiences throughout the world.

Continuity Drill – the execution of a complex series of drill movements covering foot and arms drill without orders – was pioneered by the RAF Regiment's Demonstration Flight and began life as a training aid; it later evolved into a role for The Queen's Colour Squadron. The displays require the Gunners to memorise several hundred consecutive drill movements, all of which are taken directly from the RAF Drill Manual; none are contrived merely to enhance a performance. The Queen's Colour Squadron currently holds the world record – certified by the Guinness Book of World Records – for completing the most rifle and foot drill movements in a 24-hour period.

INITIAL TRAINING

The RAF Regiment, in concert with British Army Infantry and Royal Marines, only accepts male candidates for service. If you aspire to join the RAF Regiment, you will have to undertake (for commissioned service as an officer) a Potential Regiment Officers' Acquaintance Course – PROAC – or (for non-commissioned service as a Gunner) the Potential Gunners' Acquaintance Course – PGAC – at RAF Honington. Organized through the Armed Forces' Careers Information Offices, these three-day courses would assess your level of fitness and overall suitability for undergoing Regiment training.

For those successful PROAC candidates, initial officer training conducted at RAF College Cranwell would be a pre-cursor to undertaking the Junior Regiment Officers' Course (JROC) but, for those passing the PGAC, initial RAF training is undertaken at RAF Honington before embarking on the professional Trainee Gunners' Course. Both courses would teach you how to operate a variety of personal and section-level weapons, in a wide range of environments and climatic conditions. The training is tough because it has to be. Soon after graduation, you could find yourself in the thick of an engagement with enemy forces in a distant and hostile land; the RAF

THE RAF REGIMENT

Regiment trains its people well and effectively to ensure that they have the best advantage in a conflict situation. Those on the JROC also learn to be junior commanders, developing the necessary tactics to enable them to lead their men in combat situations from the outset of their careers. Those who make the grade at the end of the long and arduous courses have the honour of wearing the Corps' coveted RAF Regiment shoulder 'flash'. On completion of the basic RAF Regiment training, individuals will then progress to further training, including specialist communications and 'close precision attack' skills as a Sniper. After graduation, you would find yourself assigned to a RAF Regiment squadron with the prospect of deploying operationally within a short period of time. However, you would return to RAF Honington occasionally to complete further training.

The RAF Regiment is fiercely proud of its heritage and its reputation for its world-class Force Protection capabilities. Do you have what it takes to serve in the RAF Regiment? For more details contact your local Armed Forces' Careers Information Office or go on-line at: www.raf.mod.uk/rafregiment for an interactive look at the Corps.

Picture of the Al Waki firefight in Basrah, Iraq, in which Cpl David Hayden won the Military Cross

THE RAF REGIMENT

Self Test Questions

1. After the Great War of 1914-18 what was the role of the Regiment.
2. How was it equipped to carry out its operational role.
3. When was the RAF Regiment formed.
4. What was thought to be its original task.?
5. In WW2 what battle in North Africa did the Regiment take part.
6. In June 1944 Europe which Army did the RAF Regt serve with.?
5. When was number No63 Squadron equipped with a short-range air defence system.
6. What was the name of the weapons used for short-range defence.
7. Who did the Regiment serve with during the Falklands conflict.
8. What was essentially their role in the Falklands.
9. Which Squadron of the RAF Regt served in the Falklands.
10. Name five theatres of operation that the Regt has served.?
11. Which is the RAF Regt parachute Squadron, and where is it based.?
12. Which is the Queens Colour Squadron.
13. What is the RAF 'STOC' what is its role.?
14. Where is the current home of the RAF Regiment.
15. When was the first Queens colour presented to the Regiment.
16. On what date was the Air Defence role transferred to the Army Royal Artillery.
17. At present there are seven field Squadrons, under whose operational command are they.
18. The Regiment on operations what is their primary responsibility.
19. When was the Queens Colour Squadron formed.
20. What is the purpose of PAGC training.?
21. What is a 'TG' course and how long does it last.?

Chapter 24

LIFE STYLE.

INTRODUCTION - FACING THE FACTS.

As a member of your ATC Unit you will have already accepted the challenge of joining the best youth organisation in the UK. Your training achievements will be measured by your progress through the classification system, your achievements and progress with the Duke of Edinburgh's Award and your record of achievement.

Your "Cadet Life" as the above paragraph relates is planned out for you according to your age and training under the guidance of your Officers and Adult Instructors.
This Chapter "Your Life Style" is not directly related to the paragraph above, but to make sure that you understand there is a greater challenge to you than any you have yet encountered, and that is for you to decide on what your Life Style is to be.

"Without challenge there is no achievement"
Making correct judgments and the right decisions on the route you take in developing your own identity is not easy. You can go with the flow and see where it leads to, or you can take charge of your life, put the effort into your career, relationships and identity.
Be observant, listen to others points of view and opinions. Learn about different cultures and their life-styles. Try and understand and possibly help others less fortunate than you.
The choice is yours!

EDUCATION FOR LIFE

Having left school you think education that it is all behind you. Hopefully, you will take up every chance that comes your way to improve your education, knowledge and skills. Being a cadet will help, but opportunities are available to everyone, no one will make you go out and look for them or do anything about it about finding them for you, have to find them yourself.

CONTINUED EDUCATION

Colleges of Further Education offer many courses to improve your levels of education and skills, to gain qualifications by day release or evening classes in subjects that most interest you.

Find out what is on offer and go about improving your own education standards. You will have to be prepared to carry out private study. That is how many thousands of students of all ages study every year through the Open University for Degrees in their chosen subjects.

SELF IMPROVEMENT

If you are seen to be making an effort to improve yourself and making the most of your life by the example you are setting, you will earn the respect of those around you. No matter what job or occupation you have at any given time, you will know that through your own efforts you are on top of it, your value as a person will have increased and so will your potential to an employer.

MANNERS - DO OTHERS SEE YOURS?

It might be a sound advice for you to look to your manners when it comes to employment or where you come into contact with people you have not met before. It is often said " its the little things that matter", for instance; when you are out and about, do you open a door for someone, do you always say "please" and "thank you" at the right time, do you know the correct way to behave at a meal table - holding your Knife, fork and spoon correctly, not sitting with your arms on the table, not talking with a mouth full of food - its the little things that matter, manners and social skills are noticed - especially by employers.

If you don't have good manners would you expect your boss to let you look after one of his customers? - Would you?

Would you expect your Squadron Commander to let you look after an important visitor if they had doubts about your manners - would you?

'MILESTONES' TO REMEMBER

Your achievements can be looked upon as 'milestones' in your life, they are stages in your learning experience. Some of the 'milestones' will not be a pleasant experience, they may be broken relationships, the start or end of a particular job, or when you have to part with something you value.

LIFE STYLE

The important outcome for you as a person, is to be able to draw lessons from them to improve your own ability, knowledge, skills, attitudes and understanding.

YOUR CONTRIBUTIONS and HELP

Does your contribution you make at home include; Dirty clothes left on the bedroom floor; dirty mark around the bath: an assault course to change your bedding? A plate growing penicillin (mould) under your bed: empty drinks tins hidden under dirty clothes acting as a booby trap for an unsuspecting parent or guardian?

Is this fair?

If you are to be a good cadet/citizen then you should not need reminding that you have to make a meaningful contribution in helping with the "chores", whether at home, at work, or in the cadet hut. It's a part of your 'life skills' to show other people that you do your share in helping others, and appreciate what others do for you.

LEAVING HOME

The 'milestone' that most of us remember vividly throughout our lives is when we leave home for the first time.

To some it is an action that is forced upon them through unhappy home circumstances, or after some row they have had, followed by an action taken on the spur of the moment. It is a difficult experience to say the least.

Even those who have had a caring family home and been a complete unit, sharing all the joys and sorrows of life, find it difficult when it comes to the time to leave.

Feelings run high and are very powerful, causing heartache and "home-sickness" which takes a lot of coping with.

Those of you who have been to Annual Camps or on courses will have already had the experience of being away from your home and normal surroundings, and will appreciate and understand these feelings.

Leaving home will not present you with quite so much of a problem, but you will be in a position to help others, who have not had your experience to cope with theirs.

CONSIDERATION FOR OTHERS

You must also consider the feelings of those you leave behind you. The parents, brothers and sisters and relatives that have watched you grow up, they will have real feelings of losing you.

It's very little to ask you to stop by sometime and say hi!, how are you doing, or if away from home - do remember to phone, text, email or write.

WHAT IT IS TO BE A UK CITIZEN

First consider that as a member of this nation you belong to a family of nations across the world - the Commonwealth.

Some parts of our history we are perhaps not so proud of such as how we initially possessed other lands. However, today the individual countries of the Commonwealth do operate independently of us in Britain, yet keep close ties in many ways through trade and other agreements and recognise Her Majesty The Queen as the head of the Commonwealth.

Our traditions that have been built up over many hundreds of years are the envy of many countries abroad, whose people visit us in their millions every year.

Let there be no doubt in your minds that many of them would gladly like an opportunity to change places with you, to become a Citizen of the UK. The role that you play as a citizen, how you use the opportunities that others do not have is entirely up to you. It is important that whatever you do, you maintain the traditions and standards that so many people have fought and died for in our past history.

YOUR FREEDOM

The freedom and the laws of the land which have been handed down from generation to generation are now in your hands. Future generations will expect you to have have taken care of this task in preserving our freedom and way of life that we all enjoy.

Our democratic system is not for your particular benefit, but for the nation as a whole. Your responsibility is to uphold the law and to assist those who's job it is to administer it.

Should our laws need changing then this is done through the democratic process by the people making representations to their local Member of Parliament.

There are those who are not satisfied with the democratic system will resort to their own remedies. Today we are often faced with people who have a mission in life, through political or other reasons, they try to make changes through subversive and terrorist activities in attempts to undermine the government of the day. This threatens our peaceful, established way of life and the prosperity of the nation.

You will no doubt be quick to recognise those who fall into this category and their associates and as a result be guarded against becoming exposed to their influences.

A CHALLENGE

There are many responsibilities that you have to accept as a citizen. One of them is to always cast your vote (when old enough at 18 years plus). It is your right and duty as a citizen to do so. You may be called upon to act as a member of a jury, you will be asked to fill in endless numbers of forms for all manner of reasons from T.V. Licences to Application Forms and Tax Forms!!

Your time will be called upon to assist with many voluntary organisations as you are already doing.

There are very few people who at some period of their lives have not given some of their spare time as a volunteer.

Consider what time and effort you are prepared to put into helping others.

INFORMATION - WE ALL NEED IT.

The ability to get the right information at the right time can make yours and other peoples lives a lot easier. There are a few simple rules about getting help, the first thing is to sort out exactly what it is you need to know, then to be able to communicate in such a way that the person you are asking will gladly want to help you - internet, library, etc.

THE RIGHT APPROACH

"Please can you help me", listen carefully, writing down what you are told. Generally people will respond always remember to thank them for their help.

You will have had to carry out many projects during your education and this is when you start to use that skill to its full, finding out for yourself and making use of all available information.

Having brought together the information the skill is then required to be able to present it in such a way that others can easily understand it.

This skill is worthwhile practising whenever you can, the reason being that if you have to make decisions that can have serious consequence for you, then treat the problem as a project.

The more you practice the more useful you will find it, even if it is only to help making the decision to spend some of your hard earned savings.

DECISION MAKING/PROBLEM SOLVING

The act of making your mind up about something, a choice made between alternative courses of action in a situation of uncertaintity. There are a number of descision process available however the most popular tends to be **listing the advantages and disadvantages of each option**. (This was popularised by Plato (classical Greek philosopher & mathematician and Benjamin Franklin one of th founding fathers of the United States).

ACHIEVEMENTS.

It is always advisable to keep records of events, happenings, progress made with the dates, you will often require to have such information throughout your life. All that you record in your Training Record Book will only be a part of your achievements as the space available will soon be used up, but it will get you started and if sensible you will always carefully record your achievements and career details with the dates and places etc., for future reference.

YOUR ROLE IN LIFE. WHERE ARE YOU GOING?

What are your "goals", what would you like to do, what would you like to achieve in the next three, five or ten years?
When you have the decided to achieve certain goals no matter how small they appear, in a fixed time, then you will do it.
List what has to be done and by when to attain those goals, then set about doing it in earnest.
Parents and other will try to influence you, be a good listener, make sure you learn from their mistakes, and draw your own conclusions.

INTERESTS and HOBBIES

Throughout your life it is important to develop interests and hobbies. Some become more than just a hobby and turn into a job or a full time occupation or provide you with an interest for life.
Many people find great satisfaction in having a deep interest in a hobby, especially when going through a difficult period in their lives, such as when losing their job or being ill for a long period, it is always something interesting to look forward to and which you enjoy.
Many people who are retired - that may seem a long way off for you - as a result of having an interesting hobby throughout their lives, have a very happy and rewarding retirement.
Many have interests in the community in which they live, taking on voluntary work helping others by belonging to local clubs or

organisations, not just as a member, but actively helping to make things happen, such as serving as a committee member.

COMMUNITY SERVICE

If you have been taking part in the Duke of Edinburgh Award Scheme, you may already be aware of a great many different organisations in the area where you live.

You will know that they all can do with a helping hand, from the care of the elderly to those who run the local youth clubs or other organisations, they need so much support and help you should never be bored! Remember the saying ' SERVICE BEFORE SELF'.

DON'T PUT YOURSELF OR OTHERS AT RISK

FITNESS HEALTH & HYGIENE

Healthy mind and healthy body - fitness, to be really fit, fit enough to take part and finish a marathon needs a lot of determination and hard training. The hard part is to finish, for some it is easy to take part and finish, but for others the effort and self discipline to take part are an example to all of us.

PARTICIPATION

It is important to take part in sporting activities of as many different kinds as possible, especially team games or activities where the joint efforts of all taking part achieve results.

The fun and excitement that you experience no matter what level of ability you attain are part of your quality of life.

If as a result of this you also become fit it is a bonus, as so few people experience the joy of being really fit, you and your team may get an added bonus by winning something.

You are probably better than you think you are - put it to the test, don't just stand on the touch line watching others, do it, be one of them.

Should you be a sports enthusiast much time and effort for practice will be required to reach any 'club standard', it is not easy to maintain the peak performance for top class levels in many sports.

While you remain an amateur, you may find yourself spending too much time training and practising as a result of which your work or other interests and social activities may suffer. Unless you are a professional sports person, you have to get the balance right, sufficient to keep fit without it taking over all your spare time.

A HELPING HAND

There is always something you can do to help if you are sufficiently interested and take the trouble to find out.

Membership of your local sports club will also involve you in the social events that most clubs have as a part of their normal activities.

This is an added responsibility that you have towards the club, to support the committee who plan and organise events for the entertainment of the members and their friends.

Membership of any club or organisation must have a commitment from their members to give full support for it to be successful, but like many things in life you will only get out of it what effort you are prepared to put into it.

Many life long friendships are forged through membership of clubs and associations. People will encourage you to find out about your own abilities, everyone has hidden talents that given the chance can lead to many new opportunities to different things in life, meet new people, improve your ability to mix with others and widen your circle of friends.

FACTS OF LIFE AND DEATH

We hope that you will make the decisions in your life that mean you don't need to use the helplines listed. However non of us are prefect so here is a list of contacts, which you may find useful.

Service	Contact	Telephone No.
Teenage Pregnancy	BrookAdvisory Centre	0800 0185 023
	Care Confidential	0800 028 2228
Bullying	Childline	0800 1111
Bereavement	Cruse Bereavement Care	0870 167 1677
	Winstons Wish	08452 030 405
	Young Persons helpline	0808 808 1677
Suicide	Samaritans	08457 909090
Eating disorders	Beat eating	0845 634 1414
	Disorders Helpline	
	Caraline	01582 457 474
Relationships	Relate	0845 130 4010
Sexual orientation	Lesbian and Gay foundation	0845 330 3030
Sexual Health	Terence Higgins Trust	0845 122 1200
Addiction	Action on Addiction	0208 554 9004
Teenage support	Teenage Support Line	0208 554 9004

Web Sites address	Service
www.bullying.co.uk	Bullying
www.teenagehealthfreak.org	Teenage General health questions
www.bpas.org.uk	British Pregnancy Advising service
www.avert.org.uk	Comprehensie website, aimed specifically at young people.
www.childline.org.uk	A listering ear when you want to talk.
www.childrenslegalcentre.com	Legal help for young people
www.efc.org.uk	Education of choice; Sex, relationships, pregnancy, abortion aimed at young people
www.likeitis.org/indexuk.html	Advice for young people
www.there4me.org.uk	Aged between 12 - 16 years old.

Chapter 25

METHODS OF INSTRUCTION

The 'Golden Rule' of successful instruction:
THE SIX P'S

PRIOR - PREPARATION AND PRACTICE
PREVENTS POOR PERFORMANCE

INTRODUCTION

Methods of Instruction, (MOI) follows the system used by the Services.. Providing you apply the well tried and practiced framework called a **Lesson Plan** you will find that instructing becomes simplified and there is less chance of you 'losing your way' in a class.

As a Senior Cadet, the skills you acquire following this system will improve your confidence; it is a skill that you may be able to put to good use in your career.

QUALITIES REQUIRED

The main qualities you need as an instructor are:

1. Enthusiasm – boredom is infectious
2. Self confidence – through following the 6 P's
3. Good knowledge of your subject. Your class soon picks up on 'Surface knowledge'.
4. Look the part – be smart
5. Good manner and bearing - look up whilst you speak, your voice will travel further.
6. Vary the pitch/strength of your voice to stress a particular point and keep the class alert.
7. Be firm but fair - encourage your class to join in – to a point!

METHOD OF INSTRUCTION

8. Never be satisfied with your standard of instruction, always look for ways to improve your presentation skills
9. The ability to instruct **clearly, completely, patiently, giving information at a suitable pace, one stage at a time.**

AVOID

The following are the **"DO NOT's"**

1. Use sarcasm to get a laugh
2. Make a fool of one of the cadets in front of the class
3. Use remarks that have a double meaning or that may offend one of the class
4. Pick on one cadet to answer questions too often
5. Do not 'cut corners' by omitting important information or assuming knowledge
6. Overload your lesson with too many aids, e.g. a projector, flip chart, overhead projector video recorder, camera and computer for one lesson will detract from subject matter. Keep it simple but effective.
7. Watch yourself for distracting mannerisms such as saying 'OK' or 'RIGHT' after each statement, scratching your nose etc. You know how it is when you are the student and your teacher/instructor's mannerisms become more interesting than the lesson.

PREPARE AND PLAN

1. What is the objective?
2. Which is the best method – lecture, lesson, discussion, exercise or demonstration.
3. Where is the instruction to take place – a small room may rule out some of the activities you may wish to use.
4. What is the size of the class?
5. What time is available?
6. What equipment and training aids are available?
7. Are the aids suitable, simple enough, large enough or even necessary?
8. What handout notes should be produced?
9. What is the present standard of the class's knowledge?
10. Prepare your list of questions and answers for this lesson and have your questions and answers ready from the previous lesson if appropriate.

METHOD OF INSTRUCTION

SKILLS LESSONS – (Drill, Skill at Arms, etc.)

Remember and use the sequence: (EDIP)

EXPLANATION – DEMONSTRATION
– IMITATION - PRACTICE

STAGE	KEY POINT
BREAK DOWN THE LESSON TO AS MANY STAGES AS YOU LIKE	IMPORTANT POINTS NOT TO BE MISSED
1	STRESS SAFETY, ANYTHING THAT CAN CAUSE DAMAGE
2	"MEMORY TICKLER" FOR SIZES, MEASUREMENTS REFERENCES, COLOURS ETC

A SIMPLE LESSON PLAN

Rule up sheets of paper using the sample as a guide, setting out the **STAGES** or **BLOCKS** of information as headings on the subject, and the **KEY POINTS** which are the important points to be made, such as safety, figures, codes, references and the correct training aid to use at this particular point, use this section as a prompt, drawing as many lines as you require. Don't forget to write large enough and clearly as you may be using your plan when standing up - **NOT** held in your hand, reading from it!

The plan is divided in to three stages:

STAGE ONE – BEGINNING

Subject: Class/Squad: Time: Location:

Dress: Stores required and Training Aids:

Time allowed:

METHOD OF INSTRUCTION

'Prelims': Roll Call: Safety Precautions: Class Formation: Seating Plan: Comfort of the Class: Lighting Levels: Standard of Visual Aids. Training aids make sure they all work and you have sufficient for the class; spare bulbs for OHP

Introduction: Make sure the class know your name.

Objective: must be clearly stated and understood, attainable in the time allowed.

Reason Why: give a realistic reason, incentive to achieve

Results: Benefits to be gained from the lesson.

Revision: Check the classes' knowledge/skills in the subject previously taught. Cadets soon forget.

STAGE TWO – THE MIDDLE

The main instruction to be taught. Time allowed – divide the subject in to several **STAGES**, select from each stage the **KEY POINTS** that you must bring out in your instruction, for example, SAFETY to ensure a complete understanding of the lesson.

CONFIRMATION

At the end of each **STAGE** of the instruction, confirm that the key points have been understood. It is important to ensure that all the class are 'kept on their toes' you must therefore **pose the question to the whole squad,** wait for a few moments for them **ALL** to think of the answer, then **select or nominate one of them to answer.**

Note: if a cadet is unable to answer the question, give a little time, then re-nominate. Correct any errors as they occur. Do not keep nominating the same cadet – even if they give the correct answers!

ASK - PAUSE – NOMINATE

METHOD OF INSTRUCTION

STAGE THREE – THE END

Invite questions from the class; if you are asked a question and do not know the answer, do not try and bluff your way out, ADMIT IT, but find out and let them know – **MAKE SURE THAT Y OU DO!**

Use your prepared questions to confirm that the class has achieved the objective of the lesson. In the case of skills based instruction you will confirm by practical assessment.

Summary: – bring out and stress the achievement of the objective. Once you have taken the time to plan and produce a Lesson Plan - stick to it - it is so much easier than getting lost for words!

Look forward: state when the next lesson will be/what the next lesson will be.

KEEP ALL YOUR LESSON PLANS – CAREFULLY FILE THEM FOR EASY REFERENCE. THE NEXT TIME YOU TAKE THAT LESSON – HALF YOUR WORK WILL ALREADY BE DONE.

TRAINING AIDS

There are various methods of presentation available today such as OHP, Power Point, Videos, etc all of which have their advantages and disadvantages.

Whatever medium you decide to use always be prpared for a 'system failure' or lack or equiment. Have a 'back up' and be prepared to improvise.

You will have to allow plenty of time to set up equipment and ensure it is all working. Likewise check that any handouts are available and set out in the order they are required. Rehearse any demonstration and check that those who may be assisting do know what and when to perform.

IMPROVISED TRAINING AIDS

Many Squadrons will have a box in their stores of 'training aids' which amongst other item will have an old blanket used as a 'cloth model' for tactical training or perhaps a lump of plasticene for teaching contours and relief for map reading. What appears to be a blood stained trophy is in fact an improvised wound for a compound fracture. If your Squadron does not have improvised Training Aids now is the time to make some. It makes a good competition as to who can produce the best and most useful aids.

METHOD OF INSTRUCTION

SELF TEST QUESTIONS

1. What is the "Framework" used for good instruction.
2. When preparing a lesson what do you have to take to do it correctly.
3. What are the qualities required of a good instructor.
4. What should you do about habits.
5. Look up when you speak, — why.
6. What do you understand by "looking the part".
7. Complete the following sentence; "Instruct, Clearly, completely one _ _ _ _ _ at a _ _ _ _
8. As an instructor how can you check your own performance.
9. What are the six "Basic Points of Instruction.
10. Name six of the ten things to do before you Prepare and Plan a lesson.
11. How do you use the "Questioning Technique".
12. If instructing a SKILL, what is the "Sequence of Instruction".
13. What do you understand by a. "A STAGE. b. "A KEY POINT".
14. A COMPLETE lesson is broken into how many parts or stages, what is the name of each one.
15. What are you doing if you are carrying out the "PRELIMS".
16. What do you do about Training Aids before a lesson.
17. If asked a valid question and you don't know the answer, what do you do about it.
18. Name three methods to confirm that all your class members have learned the lesson given.
19. Why and how should you keep the lesson plan that you have just used.
20. What is the last thing you tell a class before finishing.
21. If the lesson is on any Skill at Arms subject, (including Shooting), what is the FIRST and LAST most important action to carry out and who takes part in it.

ABBREVIATIONS IN COMMON USE – PLEASE ADD/DELETE AS NECESSARY

ACCGS	Air Cadets Central Gliding School
ACPNTS	Air Cadet Pilot Navigation Training Scheme
ACLO	Air Cadet Liaison Officer
ACO	Air Cadet Organisation
ACP	Air Cadet Publication
ADC	Aide de Camp
Adjt	Adjutant
Adv Trg	Adventure Training
AEF's	Air Experience Flights
AEG	Air Experience Gliding
AFIS	Aerodrome Flight Information Service
AGL	above ground level
AGT	Advanced Glider Training
AIC	Aeronautical Information Circular
Air Cdre	Air Commodore
AIS	Aeronautical Information Service
AME	Authorised Medical Examiner
Amsl	above mean sea level
AOC	Air Officer Commanding
AP	Air Publication
ASP	Aircraft Servicing Platform
AWO	Adult Warrant Officer
AWOL	Absent Without Leave
A&T	Administration and Training
ATC	Air Training Corps/Air Traffic Control
ATCC	Air Traffic Control Centre
AVM	Air Vice Marshal
BRC	British Red Cross
C of E	Certificate of Experience
C of T	Certificate of Test
CCF	Combined Cadet Force
Cdt	Cadet
CI	Civilian Instructor
CO	Commanding Officer
Cpl	Corporal
CTA	Control Area
CTC	Cadet Training Centre
CTR	Control Zone
CWO	Cadet Warrant Officer
D/F	Detached Flight
DP	Drill Purposes
DPM	Disruptive Pattern Material
ETA	Estimated Time of Arrival
ETD	Estimated Time of Departure
Eqpt	Equipment

ABBREVIATIONS IN COMMON USE – PLEASE ADD/DELETE AS NECESSARY

FFI	Free From Infection	
Fg Off	Flying Officer	
FIR	Flight Information Region	
FIS	Flight Information Service	
FL	Flight Level	
Flt Lt	Flight Lieutenant	
Flt	Flight	
Flt Cdr	Flight Commander	
FS	Flight Sergeant	
GIC	Gliding Induction Course	
GMA	Grid Magnetic Angle	
Gp Capt	Group Captain	
GP	General Purpose	
GN	Grid North	
GMA	Grid Magnetic Angle	
GRP	Glass Reinforced Plastic	
GS	Gliding Scholarship	
HE	High Explosive	
HQAC	Headquarters Air Cadets	
HQ	Headquarters	
ICAO	International Civil Aviation Organisation	
I/C	In Command	
ICE	Individual Compass Error	

IFR	Instrument Flight Rules
IMC	Instrument Meteorological Conditions
IR	Instrument Rating
Kg	kilograms
Km	Kilometer
MATZ	Military Aerodrome Traffic Zone
Mb	millibars
MOD	(Air) Ministry of Defence (Air Force Department)

MT	Motor Transport
MTO	Motor Transport Officer
MN	Magnetic North
NATS	National Air Traffic Services
NBC	Nuclear Biological Chemical
NCS	Network Control Station
NDS	Network Directing Station
Nm	nautical miles
NSP	Normal Safety Precautions
NCO	Non Commissioned Officer
NOTAM	Notice To Airmen
NRA	National Rifle Association
No	Number
Obs	Observation
OC	Officer Commanding

ABBREVIATIONS IN COMMON USE – PLEASE ADD/DELETE AS NECESSARY

OC Sqn	Officer Commanding Squadron		SASO	Senior Air Staff Officer
OS	Ordnance Survey		Sgt	Sergeant
OASC	Officer and Aircrew Selection Centre		SOA	Senior Officer Administration
PA	Personal Assistant		Sqn	Squadron
PEdO	Physical Education Officer		Sqn Cdr	Squadron Commander
PIC	Pilot In Command		Sqn Ldr	Squadron Leader
Plt Off	Pilot Officer		SRA	Special Rules Area
Pm	Post Meridian		SRO's	Squadron Routine Orders
PPL	Private Pilot's Licence		SRZ	Special Rules Zone
PRO	Public Relations Officer		SSO's	Squadron Standing Orders
PSO	Personal Staff Officer		SSO	Senior Staff Officer
RAS	Radar Advisory Service		SVFR	Special Visual Flights Rule
RAFRO	Royal Air Force Reserve of Officers		TAF	Terminal Aerodrome Forecast
			TMA	Terminal Manoeuvring Area
RAFVR (T)	Royal Air Force Volunteer Reserve (Training Branch)		TOET	Test Of Elementary Training
Rgnl Co ndt	Regional Commandant		Trg Off	Training Officer
RHQ	Regional Headquarters		TX	Transmit
RIS	Radar Information Service		UIR	Upper (Flight) Information Region
RSO	Regional Staff Officer		UK AIP	United Kingdom Aeronautical Information Publication
RT	Radiotelephony		VFR	Visual Flight Rules
RV	Rendezvous		VGS	Volunteer Gliding School
Rx	Receive		VMC	Visual Meteorological Conditions
			VOP	Voice Operating Procedures

ABBREVIATIONS IN COMMON USE – PLEASE ADD/DELETE AS NECESSARY

Wg Cdr	Wing Commander
WHQ	Wing Headquarters
WO	Warrant Officer
WSO	Wing Staff Officer
WAdO	Wing Administrative Officer

PERSONAL INFORMATION

Name	
Address	
Post Code	Tel No	Email

Name	
Address	
Post Code	Tel No	Email

Name	
Address	
Post Code	Tel No	Email

Name	
Address	
Post Code	Tel No	Email

Name	
Address	
Post Code	Tel No	Email

PERSONAL INFORMATION

Name	
Address	
Post Code	Tel No	Email

Name	
Address	
Post Code	Tel No	Email

Name	
Address	
Post Code	Tel No	Email

Name	
Address	
Post Code	Tel No	Email

Name	
Address	
Post Code	Tel No	Email